THE
SON OF MAN
IN MARK

THE
SON OF MAN
IN MARK

A Study of the
background of the term "Son of Man" and its use
in St Mark's Gospel

MORNA D. HOOKER

MONTREAL
McGILL UNIVERSITY PRESS
1967

Made and printed in Great Britain by
William Clowes and Sons, Limited
London and Beccles

Contents

Foreword

A great deal of this study was written during the two years 1959–61, when I held the position of Research Fellow in the University of Durham; I am grateful for the opportunities which this afforded me.

I should like to express my thanks to the Reverend Professor C. K. Barrett, for his encouragement and unfailing willingness to discuss the problem of "the Son of man" with me. I am also grateful to my father for help in proof-reading and in compiling the indexes, and to Mr Robin Myerscough for assistance with the indexes.

December 1966.   M. D. HOOKER

Acknowledgements

Thanks are due to the following for permission to quote from copyright sources:

Newman Press and The Mercier Press Ltd: *The Trial of Jesus*, by J. Blinzler.

S.C.M. Press Ltd., 1965 and The Westminster Press, U.S.A., 1965: *The Son of Man in the Synoptic Tradition*, by H. E. Tödt (translated by D. M. Barton).

Biblical quotations from the *Revised Standard Version* of the Bible, copyrighted 1946 and 1952 by the Division of Christian Education of the National Council of the Churches of Christ in the United States of America, are used by permission.

Abbreviations

PERIODICALS

B.J.R.L.	*Bulletin of the John Rylands Library*, Manchester
E.T.	*The Expository Times*, Edinburgh
J.B.L.	*Journal of Biblical Literature*, Philadelphia, U.S.A.
J.T.S.	*Journal of Theological Studies*, Oxford
N.T.S.	*New Testament Studies*, Cambridge
S.J.T.	*Scottish Journal of Theology*, Edinburgh
V.T.	*Vetus Testamentum*, Leiden
Z.A.T.W.	*Zeitschrift für die alttestamentliche Wissenschaft*, Giessen
Z.N.T.W.	*Zeitschrift für die neutestamentliche Wissenschaft*, Giessen
Z.Th.K.	*Zeitschrift für Theologie und Kirche*, Freiburg
S.N.T.S. Bulletin	*Bulletin of the Studiorum Novi Testamenti Societas*, Oxford

BOOKS

Arndt-Gingrich, *Lexicon* W. F. Arndt and F. W. Gingrich, *A Greek-English Lexicon of the New Testament and Other Early Christian Literature*. Translation of W. Bauer's *Wörterbuch*, Chicago and Cambridge, 1957.

Brown-Driver-Briggs F. Brown, S. R. Driver, and C. A. Briggs, *Hebrew Lexicon of the Old Testament*, Oxford, 1907.

Blass-Debrunner F. Blass, rev. A. Debrunner, *Grammatik des neutestamentlichen Griechisch*, 8th edn, Göttingen, 1949, trans. R. W. Funk, Cambridge, 1961.

Beginnings *The Beginnings of Christianity*, part I, 5 vols., ed. F. Jackson and K. Lake, London, 1920–33.

Bultmann, R., *Geschichte Die Geschichte der synoptischen Tradition*, 2nd edn, Göttingen, 1931, trans. J. Marsh, Oxford, 1963.

Fuller, R. H., *Mission and Achievement* The Mission and Achievement of Jesus, London, 1954.

Higgins, A. J. B., *Son of Man* Jesus and the Son of Man, London, 1964.

Liddell and Scott H. G. Liddell and R. Scott, *A Greek-English Lexicon*, rev. H. Stuart Jones, 9th edn, Oxford, 1958.

Loisy, A., *Synoptiques* Les Évangiles Synoptiques, Paris, 1907.

Moulton and Milligan J. H. Moulton and G. Milligan, *The Vocabulary of the Greek Testament Illustrated from the Papyri and other Non-Literary Sources*, London, 1930.

S'.-B., *Kommentar* H. L. Strack and P. Billerbeck, *Kommentar zum Neuen Testament aus Talmud und Midrasch*, 4 vols., Munich, 1922–8.

Tödt, H. E., *Menschensohn* Der Menschensohn in der synoptischen Überlieferung, Güttersloh, 1959, trans. D. M. Barton, London, 1965.

T.W.N.T. Theologisches Wörterbuch zum Neuen Testament, ed. G. Kittel and G. Friedrich, Stuttgart, 1933.

Commentaries are referred to by the title of the biblical book after the first reference.

E. Tr., English translation

INTRODUCTION

1

Introduction

In the year 1959 A. J. B. Higgins, writing in the T. W. Manson memorial volume of essays,[1] referred to "the bewildering mass of material on the Son of Man problem" which had appeared since the publication of Professor Manson's own book, *The Teaching of Jesus*, in 1931. Since Dr Higgins' essay was written, the material has continued to pour from the Press at an ever-increasing rate, making the study of this topic even more complex and bewildering; no subject in the realm of New Testament scholarship has been more debated. One thing, however, does emerge clearly from the confusion: in the last few years there has been a considerable shift in opinion, and an ever-increasing number of scholars are upholding the view that Jesus did not use the term "Son of man" as a self-designation. The change is illustrated by Dr Higgins himself, who in 1959 wrote,[2] "There is still to be found the opinion that Jesus did not allude to himself as Son of Man at all", an opinion which he apparently did not then consider tenable, but who in 1964 was himself championing this view;[3] an even more dramatic change is seen in the case of R. H. Fuller, who in his earliest book, *The Mission and Achievement of Jesus*, published in 1954, maintained that Jesus used the term "Son of man" as a self-designation, but in his most recent study, *The Foundations of New Testament Christology*, published in 1965, has presented us with a completely revised interpretation.

Higgins and Fuller are only two of the many scholars who, though varying widely in their interpretation of the term "Son of

---

[1] *New Testament Essays*, ed. A. J. B. Higgins, 1959, pp. 119-35.
[2] Op. cit., p. 124.
[3] A. J. B. Higgins, *Son of Man*.

man", have arrived at what is basically the answer given by Bultmann[1] to the problem. Others include John Knox,[2] F. Hahn,[3] and H. E. Tödt.[4] All these scholars agree in their conclusion that Jesus spoke of an eschatological figure, the Son of man, and that the early Church made the steps of identifying Jesus himself with that figure and of creating non-eschatological "Son of man" sayings. A still more radical approach to the problem has been made by P. Vielhauer[5] and H. Conzelmann,[6] who regard all the "Son of man" sayings in the gospels as creations of the Church.

One exception to the recent trend in this study is E. Schweizer.[7] Contrary to the general consensus of opinion that the most primitive sayings are those which speak of the Son of man in terms of eschatological events, Schweizer maintains that this group is in fact the least trustworthy, and that the most important group is that which contains the sayings about the humble life of the Son of man on earth. The third group of sayings, which predict the passion and resurrection of the Son of man, are generally dismissed as *vaticinia ex eventu*; nevertheless, although these sayings have been elaborated, Schweizer feels that the tradition of the Son of man being "handed over" is very early, and he concludes that "it is probable that Jesus spoke of himself as the Son of man who was to be humiliated and rejected by men, yet exalted by God".[8]

In spite of recent support for Bultmann's position, therefore, there is no agreed solution to the problem. Until some clear answer emerges, it is perhaps understandable and excusable if many English scholars, with typical conservatism, continue to cling to the old belief, which goes back at least as far as the gospels, that Jesus did speak of himself as Son of man.

But *will* some clear answer to the problem emerge? Will the methods of form-criticism and tradition-criticism ever solve the

---

[1] See *Theology of the New Testament*, I, 1958, pp. 26–32.
[2] *The Death of Christ*, 1959, pp. 31–125.
[3] *Christologische Hoheitstitel, Ihre Geschichte im frühen Christentum*, 1963, pp. 13–53.
[4] *Der Menschensohn in der synoptischen Überlieferung*, 1959, E.Tr. 1965.
[5] "Gottesreich und Menschensohn in der Verkündigung Jesu", *Festschrift für Günther Dehn*, ed. W. Schneemelcher, 1957, pp. 51–79; "Jesus und der Menschensohn", *Z.Th.K.*, 60, 1963, pp. 133–77.
[6] "Gegenwart und Zukunft in der synoptischen Tradition", *Z.Th.K.*, 54, 1957, pp. 277–96.
[7] Schweizer's position is set out in "Der Menschensohn", *Z.N.T.W.*, 50, 1959, pp. 185–209. See also "The Son of Man", *J.B.L.*, 79, 1960, pp. 119–29, and "The Son of Man Again", *N.T.S.*, 9, 1963, pp. 256–61.
[8] "The Son of Man", *J.B.L.*, 79, 1960, pp. 120f.

problem satisfactorily? It looks as if the answer is "No". The same principles and methods lead one scholar to trace the title "Son of man" to Jesus, another to attribute it to the Church, and a third to trace the term itself to Jesus, but its use as a Christological title to the community. The attempt to trace the history of the tradition through all its stages from Jesus to the Church cannot be made objectively, for scholars differ in their understanding of the term "Son of man" itself, in the place which they allow to the creative activity of the Church, and in the relative importance which they give to the objections which can be brought against every solution. The form-critical method in itself cannot solve the problem.

It is certainly not our intention in this study to attack the form-critical method. Form-criticism has established itself as an invaluable tool which can tell us a great deal about the history of the gospel material. But when the same method provides different answers to a problem, then other methods of approach have to be taken into consideration. Important as the study of sources, forms, and tradition is, it may be that this alone cannot provide the answer to the problem of the origin of the use of the term "Son of man" in the New Testament.

When we examine the methods which are employed in answering this particular question, we find that the application of the various disciplines can take us only part of the way. This is acknowledged by R. H. Fuller, in his recent discussion in *The Foundations of New Testament Christology*. We find him confident in allocating the "suffering" sayings to a comparatively late stratum on the basis of source criticism, but hesitant about the remaining two groups. He writes:[1]

> the strict application of traditio-critical principles will not allow us to eliminate the "present" and "future" Son of man sayings from the authentic *logia*.

Nevertheless, in spite of this conclusion, Fuller is driven—reluctantly—to eliminate the "present" sayings for two reasons; firstly, because he agrees with Bultmann that there is an inconsistency between the "present" and the "parousia" sayings, and secondly, because "it is impossible to account for these sayings within the framework of Jewish apocalyptic, where the Son of man is a

---

[1] *The Foundations of New Testament Christology*, p. 121, cf. p. 120.

transcendent figure coming on the clouds of heaven.[1] Here we have moved beyond "the strict application of traditio-critical principles" to a judgement made upon the basis of a particular interpretation of the term "Son of man".

Another example of the limitations of the form-critical approach is found in Dr Higgins' book. Having come to the conclusion that Jesus did not identify himself with the Son of man, he turns in his final chapter to a consideration of the question of Jesus' own self-understanding. At this point, Higgins abandons the application of the principles of tradition-criticism, and lapses into an extraordinarily imaginative attempt to reconstruct the mind of Jesus, entirely out of harmony with the methods of critical scholarship which he has been claiming to use in the rest of his book. Having ruthlessly eliminated all traces of any self-identification with the Son of man from Jesus' words, Higgins maintains that "on earth Jesus believed himself to be God's Son acting as the Servant of God foretold in prophecy",[2] and that "he fulfilled consciously the rôle of the Suffering Servant, and especially in his death 'for many' ".[3] This interpretation of the mind of Jesus will seem to many to be a strange reversal of the gospel evidence, and it is certainly one which is based on judgements other than those of form-criticism.

One factor which needs to be considered is the often unnecessarily negative way in which the critical method is applied. We find Fuller writing:[4]

> [Following the form-critical method] means, among other things, that where a saying or a tradition about Jesus in the gospels reflects the theology of the post-resurrection church, that saying or tradition must be placed to the credit of the church, rather than to Jesus himself, or to his original history.

There would seem to be a grave danger in this interpretation of the form-critical method if it means, as Fuller takes it to mean, that we eliminate such sayings from the words of Jesus. For though it may lead us to a much fuller and deeper understanding of the theology of the Church, it may well lead also to a distortion of our understanding of Jesus. If we place a saying or tradition to the *credit* of the Church, are we necessarily obliged to *debit* it from our picture of Jesus? In some cases, of course, we ought to do so: but in

[1] Ibid., p. 124.   [2] *Son of Man*, p. 197.   [3] *Son of Man*, p. 207.
[4] Op. cit., p. 116.

others, it could be that the Church and Jesus are in agreement—
that his understanding overlaps that of the community. If we
credit to Jesus himself only those sayings which seem to be out of
character with the beliefs of the Church, then we may well eliminate material which is of great importance for our understanding
of Jesus. To reduce the number of "authentic" *logia* to such an
extent may produce a picture of Jesus which is so unbalanced as to
be misleading, for we shall have eliminated not only later accretions,
but also the material which could possibly be common to Jesus and
the Church, and which may explain the continuity between them.

The danger of this method of selection is especially great in the
case of the "Son of man" *logia*, where we have different types of
sayings. To remove two out of the three groups, with Bultmann
and Tödt, may be a solution of the apparent inconsistency, but it
may be too simple. The method appears even more risky when we
realize that the group of sayings with which they are left, and which
forms the basis of their reconstruction of the authentic *logia* of
Jesus, is the group of eschatological sayings—in other words, those
which are most likely to reflect the beliefs of the early Church,
since the believing community clearly identified Jesus with the
coming Son of man. As far as an analysis of these sayings is concerned, it would seem that Schweizer is more loyal to the principles of form-criticism than Bultmann himself, since he treats this
group as untrustworthy, and places more confidence in the group
of sayings which depict the Son of man as a humble figure on earth.

There would seem, then, to be a great danger of distortion if we
hastily eliminate too many of the sayings. It may be that the
different kinds of sayings reflect different aspects of the function
of the Son of man, and that these are integral parts of the concept,
not inconsistent elements. We should perhaps take into consideration all three strands of the "Son of man" tradition, and not try to
reduce them to one element, any more than one would attempt to
reduce a rope to a single cord. It is possible that the inconsistency
lies in our own interpretation rather than in the sayings themselves,
and that we need all three groups to lead us back to the truth about
the Son of man.

Our purpose in this book is therefore not to analyse the various
groups and sources, but to study the problem of the Son of man
from another angle: we wish to study the impact which the "Son
of man" sayings make when we look at one gospel—St Mark's. In

doing this we are obviously primarily concerned with the Son of man as understood (or partially understood) by Mark himself, and the picture which emerges can only be a part of the truth about the Son of man. At the same time, however, it is legitimate to ask whether the various "Son of man" sayings can be admitted to a consideration of Jesus' own use of the term, and can have a setting within the life of Jesus, as well as within the faith of the Church. If we find a consistent pattern in the Marcan sayings, then it will also be legitimate to ask whether this throws any light on Jesus' own use of the term. Obviously such a study in itself cannot solve the problem of Jesus' own understanding, and this is not its purpose. The Marcan pattern is, however, one element in the total picture of the "Son of man" sayings, and as such deserves consideration. It may be that we can also use it to point tentatively towards a conclusion to the larger problem of Jesus' own use of the term.

Before examining the gospel, however, we must first examine the background of the term, for this is important for our study. It is surprising how many writers recently have assumed that its meaning is obvious, and have based their interpretation of the "Son of man" sayings upon their own understanding of the term, ignoring the background material. We therefore begin with an examination of this background in Jewish literature.

PART ONE

BACKGROUND

2

The
"One Like a Son of Man"
in Daniel 7

1. MAN AND BEAST

Who or what is the figure like a Son of man in Dan. 7.13? The fact
that the phrase "Son of man" is used here as a comparison suggests that, whatever else he may or may not be, he is not a mere
"Son of man".[1] It has, indeed, been maintained that the comparison has no inherent value, and merely serves to develop the
mysterious atmosphere of apocalyptic vision.[2] In opposition to this
view, C. H. Kraeling[3] rightly pointed out that while the comparative is used four times in chapter 7, it is not found with the symbols
employed elsewhere in Daniel; moreover, the comparative is retained with the human figure in both 1 Enoch and 2 Esdras. Kraeling
goes on, however, to argue that the comparative particle in v. 13
indicates that the figure is a member of the human race possessing
certain unusual features, rather than a member of some other
group of beings, possessing a few human characteristics.[4] In support of this he maintains that the comparative here is paralleled by
that used in vv. 4, 5, and 6, where it "is used to allow for the
superadded peculiarities of the beasts, not to distinguish them

---

[1] This confirms the impossibility of the messianic interpretation, which is in
any case incompatible with Daniel's own explanation.
[2] See P. Volz, *Die Eschatologie der jüdischen Gemeinde in neutestamentliches
Zeitalter*, 1934, pp. 11f.
[3] C. H. Kraeling, *Anthropos and Son of Man*, 1927, pp. 142f. Cf. J. A. Montgomery, *A Critical and Exegetical Commentary on the Book of Daniel*, 1927, p.
318.
[4] Op. cit., pp. 143f.

generically from the animal whose name they bear". This argument appears to be unnecessarily forced and over-subtle. It is stretching language and reason alike to say that a beast which is "like a leopard, with four wings of a bird on its back and . . . four heads" is merely a leopard with "superadded peculiarities"! The correct interpretation is surely the obvious one: Daniel sees in his vision various animals which, naturally enough, bear certain resemblances to ordinary animals; they are more like a lion, a bear, or a leopard than anything else he knows, but no zoologist would agree to classify them in these categories. Similarly the figure which he sees in v. 13 is "like a Son of man", but the phrase allows for fundamental differences as well as certain similarities.[1]

Kraeling's argument is offered in support of the view that Daniel's figure is linked with the Anthropos of Iranian belief. Various scholars have endeavoured to trace the "one like a Son of man" to some form of the idea of a primal or heavenly man,[2] and the attempt is justified, in so far as both belong ultimately to the same mythological pattern of thought. Too little is known, however, about the date and extent of the Urmensch speculations for us to place any confidence in theories which suggest that the author of Daniel 7 deliberately borrowed traits from a well-known figure of this nature. Evidence is too slight to justify assumptions such as that made by Mowinckel, who, on the basis of the fact that Daniel's figure comes with the clouds of heaven, declares that:[3]

We can conclude from Dan. vii. that about 200 B.C. or earlier there was *in Judaism* a conception of a heavenly being in human form ("one

[1] A. Feuillet, "Le Fils de l'homme de Daniel et la tradition biblique", *Revue Biblique*, 60, 1953, pp. 186f, rightly stresses that the use of the comparative particle shows that the beasts, though real, differ from the species to which they are likened. He notes a similar differentiation with regard to the angelic figures in 8.15 and 10.16, and maintains that there is a difference between the terms of comparison used there and that in 7.13. On this last point he is correct, but the parallel to the description of the beasts is to be found in 7.13, and not in 8.15 and 10.16, 18, where the angelic being is compared to an appearance (מַרְאֶה) or likeness (דְּמוּת) of a man. In 7.13, on the other hand, a direct comparison is made, as is done in vv. 4–6. The fact that the beasts are classified as such should not be allowed to confuse the issue: the enumeration of the beasts could be omitted from vv. 4–6 (thus giving an exact parallel with v. 13) without affecting the comparison in the slightest way, but it serves to emphasize their common origin and their distinction from the man-like figure. While there are many varieties of animals, however, man is unique, and it is thus impossible to classify him by writing "a —— like a Son of man".

[2] See the discussions of various views by J. M. Creed, "The Heavenly Man", *J.T.S.*, 26, 1925, pp. 113–36; C. H. Kraeling, op. cit.; W. Manson, *Jesus the Messiah*, 1943, pp. 174–90.

[3] S. Mowinckel, *He That Cometh*, E.Tr. 1956, p. 352 (italics mine).

like a man"), who, at the turn of the age, the dawn of the eschatological era, would appear, and would receive from God delegated power and authority over all kingdoms and peoples.

Even if the author did have such a "heavenly being" in mind, the ideas which he borrowed have been so radically changed in his use of them that it is doubtful whether they could have been of any great significance to him, and even more doubtful whether they would have conveyed any particular significance to his readers. His concern—and theirs—is not with a heavenly man, but with the fortunes of Israel.

If the "one like a Son of man" is not a human being, however, either he is, like the figure in 10.16, an angelic being, or he stands for a group of people—a metaphorical device already employed in Ps. 80.18 (17). Although Daniel himself twice makes clear that the latter interpretation is correct,[1] some scholars have argued in favour of the former solution. R. H. Charles combined them;[2] beginning from his statement that "In apocalyptic visions where men are symbolized by beasts, angels and other supernatural beings are symbolized by men", he maintained that the expression must therefore represent "a supernatural being or a body of beings". Since he accepted Daniel's own explanation in vv. 18, 22, 25, and 27 that the figure represents "the saints of the Most High",[3]

---

[1] Dan. 7. 18, 27.

[2] *A Critical and Exegetical Commentary on the Book of Daniel*, 1929, p. 187.

[3] M. Noth, developing a thesis of O. Procksch, has recently challenged the traditional interpretation of the phrase "the saints of the Most High" as a reference to Israel, and maintains that it denotes heavenly beings. In "Die Heiligen des Höchsten", *Gesammelte Studien zum Alten Testament*, 2nd edn, 1960, pp. 274–90, reprinted from the Mowinckel *Festschrift*, 1955, he argues that in the Old Testament the term "the holy ones" is almost invariably used to denote heavenly beings, and that the phrase "the saints of the Most High" in Dan. 7 should be given the same meaning. He finds further support for this interpretation in CD XX 8. The expression found in Dan. 7.27, "the people of the saints of the Most High" should also not be understood of Israel, since it refers to the company of holy ones; vv. 21f do seem to refer to the pious in Israel, but this is probably a later interpolation. Noth's thesis has been examined by L. Dequeker (in J. Coppens and L. Dequeker, *Le Fils de l'homme et les Saints du Très Haut en Daniel*, VII, 1961, pp. 33–54), who cites material from Qumran in further support. Noth's view has also been accepted with enthusiasm by J. Barr, writing on Daniel in the new *Peake's Commentary on the Bible* (ed. M. Black and H. H. Rowley, 1962), p. 598, but has been treated with caution by N. W. Porteous, *Das Danielbuch*, 1962, pp. 90f.

Although the majority of the occurrences of קְדֹשִׁים in the Old Testament support Noth (e.g. Ps. 16.3; 89.6, 8 (5, 7); cf. also S. Mowinckel, *He That Cometh*, p. 380; F. M. Cross and D. N. Freedman, "The Blessing of Moses", *J.B.L.*, 67, 1948, p. 199), there are exceptions to be found in Ps. 34.10 (9);

Charles was forced to conclude that "the faithful remnant of
Israel are to be transformed into heavenly or supernatural beings".
Earlier, N. Schmidt[1] had suggested, on the analogy of the man-
like figures in 8.15,16 and 10.16,18, that the "one like a Son of
man" must also be an angelic being—in this case Michael, the
heavenly representative of Israel.

Such reasoning, however, produces a too-neat solution to our
problem. The useful convention that animals represent men and
men represent supernatural beings no doubt holds good for later
apocalyptic, but it is doubtful whether it was already a recognized formula when Dan. 7 was composed. Moreover, there is an

---

Dan. 7.21f and 8.24. Exceptions are also noted by Dequeker in the Dead Sea
Scrolls (I QM IX 7f; X 9–11), and the interpretation of other passages which he
lists in support of Noth is often debatable (e.g. CD XX 8; I QSb I 5; I QM VI 6)
or depends on a textual emendation (I QSb III 5f; IV 22–6). The idea of holiness
is not confined to angels, as Noth and Dequeker themselves recognize, but is
extended to the people of God, who also share his holiness; in the Similitudes of
Enoch, too, we find the term "holy" applied to both angels and elect (cf. 1 Enoch
39.4f). It is possible that this use is a later development, but we find it already
in the book of Daniel itself, in 7.21f and 8.24; these passages are themselves
strong support for the traditional interpretation of the phrase. Noth and Dequeker
both explain this difficulty by linking their exposition with a theory of editorial
recensions: the interpretation of the phrase in Dan. 7.21f, therefore, reflects the
outlook of a later editor. This is possible, though one must always use theories
about later editorial additions with caution.

Various objections to the theory have been discussed recently by J. Coppens
in "Les Saints du Très-Haut sont-ils à identifier avec les Milices Célestes?",
Ephemerides Theologicae Lovanienses, 39, 1963, pp. 94–100 (see also the remarks on the same subject in his discussion of Porteous' book in the same issue,
pp. 91–3). Coppens is able to deal with many of the difficulties, but the greatest
stumbling-block is the paucity of evidence: CD XX 8 remains the only real
parallel to the phrase "the saints of the Most High", and its meaning is disputed.
The evidence of the use of the simple קְדוֹשִׁים is inconclusive,and Coppens himself distinguishes between the expression "saints of the Most High" and the
term "saints" in Dan. 7. 21, 22, 25b; he understands the latter to designate "les
Israélites pieux, restés fidèles à Yahvé" (op. cit. p. 94). Elsewhere ("Les Saints
dans le Psautier", *Ephemerides Theologicae Lovanienses*, 39, 1963, pp. 485–500),
he traces in the Psalms a development from an earlier use of קְדוֹשִׁים to denote
supernatural beings to the later extension of the term to the faithful in Israel. In
these circumstances one still inclines towards the traditional interpretation of
the phrase "the saints of the Most High", an interpretation which is supported
by the context of the phrase in Dan. 7. In any case, it would seem that in its
present form Dan. 7 uses this term, as well as the simple "the saints", of the
righteous within Israel. For a similar judgement, see D. S. Russell, *The Method
and Message of Jewish Apocalyptic*, 1964, pp. 325f, and cf. W. Baumgartner,
"Ein Vierteljahrhundert Danielforschung", *Theologische Rundschau*, Neue
Folge, 11, 1939, p. 216.
[1] "The 'Son of Man' in the Book of Daniel", *J.B.L.*, 19, 1900, pp. 22–8.
See also F. C. Porter, *The Messages of the Apocalyptical Writers*, 1905, pp. 131–4,
G. H. Box, *The Ezra-Apocalypse*, 1912, p. 283, and the discussion of F. Stier's
views by J. Coppens in "Le Fils d'homme Daniélique, vizir céleste?", *Ephemerides Theologicae Lovanienses*, 40, 1964, pp. 72–80.

enormous difference between that chapter and the automatic symbolism of a passage such as 1 Enoch 83—90, where various animals are simply substituted for the names of biblical characters. There are traces of this sort of symbolism in the later chapters of Daniel, but it is doubtful whether one can justifiably use it as a basis to explain the far more impressive and original imagery of chapter 7.[1]

A more profitable line of enquiry is an examination of those passages in Daniel where human characteristics are attributed to figures which in other respects are to be classified as "beasts". Thus in Dan. 7 itself we find that the first beast "was lifted up from the ground and made to stand upon two feet like a man; and the mind of a man was given to it" (v. 4). Exactly the same idea is to be found in the account in Dan. 4 of Nebuchadnezzar's dream and its sequel. In spite of the added confusion of the tree metaphor the contrast is clear: Nebuchadnezzar's mind is changed from a man's to a beast's; he lives with the animals in the fields and behaves like them, until his reason is restored. Now it is obvious that the contrast between human and beastly in these two passages has nothing to do with the later apocalyptic convention which we have been discussing; the author certainly has no intention of suggesting that either Nebuchadnezzar or his kingdom ever possessed a supernatural mind or heart. Nor does the context suggest that the change represents a gradual "humanization".[2] What the context does suggest—at least in the former passage—is that the change from a man's mind to a beast's typifies Nebuchadnezzar's loss of reason.

Once again the obvious solution has a good claim to being the correct one. But it is the interpretation which the author gives to this change that supplies the clue to its importance. For it is made quite clear that the reasons for Nebuchadnezzar's downfall and disgrace were his self-glorification and pride in his own achievement (v. 30). Moreover, his self-delusion, which is its own punishment, is to continue until he has learned "that the Most High rules the kingdom of men and gives it to whom he will" (v. 32; cf. vv. 17 and 25). His reason and kingdom are both restored to him when he

---

[1] Even in 1 Enoch 83—90 the convention that men = angels, animals = men is not consistently maintained. Thus in 89.1 Noah is changed from a bull into a man, presumably so that he can build the ark (thus R. H. Charles, *The Book of Enoch*, 1912, p. 190). In v. 9 of the same chapter, however, he appears to have changed back into a bull. Similarly Moses, who is represented as a sheep, changes into a man in 89.36 in order to build the tabernacle.

[2] Cf. J. A. Montgomery, *Daniel*, pp. 287f; R. H. Charles, *Daniel*, p. 176.

recognizes that dominion belongs to God, and that in his sight "all the inhabitants of the earth are accounted as nothing" (vv. 34–7). In the absence of any evidence outside Dan. 4 for Nebuchadnezzar's madness, it would be possible to argue that Daniel's description is entirely metaphorical, a pictorial representation of Nebuchadnezzar's self-vaunting and folly. But whether primary or secondary, the idea that man by his self-glorification and rebellion against God's dominion reduces himself to the level of an animal is fundamental.[1] It should be noted that before its fall, the "tree" sheltered both beasts and birds. With this we may compare the interpretation of Nebuchadnezzar's dream in Dan. 2, where he is said to be the head of gold in the visionary image; Daniel declares that God has given to Nebuchadnezzar "the Kingdom, the power, and the might, and the glory", and has placed in his hand "the sons of men, the beasts of the field, and the birds of the air, making [him] rule over them all" (vv. 37f). According to chapter 4, it is when Nebuchadnezzar forgets that his kingdom and glory are God-given that he loses his dominion, not only over men, but over birds and beasts as well, and is reduced to the level of the beasts.

The same emphasis on self-magnification is found in the later visions of Daniel. Thus in chapter 8 we read repeatedly of the animals and their horns that they magnified themselves.[2] Similarly, chapter 11 speaks of men who exalt themselves and seize kingship which is not theirs by right.[3] As for the beasts in chapter 7, it is self-evident that they—with the partial exception of the first—are in rebellion against God and have seized power for themselves.[4] This connection between man's rebellious self-sufficiency and animal life is found also in the Psalms. Thus in Ps. 73.21f, the psalmist confesses that his bitterness, brutish stupidity, and ignorance had made him as a beast before God. Again, in Ps. 49.21 (20), we find it stated that "Man that is in honour, and understandeth not, is like the beasts that perish".[5] A similar statement appears in v. 13 (12),[6] and this is followed by a passage which distinguishes between the psalmist, whose life is apparently to be

---

[1] Cf. the use made of the same idea by Jesus in Luke 15. 11–32.
[2] Vv. 4, 8, 11, 25.   [3] Vv. 12, 18, 21, 36.
[4] Note also the "big things" spoken by the little horn in vv. 8 and 11.
[5] R.V. translation.
[6] The LXX and Syriac have the same reading as in v. 21. The Hebrew text reads יָלִין, abideth, and not יָבִין, understandeth, as in v. 21.

spared, and those who are now foolishly self-confident, but who are in fact appointed like sheep to Sheol.

The fundamental basis of the antithesis between human and beastly in Daniel would thus seem to be man's attitude to God. Those who recognize his dominion and are subservient to his will can be described as having human characteristics, while those who rebel against his authority are akin to beasts. This distinction holds good even in the latter part of Daniel, since it is not only the "heavenly beings" which are described as being human in form; Daniel himself is several times addressed as "man".[1] The conventional apocalyptic symbolism would indeed appear to have grown out of the imagery which is used in Dan. 7, but to understand the latter we must look not forward but backward, to its origins.

2. THE MYTHOLOGICAL BACKGROUND

The recognition that with Daniel we pass from prophetic to apocalyptic has perhaps tended to obscure this book's true position in Hebraic thought. For while it is correct to describe the author as an apocalyptist, he nevertheless still stands very close to the prophetic movement out of which apocalyptic grew, and his book forms a bridge between the two, so that his thought must be considered in relation to both.[2] It is clear that the ideas expressed in Dan. 7 are a re-interpretation of those found in the psalmists and in the later prophets, especially Deutero-Isaiah, depicting Yahweh's victory over Israel's enemies and the nation's restoration in terms of creation mythology.[3] The difference is that apocalyptic vision has replaced prophetic metaphor: the wheel has come full circle, and Tiamat and Leviathan have once again taken on concrete shape.

The pattern of the vision in Dan. 7 has been shaped by the primitive myth of creation; the emergence of the beasts from the sea, their defeat by Yahweh, and the bestowal of dominion on a human figure, are all motifs taken from this background. This does

---

[1] Dan. 8.17; 10.11, 19.

[2] S. R. Driver, *The Book of Daniel*, 1900, pp. lxxxvif, on Dan. 7: "This representation of the future kingdom of God, though it differs in details, and displays traits marking the later age to which it belongs, is, in all essential features the same as that which is found repeatedly in the earlier prophets."

[3] S. Mowinckel believes that the connection in Deutero-Isaiah is the result of his use of the ritual of an enthronement festival. See *He That Cometh*, pp. 138–43.

not necessarily mean, of course, that Daniel used the priestly account of the creation in Genesis as the basis of his description;[1] some of his details are nearer to the ideas underlying the Babylonian Epic of Creation.[2] It has, indeed, been suggested that Daniel is largely dependent upon Babylonian sources for his imagery.[3] Creation mythology played a central rôle in the Babylonian cultus, and it is quite possible that Daniel has borrowed traits from that tradition. Much more significant, however, is the fact that a similar pattern of thought was already an integral part of Hebrew religion.[4] Many scholars have argued, on the basis of this fact, that Israel played a full rôle in the myth and ritual pattern of the Ancient East, and that the ritual combat between the King-god and the monster, the triumphant procession and the sacred marriage, were all to be found in pre-Exilic Israel.[5] A. Bentzen, indeed, has argued that the imagery of Dan. 7 is based directly on this Enthronement Festival.[6] Whether or not such a festival ever existed, the evidence which its advocates have brought forward shows that the myth, if not the ritual, had been absorbed into Hebrew thought. While Daniel may possibly have been influenced by foreign cults, he did not introduce anything which was alien to Hebrew tradition: the motifs which he employs already have their place in the life of the nation.[7]

Daniel's affinity with earlier Hebrew thought is illustrated by the character in which he portrays the beasts: they are still the powers of chaos, revolting against God's rule, but now they are no longer

---

[1] This is the position maintained by A. M. Farrer, *A Study in St Mark*, 1951, pp. 258–62. See his whole chapter, pp. 247–64.

[2] In particular, the beasts brought up from the sea by the four winds bear more resemblance to the sea-monsters of mythology than to the birds, animals, and fish of Gen. 1.28. Cf. R. H. Charles, *Daniel*, p. 175; E. W. Heaton, *The Book of Daniel*, pp. 92–6, 169–76.

[3] See, e.g., H. Gunkel, *Schöpfung und Chaos in Urzeit und Endzeit*, 1895, pp. 323–35; C. H. Kraeling, *Anthropos and Son of Man*, pp. 128–65.

[4] See, e.g., Ps. 74.12–17 and 89.10f (9f). Cf. H. Gunkel, op. cit., pp. 3–170.

[5] See, e.g., *Myth and Ritual*, essays ed. by S. H. Hooke, 1933, and Hooke's essay on "The Myth and Ritual Pattern in Jewish and Christian Apocalyptic" in *The Labyrinth*, 1935. Cf. S. Mowinckel, *The Psalms in Israel's Worship*, E.Tr. 1962, I, pp. 130–40.

[6] *King and Messiah*, E.Tr. 1955, pp. 73–80. Bentzen writes (p. 75): "The vision of chapter 7 is an eschatological representation of the ancient Enthronement Festival."

[7] Cf. J. A. Emerton, "The Origin of the Son of Man Imagery", *J.T.S.*, new series, 9, 1958, p. 228: "It would probably be a mistake to think simply of direct Babylonian influence on Daniel. The O.T. has a number of references to a struggle between Yahweh and Rahab or Leviathan, the chaos dragon, and it is, therefore, probable that any foreign influence was mediated through the O.T. tradition."

natural forces but nations. In depicting Israel's enemies as wild
beasts, Daniel is once again following the tradition of prophets and
psalmists.[1] The dignity of man as against the beasts is also found
in biblical thought—not only in Gen. 1, but also in Ps. 8. Moreover,
in Ps. 80, Israel—or possibly the king as Israel's representative—
is described as "the man of thy right hand, the son of man whom
thou hast made strong for thyself". This verse follows immediately after a description of Israel as a vine which is planted in a
vineyard ravaged by a wild boar. It is perhaps significant that the
psalmist does not in fact combine these two images, and draw the
obvious contrast between the hostile nations as wild beasts and
Israel as a man. They belong here to two distinct metaphors which
are not mixed, although the one follows immediately after the
other, and may well have been suggested by it. Similar ideas seem
to lie behind the Hebrew text of Ezek. 34.31. Throughout the
chapter the prophet has described the people of Israel in terms of
sheep, their leaders as shepherds and their enemies as wild beasts.
The final verse reads: "You are my sheep, the sheep of my pasture; you are men, and I am your God." Some commentators[2]
follow the LXX in deleting the word for men (אָדָם) and thus
avoid the awkwardness of the Hebrew, but the word's difficulty
supports its genuineness. It may well be that the prophet felt that
ultimately his metaphor, while representing fairly the treatment the
people received from their neighbours and rulers, was inadequate
to express Israel's true relationship with Yahweh. Once again the
twin ideas that the people's enemies are wild beasts and that Israel
is man are linked, but not combined. Turning to Dan. 7, therefore,
it is not surprising to find that Israel's enemies are depicted as wild
beasts, nor to discover, associated with this imagery but not directly
combined with it, the complementary conception of Israel represented by one like a Son of man.

This contrast between man and beast is clear enough. There is,
however, a further important distinction to be noticed in Daniel's
vision, this time in the nature of the beasts themselves. While the
first three are described as being, in general, "like a lion", "like a
bear", and "like a leopard", the fourth is so extraordinary, and so
terrible, that the author can find no words or similes adequate to

---

[1] E.g. Ps. 68.31 (30); 74.18f; Ezek. 29.3f. Cf. Ps. 57.5 (4).
[2] E.g. G. A. Cooke, *The Book of Ezekiel*, 1936, p. 379.

describe it. Moreover, while the other beasts are suffered to sur-
vive for a time, the last monster is slain and its body destroyed with
fire. This fourth beast, indeed, as well as being "different from all
the beasts that were before it", plays a far more important part in
both the vision and the interpretation than its predecessors, and it
may be asked why such especial emphasis is placed upon it. A partial answer is undoubtedly supplied by the fact that it was under
this "beast" that the author's contemporaries were suffering, and
so it naturally filled the centre of the stage. Far more significant,
however, is the close relationship which this monster has with the
primeval dragon of mythology, slain by Marduk in Babylonian
tradition and by Yahweh in the Hebrew counterpart.[1]

An examination of the relevant Old Testament passages, however, suggests that once again the background to Daniel's imagery
is to be found there, rather than in Babylonian tradition. Closest
to the original myth are Job 9.8,13 and 26.12, where Yahweh's
defeat of the sea monster, Rahab, is still interpreted in terms of
creation. The same conception underlies the extension of the myth
in Ps. 74.12–17 and 89.10(9)f and Isa. 51.9f,[2] where Yahweh's
prowess in defeating sea and dragon, Leviathan and Rahab, is used
as a basis for an appeal for a similar show of strength in the present
historical situation. The final stage of development was to interpret
the myth in terms of history, and equate the mythical with the
historical. Thus in Isa. 27.1, Jer. 51.34–7, and Ezek. 29.3f, the
battle between Yahweh and chaos is thrown into the future:
Leviathan and Rahab have become Egypt and Babylon, whose final
destruction is as certain as that of the monsters in the myth. The
parallel with Daniel's use of the fourth beast is exact.

We can thus trace two distinct but interwoven themes in Daniel
and in other parts of the Old Testament. One is the conflict between the people of Israel and their enemies, represented as wild
beasts: the other is the conquest of chaos by Yahweh. The inter-

---

[1] Daniel does not describe the fourth beast in great detail, but what he does
tell us may perhaps be significant: apart from the general information that it was
"terrible and dreadful and exceedingly strong", we are told only that "it had
great iron teeth". Cf. with this the description of Leviathan in Job 41.6 (14) ff,
which also refers to the terror of the animal's teeth. Cf. also the description of
Tiamat's monsters in the Babylonian Epic of Creation, *Enûma Elish*, tablets I,
lines 133ff, II, 20ff, III, 24ff and 82ff; the strength and terror of the "ferocious
dragons" is depicted, and they are said to be "sharp of tooth" (see the translation in A. Heidel, *The Babylonian Genesis*, new edn, 1963).

[2] But cf. A. Heidel, op. cit., pp. 102–14, who argues that these passages do
not reflect the Marduk-Tiamat conflict.

dependence of these two themes is plain: Yahweh's struggle with the monster and the people's battle with their enemies are one, and it is God's victory which ensures the well-being of the people. But though the themes may be parallel, they are not identical. For while the powers of chaos may be reinterpreted in terms of Israel's enemies, Yahweh and the nation remain distinct. Thus the emphasis is upon Yahweh as active and triumphant, working for the salvation of his people, and upon the nation as saved from the power of its enemies: the relationship is a three-cornered one, involving Yahweh, Israel, and the enemies.

Now these related themes of conflict are precisely those which play such an important part in the "myth and ritual pattern" which some scholars suppose to have dominated the religious thought of the ancient Near East. It is clear, however, that in the person of the divine king, where such exists, these two ideas are not merely related, but coalesce. This happened in the Babylonian ritual, where the king played a dual rôle, acting both as representative of the people and as manifestation of the god. It has been suggested that a similar blurring of the three-cornered relationship took place in Israel. It is highly dubious, however, whether the Hebrews ever regarded their king as divine. Those who maintain that they did explain the lack of evidence for the belief as the result of a purge by the prophetic movement which destroyed the pattern.[1] This allows very little time, however—a mere 300 years or so between the establishment of the monarchy and the rise of the prophets—for the suggested beliefs and ritual to become integrated into Hebrew thought. A king chosen from the people, whose position was little more than that of a glorified tribal chieftain, does not become divine in a single day; belief in divine kingship—if it ever existed in Israel—must have been a gradual development, and of limited duration.

Evidence that the king was ever regarded as divine, or that he ever played the part of Yahweh in a ritual combat such as was performed in Babylon, is scanty and highly debatable.[2] While much of Israel's culture may be traced to a common origin with that of

---

[1] See, e.g., S. H. Hooke, *The Labyrinth*, p. 216; J. Morgenstern, "The King-God among the Western Semites and the Meaning of Epiphanes", *V.T.*, 10, 1960, p. 190.
[2] Cf. A. R. Johnson, *Sacral Kingship in Ancient Israel*, 1955; "Divine Kingship and the Old Testament", *E.T.*, 62, 1951, pp. 36–42; C. R. North, "The Religious Aspects of Hebrew Kingship", *Z.A.T.W.*, 50, 1932, pp. 21–38; S. Mowinckel, *He That Cometh*, pp. 82–9.

Babylon, it would appear that the idea of the king as a manifestation of the deity was never to any real extent taken over. This may
perhaps be because the most important period of contact took
place long before Israel possessed a monarchy, so that the beliefs
attached to the king were irrelevant; or it may be because Israel's
relationship with the Near Eastern culture pattern was through a
nation which had itself not developed the idea of divine kingship.[1]

Evidence for a "ritual lament" by the king, on the other hand,
is much less speculative, and there is a considerable quantity of
material in the Psalms[2] which can legitimately be interpreted in
this way.[3] It can equally well be regarded as an appeal by the king
for help in a particular historical situation.[4] For our purpose it is
unnecessary to decide which is the correct interpretation: in either
case, the king acts as representative of the people, and appeals to
Yahweh for help. The three-cornered relationship between
Yahweh, Israel, and the powers of destruction is preserved, and it
is Yahweh who saves, the king, symbol of his people, who is delivered.

It is precisely this relationship which reappears in Daniel's
vision. On the one hand, we have the initial victory of the hostile
powers who have conquered and crushed Israel; their triumph is
temporary, however, for the decree of the divine court is followed

---

[1] The support which was presumed to have been found in the Ras Shamra
tablets for the existence of a belief in divine kingship among the Canaanites has
been questioned recently by R. de Langhe in his essay on "Myth, Ritual and
Kingship in the Ras Shamra Tablets", *Myth, Ritual and Kingship*, ed. S. H.
Hooke, 1958, pp. 122–48. De Langhe is not convinced that the material is cultic,
although in the next essay G. Widengren, writing on "Early Hebrew Myths and
Their Interpretation" (pp. 149–203), writes (p. 156): "The chief value of the
Ugaritic texts . . . lies in the fact that they so clearly exhibit the ritual aspects
of myth." O. R. Gurney, in an essay on "Hittite Kingship" in the same volume
(pp. 105–21), feels that the evidence is against a belief in divine kingship among
the Hittites.

[2] E.g. Ps. 13; 22; 54; 59; 69—71; 74; 88; 89.39–53(38–52).

[3] As by A. R. Johnson, op. cit., and in "The Rôle of the King in the Jerusalem
Cultus", *The Labyrinth*, ed. S. H. Hooke, pp. 71–112; cf. I. Engnell, in "The
'Ebed Yahweh Songs and the Suffering Messiah in 'Deutero-Isaiah' ",
B.J.R.L., 31, 1948, pp. 56f, and *Studies in Divine Kingship in the Ancient Near
East*, 1943, p. 210, n. 2.

[4] The historical emphasis in the Psalms is of great importance, and it should
not be overlooked by those who place them in a ritual setting. Thus A. R.
Johnson, in *The Labyrinth*, pp. 95–7, writing of Ps. 46, maintains that it is as the
sun-god, Elyon, that Yahweh triumphs over the powers of darkness and saves
his people at dawn. His evaluation of the background may be correct, but it must
not be forgotten that God's re-creative work, as it is described in this psalm, is
to be seen in history, not in ritual, and that the recurrent refrain is not a reference
to the sun-god, but speaks of Yahweh of hosts, the God of Jacob. Cf. S. Mowinckel,
The Psalms in Israel's Worship, I, pp. 241–6, *He That Cometh*, pp. 86f, 454f.

by their defeat and subjugation, and dominion over them is given to the Son of man, representing the faithful remnant of Israel. On the other hand, we have the motif of Yahweh's conquest over chaos symbolised by the fourth beast, who, at this final battle, must be slain and destroyed. As in other applications of the myth, whether cultic or historical, it is the people who suffer initial defeat, and Yahweh who gains victory; the rule of the righteous is restored to them, but it is the gift of God, not the result of their own achievement.[1] It has, indeed, been suggested that the fourth monster is in fact killed by the Son of man,[2] but there is nothing in the text to support such a theory. It is, of course, equally true that the text does not say that the fourth beast was slain by the "one that was ancient of days"; the omission, however, is undoubtedly the result of a desire to avoid crude anthropomorphism in a context which has passed beyond prophetic metaphor to visionary experience: that the beast's destruction is the direct consequence of the divine judgement is irrefutable.

This idea of the heavenly judgement is another feature in the reinterpretation of the myth which is found also in the Psalms. Again and again we find there that Yahweh's kingship and his judgement are linked.[3] Psalms which extol his activities, such as 89, speak of his victory over alien forces, the establishment of his throne in righteousness and justice, and his exaltation of Israel and her king;[4] those which appeal for help, or speak of deliverance, give as the basis of their appeal, or the reason for recovery, the individual's integrity and right relationship with God.[5] The sequence of thought is logical, since God's decisive action must be at once the re-establishment of his kingship and the manifestation of his righteousness, which punishes the wicked and rewards the humble. Daniel's vision is a pictorial representation of an idea which pervades the psalter, whether it is expressed there in historical, cultic or eschatological terms.

---

[1] The saints of the Most High have the same passive rôle in the explanation of the vision. The context of the ambiguous words וְדִינָא יְהִב לְקַדִּישֵׁי עֶלְיוֹנִין in 7.22 suggests that they should be understood as meaning "and judgement was given for the saints of the Most High".

[2] E.g. J. A. Emerton, "The Origin of the Son of Man Imagery", *J.T.S.*, new series, 9, 1958, p. 232. The passive rôle of the Son of man is a further argument against the suggestion that Daniel has been influenced by the Urmensch figure.

[3] Cf. Ps. 96—99.   [4] See also Ps. 47; 98; 105.

[5] See Ps. 7; 9; 17; 18; 94. Salvation is also said to be conditional on right behaviour; see Ps. 15; 26; 37.

3. THE RESTORATION OF ISRAEL

A feature in Daniel's vision which has aroused considerable discussion is the fact that the "one like a Son of man" does not make his appearance on the scene until comparatively late—not, in fact, until after the destruction of the fourth beast. In the exposition, however, the saints are present from the beginning, first in the power of their enemies, and finally exercising rule over all nations. Why, then, is there this apparent disagreement between the vision and Daniel's own explanation?[1]

In attempting to understand this problem it must be remembered that this "disagreement" is bound to arise in any endeavour to recast mythological concepts in terms which can in any sense be considered as historical. The inconsistency is not confined to Daniel, but is inherent in all attempts to express the continuation of a remnant in terms of creation mythology. The significant difference between the original myth and its application is that in the latter, man himself is already in existence. Thus the inconsistency between vision and interpretation in Daniel arises because the former takes its terms from a mythology which speaks of man's creation as subsequent to the rule of the beast, while the latter speaks of "historical" events in which man plays a part. Yahweh's ancient conquest of the dragon is re-enacted on the plane of history, just as it was re-enacted in the situation—whether cultic or historical—reflected in the Psalms. In neither case, however, can the re-enactment be an exact repetition of events; for while the original order was (1) The temporary triumph of chaos; (2) Yahweh's victory and enthronement; (3) The creation of man,

[1] A. M. Farrer, *St Mark*, p. 260, argues that the late appearance of the Son of man in Dan. 7 is due to the author's dependence on Gen. 1 as his model: just as Adam appears after the "decree" in Gen. 1.26 and as a consequence of it, so here the Son of man appears only after a comparable decree. There is, however, no real parallel between the declaration of Yahweh's intention to create man in Gen. 1.26, and the judgement of the beasts in Dan. 7.11f. If there is any connection between the two accounts, it would seem rather to lie in the "decrees" made *after* the appearance of Adam and the Son of man, in both of which man is expressly given dominion and authority. Obviously this authority can be given to man only when he already exists, and therefore the fact that v. 28 follows v. 27 in Gen. 1, and v. 14 follows v. 13 in Dan. 7 is of no significance. Indeed, the "chronology" of the vision—if, indeed, it is permissible to argue in these terms at all—departs radically from Gen. 1, since the actual (and not merely the intended or implied) subjugation of the beasts takes place before the one like a Son of man appears on the scene.

any re-enactment of the primitive conflict must take man's existence into account. In the myth, man's creation is the final event, but in history the primeval battle is reflected in the conflict between the nation and its enemies: thus man, whose existence is the outcome of Yahweh's victory, becomes, on the empirical level, one of the contestants in the preceding battle!

The ideas connected with the re-enactment of the myth are thus not so much those of re-creation, but rather of restoration. The New Year festival, where it existed, depicted not a re-creation of the people but a restoration—their deliverance from the powers of chaos, which annually raised their heads and threatened the life and welfare of the nation. Deutero-Isaiah, describing the Exodus in terms of the creation, speaks of the destruction of Rahab and the dragon: we might expect him to go on to speak of the creation of Israel, but instead he speaks of the people's redemption:[1] their creation goes further back than the Exodus—to Abraham their father.[2] The Restoration, the new Exodus, is described in similar terms: the sea will be divided and the wild beasts subdued.[3] Once again, however, Israel is already in existence: the nation will therefore pass through the waters of chaos,[4] and the re-creation of nature is designed for the benefit of the people whom Yahweh has already created and chosen.[5] In Dan. 7, too, man himself is already in existence, in the shape of the saints of the Most High. No mention is made of his re-creation, or even of giving him a new heart; for though he is in a sorry plight this is due, not to powers of sin within, but to human enemies who have crushed him beneath their feet (v. 7). The powers of chaos have burst their bonds and man is in their power: only God can subdue them again and restore the kingdom to man.

It is because Daniel is speaking in terms of restoration rather than of re-creation that there is an apparent disagreement between his vision and the subsequent interpretation. The vision, faithful to the creation mythology, depicts the appearance of man as subsequent to the destruction of the beast; the interpretation admits that he has existed all along. Both are correct. The apocalyptic imagery is correct in depicting the revolt of powers hostile to God as the partial reversal of his work of creation: his intention to give the kingdom to man is temporarily thwarted by the rebellion of the

---

[1] Isa. 51.9-11.   [2] Isa. 51.1f, cf. 52.4.   [3] Isa. 43. 15-20.
[4] Isa. 43.1-3.   [5] Isa. 43.20f.

beasts. But Daniel's interpretation of the myth is equally correct:
even though the saints may not yet enjoy the authority which they
were intended to exercise, they are nevertheless already in existence, and what is needed is not man's re-creation but his restoration to power.

Although the absence of the "one like a Son of man" from the
first part of the vision has so frequently attracted comment, a
parallel feature—the absence of the "beasts" in the final part—
appears to have been overlooked. This omission is surely of considerable significance, however, for while mythology has no room
for man in the first part of the vision—and, moreover, the author
may well have felt that a description of the beasts trampling on man
would not have been fitting—it is surprising to find in the final
section that the beasts are not mentioned as the subjects of the
Son of man, especially as it has been stated in v. 12 that their
lives are to be spared for a time. Thus the interest in the first part
of the vision is centred entirely on the beasts, not on their victims,
and in the final part it is centred on the one like a Son of man, and
his subjects merely serve to emphasize his authority. Since man is
not mentioned before the judgement, and the beasts are not mentioned afterwards, the contrast is not between a time when the
beasts rule over man and a time when man rules over the beasts.
Rather the comparison is between the whole picture before the
judgement and the whole picture afterwards, between the nature
of the dominion of the beasts on the one hand, and that of the Son
of man on the other. Thus we find that the beasts, who seize power
for themselves and trample their victims underfoot, are justly
condemned by God, while the one like a Son of man is given
dominion over the nations, and his rule is authorized by God. The
beasts, representing the powers alien to God, are pictured as rising
from the sea; the Son of man, inheritor of God's promises to
Adam, is seen coming with the clouds of heaven.[1] The kingdom

[1] Cf. H. H. Rowley, *Darius the Mede and the Four World Empires in the Book
of Daniel*, 1935, p. 62, n. 2. There is controversy over both the meaning and
the reading of this phrase. Various attempts have been made to explain the
presence of the clouds, which elsewhere in the Old Testament appear only as
natural phenomena or in theophanies. Mowinckel, *He That Cometh*, pp. 352,
420–37, traces them to the Anthropos tradition. A. Feuillet, "Le Fils de l'homme
de Daniel et la tradition biblique", *Revue Biblique*, 60, 1953, pp. 170–202, 321–
346, links the Son of man with the human figure of Ezek. 1, and regards both as a
visible manifestation of God's glory. J. A. Emerton, op. cit., sees the clouds as
evidence that the figure of the Ancient of days and of one like a Son of man were,
in the original myth, El Elyon and Baal-Yahweh. R. B. Y. Scott, "Behold He

of the beasts is only temporary; that of the Son of man is to endure for ever. The real basis of the contrast is brought out quite clearly by Daniel himself in the explanation given in vv. 17 and 18. His simple interpretation mentions only two features: one is the statement that the four beasts are four kings who will rise from the earth; the other is the assurance that the saints of the Most High will receive the kingdom for ever and ever. In these two sentences Daniel sums up the heart of his contrast between the kingdoms of this earth and the kingdom which is from above.

Although the contrast between man and beast is clearly drawn, therefore, it is not made directly: rather it is seen in the relationship which each has to God. As we have already noted,[1] the twin ideas of Israel's enemies as beasts and Israel as Son of man are linked together but are successive rather than simultaneous: the dominion of man can only follow the subjection of the beast, and if our interpretation of the significance of the beastly character is correct, then their subjection perhaps implies that they are no longer beasts. The central issue is not whether man is "over" or "under" the beasts, but which of them has dominion.

In so far as the phrase "Son of man" is used to convey dignity, and not in connection with the preceding defeat, there is justification for those who say that the Son of man in Daniel does not suffer.[2] In fact, however, such a statement is a dangerous half-truth and conceals the author's real meaning. He may well have felt that the human figure was an inappropriate symbol for the people of Israel during their tribulation,[3] but the Son of man clearly represents in some way the saints of the Most High, and there can be no doubt at all that they suffered. There is, it is true, only one brief reference to their experiences in the vision—in v. 7 —but this was sufficient to make the author's meaning clear. There was no need for him to elaborate the theme or to emphasize the severity of their sufferings, for they were only too much in evidence, and were indeed the very cause of the book's existence. The Son of man may symbolize the victory of the saints and not their suffering,

---

Cometh with Clouds", *N.T.S.*, 5, 1959, pp. 127–32, holds that the phrase refers to the whole scene, not simply to the Son of man. A comparison with Ps. 8, however—and we may perhaps add Ezek. 28.12–15—suggests that there is no real reason why the clouds should not be extended to "Man" in this context.

[1] Above, p. 19.

[2] E.g. W. Manson, *Jesus the Messiah*, pp. 7f.

[3] Cf. Ps. 22.7(6), where the indignity of the one "scorned by men and despised by the people" is such that he speaks of himself as "a worm, and no man".

but unless we detach him from them and regard him as a separate figure with independent experiences we cannot dissociate him from what happens to them.[1] There is no justification for the assumption made by many scholars that the saints "become the Son of man in being enthroned; or, Son of man in the name of the dignity which they put on".[2] The vision must be interpreted in terms of Daniel's explanation, and not vice versa, and if the details of the one do not tally with those of the other, then the solution should be sought in the comparative inflexibility of the author's mythological material, rather than in suggestions of metaphysical metamorphoses. There is no indication that any change has taken place in their nature between v. 7 and v. 13. Indeed, if we are going to argue in chronological terms at all—and it is doubtful whether they are in fact appropriate—then we must note that in v. 13, where the Son of man is actually mentioned, he has not yet been glorified: his human form may mark him out as destined for dominion, but this has not yet been given to him, so that it would seem that the Son of man represents the saints of the Most High before their glorification as well as after.[3] We cannot, therefore, speak of the saints "becoming" the Son of man. Rather, they "become" what they have always been: their rightful authority has been usurped by the beasts, whose rebellion against God inevitably included the denial of dominion to his chosen ruler, man. Now, however, Yahweh's original purpose in creation is renewed, and man is again to be given sovereignty.

The suggestion that the Son of man does not suffer therefore rests upon a false understanding of his relationship with those he represents. For when Daniel describes Israel as Son of man he is not imagining some new dignity which is to be conferred upon the nation: rather he is revealing what Israel has in fact been all along, and is already acknowledged to be in the heavenly sphere. The fact has been hidden because the beasts were in revolt and did not

---

[1] Cf. W. D. Davies, *Paul and Rabbinic Judaism*, 2nd edn, 1955, p. 280 n: "The Son of Man in Daniel is a suffering figure—he represents the Saints of the Most High who are persecuted; cf. Dan. 7.21, 25; the whole context points to a suffering Son of Man."

[2] A. M. Farrer, *St Mark*, p. 260.

[3] Cf. C. F. D. Moule, "From Defendant to Judge—and Deliverer: an Enquiry into the use and limitations of the theme of Vindication in the New Testament", *S.N.T.S. Bulletin* III, 1952, p. 45: " 'The Son of Man' already means the representative of God's chosen people, destined through suffering to be exalted".

acknowledge Israel as the world's rightful ruler, and spectators could therefore be excused for not recognizing the nation as the heir of Adam. It is false to say that Israel "becomes" Son of man after being vindicated; the vindication takes place precisely because Israel is already the true Son of man to whom dominion belongs by right. The enthronement of the Son of man means that the dominion of Adam is restored to the rightful owner, and the saints are seen to be what they have always been—the inheritors of God's promises, the elect and true "Man", in contrast to those whose sin and rebellion has reduced them to the level of beasts. Moreover, apocalyptic vision, like the prophetic "symbolism" which it replaces, is not merely an expression of an individual's conviction about the future: as future events in some degree take place already in the prophet's action, so, to an even greater extent, the apocalyptist's vision of the future is already present in the heavenly world.[1] The saints who are now crushed on earth are already recognized in heaven as those to whom the dominion belongs, and stand even now before the throne of the Most High. The appearance and enthronement of the Son of man are thus seen to be integral parts of the whole book of Daniel, for the author's conviction that God will intervene on behalf of his saints, and that he will end their sufferings and give them the kingdom, is here given its most dramatic expression. Moreover, the beasts and the human figure are not mere symbols which reveal or disguise—according to the readers' knowledge—the real characters in the drama. Daniel's vision is not simply a fanciful and pictorial representation of a pious hope that everything will come right in the end, but a revelation which conveys a message of significance to a tortured people. Daniel offers a message of hope to despairing men; but it is important to notice the basis of this hope. It is not merely a hope that Israel will one day become Son of man, but a certain conviction based on the fact that Israel is already Son of man. It is precisely because the nation is the one to whom dominion and authority belong, that Daniel can confidently promise a glorious future: these things will come to the saints in Israel because they are the inheritors of the promises of God. The foundation of Daniel's confidence for the future is his faith that the righteous in Israel are the true Son of man, a fact which is known already in heaven, is now revealed to the elect, but will be known to others only at the End.

[1] Cf. C. K. Barrett, "New Testament Eschatology", *S.J.T.*, 6, 1953, pp. 138f.

It is because the saints are the Son of man, and because the kingdom is thereby theirs by right, that their ultimate victory over the beasts is assured.

Israel may thus fairly be described, not as Son of man *futurus* or *designatus*, but rather as Son of man *absconditus* and even *passurus*.[1] It is easy to understand, however, why, when the "one like a Son of man" ceased to be understood of Israel and became a distinct and separate figure, he was thought of in connection with the glory of the future, and not the sufferings of the present. Both because it was a title fitting for one given authority by God, and because the emphasis was thrown more and more upon the future glory, in contrast to the all too familiar reality of the present, the Son of man grew apart from the concepts of suffering and humiliation. Men failed to realize that in this vision of Daniel it is "written of the Son of man, that he should suffer many things and be treated with contempt."[2]

4. APPENDED NOTE:

THE TERM "SON OF MAN" IN THE REST OF THE OLD TESTAMENT

Apart from its use in the book of Ezekiel, the phrase בֶּן־אָדָם is found rarely in the Old Testament. Its chief use is in synonymous parallelism,[3] and the expression thus belongs, outside Ezekiel, to the language of poetry.[4] On no fewer than six of the twelve occasions when it is used in this way,[5] the phrase depicts man in his weakness and frailty in contrast to the might and character of God —a contrast which is often found, also, in the use of the words

---

[1] The terms are those used of the Messiah by C. K. Barrett in discussing the hidden Messiahship of Jesus, *The Holy Spirit and the Gospel Tradition*, 1947, p. 119.

[2] Mark 9.12.

[3] It is parallel with אִישׁ in Num.23.19; Job 35.8; Ps. 80.18 (17); Jer. 49.18, 33; 50.40; 51.43; with אֱנוֹשׁ in Job 25.6; Ps. 8.5 (4); Isa. 51.12; 56.2; and with נְדִיבִים in Ps. 146.3. Another doubtful use is in Job 16.21, parallel with גֶּבֶר; but here we should perhaps read וּבֵין.

[4] Jer. 49.18 and 50.40 are no exceptions, even though they now appear in prose contexts. Cf. 49.33 and 51.43.

[5] Num. 23.19; Job. 25.6; 35.8; Ps. 8.5 (4); 146.3; Isa. 51.12. The proportion is, in fact, greater than the figures suggest, since four of the remaining six passages—those in Jeremiah—appear to be repetitions of a single refrain.

with which בֶּן־אָדָם is paralleled.[1] In Ps. 8, a psalm which reflects the same ideas as those in Gen. 1, the phrase is applied to man in contrast to God on the one side, and to the beasts over which he rules on the other, and is thus used to express man's true relationship both with God and with the rest of creation.[2] In view of its rarity elsewhere, the frequency with which the phrase is used in Ezekiel is all the more impressive. There and in Dan. 8.17 (where it has been taken from Ezek. 2.1), the phrase is used in the vocative to address Ezekiel and Daniel, and it is noteworthy that it is applied to two men who have had visions of heavenly things, a fact which suggests that this special use arises quite naturally out of those features which are characteristic of its use elsewhere in the Old Testament—namely its poetic nature and its expression of the contrast between man and God. There seems no reason to suppose that the phrase here has any more particular significance.[3]

The plural form of the phrase, בְּנֵי־אָדָם, is more widely used, mostly as a poetic phrase for mankind. It is found in poetry and passages of elevated language,[4] and is used extensively in the Psalms, often emphasizing the position of man in relation to God;[5] it is thus close in use and meaning to the singular form, though it is not confined to passages of synonymous parallelism.[6] Of particular interest for our investigation is its use in Dan. 10.16 to describe one of the angelic beings of Daniel's vision: he is said to be "in the likeness of the sons of men".[7] On two occasions the phrase is used with the parallel expression בְּנֵי־אִישׁ; then it has a slightly

---

[1] Cf., e.g., Job 9.32; 32.13; Hos. 11.9 (אִישׁ): 2 Chron. 14.10(11); Job 9.2; 10.4f; 33.12; Ps. 9.20f (19f); 103.15 (אֱנוֹשׁ): Job 12.21; 34.18 (נְדִיבִים).

[2] Cf. M. Black, "Unsolved New Testament Problems: The 'Son of Man' in the Old Biblical Literature", E.T., 60, 1949, p. 11: "Originally a poetic synonym for man as such, 'son of man' might refer to him both in his creaturely insignificance before God, but also in his divinely appointed human dignity over against the rest of creation."

[3] Cf. the similar vocative use of אִישׁ in Dan. 10.11,19.

[4] It appears in the words of Yahweh in 2 Sam. 7.14 and Ezek. 31.14; in a prayer in Jer. 32.19; and in a vision in Dan. 10.16.

[5] E.g. Ps. 11.4; 14.2; 36.8(7); 66.5; 89.48(47); 90.3; 107.8,15,21,31; 115.16. Note also Ps. 57.5(4), where the sons of men stand in contrast to the "lions" which devour them.

[6] It is used in parallelism in Deut. 32.8; 2 Sam. 7.14; Ps. 21.11(10); Prov. 8.4,31; Isa. 52.14; Mic. 5.6(7).

[7] An alternative reading gives the singular, בֶּן־אָדָם, but the plural is more likely.

different meaning, and the two represent "the low and the high" among men.[1] This phrase בְּנֵי־אִישׁ occurs elsewhere with the general meaning "sons of man",[2] but in Gen. 42.11,13, it is used with a more specific meaning, to denote the sons of a particular man, and this is the normal use of the singular form, בֶּן־אִישׁ.[3]

A third phrase, בֶּן־אֱנוֹשׁ, occurs only once, in Ps. 144.3, in synonymous parallelism with אָדָם, and with the meaning which בֶּן־אָדָם has elsewhere. The plural form of the equivalent Aramaic phrase, בְּנֵי־אֲנָשָׁא, is used in Dan. 2.38 and 5.21, with the meaning "mankind", and the singular, בַּר אֱנָשׁ, is the term used in Dan. 7.13.

---

[1] Ps. 49.3(2); 62.10(9). The remaining uses of בְּנֵי־אָדָם are Ps.12.2(1),9(8); 31.20(19); 45.3(2); 53.3(2); 58.2(1); Prov. 15.11; Joel 1.12.
[2] Ps. 4.3(2); Lam. 3.33.
[3] Lev. 24.10; 1 Sam. 17.12; 2 Sam. 1.13; 17.25; 1 Chron. 11.22.

3

The Son of Man
in 1 Enoch

1. STRUCTURE OF THE BOOK

Controversy about the value of the evidence of the book of Enoch
has raged long and fiercely. At the one extreme stands Rudolf
Otto, who found here the key to Jesus' thought and work;[1] at the
other stands J. Y. Campbell, who dismissed the book as "a conglomeration of fragments of different kinds and diverse origins",
known to us only in manuscripts which are hopelessly corrupt, a
work moreover which is at the best of doubtful religious value,
and therefore unlikely, even if he knew it, to have influenced
Jesus.[2] While it is true that the evidence of Enoch must be treated
with caution, recent study has suggested that there is much valuable pre-Christian material in Enoch, including possibly the
Parables.[3] Moreover, Sjöberg has convincingly demonstrated that
chapters 37—71 are far more of a unity than previous scholars had
allowed.[4] We shall begin our examination, therefore, by treating
the Parables tentatively as a whole, leaving on one side for the
moment the question of sources, and merely noting those sections
which are obvious additions.[5]

Nevertheless, our starting-point will be an analysis of the

---

[1] *The Kingdom of God and the Son of man*, E.Tr. 1938.
[2] "The Origin and Meaning of the Term Son of Man", *J.T.S.*, 48, 1947, pp.
145–55.
[3] Cf. J. Bowman, "The Background of the Term 'Son of Man'", *E.T.*, 59,
1948, pp. 283–8; M. Black, "The Eschatology of the Similitudes of Enoch",
J.T.S., new series, 3, 1952, pp. 1–10.
[4] E. Sjöberg, *Der Menschensohn im Äthiopischen Henochbuch*, 1946, pp. 24–33.
[5] These are the "Noachic" fragments in 39.1–2a; 54.7—55.2; 60; 65.1—
69.25. Chapter 59 appears to be out of place, and may be secondary. Cf. E.
Sjöberg, op. cit., p. 33.

Parables which will lay more weight on the distribution of names than the most drastic of the theories which regard them as evidence for two main sources underlying the present text. For in spite of the suggestion made by Beer[1] and developed by Charles[2] that, in addition to the "Noachic" fragments, two sources can be distinguished, one speaking of the "Son of man" and the other of the "Elect One", and in spite of the fact that scholars have mostly followed them in regarding the material in its present form as a mosaic, discussion of the figure of the "Son of man" has not generally drawn any distinction between these two titles, but has regarded passages referring to the "Elect One" and those which speak of the "Son of man" as descriptive of the same figure. Even Charles could find little difference in the attributes predicated of the central figure in the supposed sources.[3]

The distribution of the various titles throughout the Parables can best be seen in tabular form (see opposite).

From this table one significant feature about the distribution of the titles is at once clear: the two most important—"Son of man" and "Elect One"—are each confined to certain blocks of material, which we may define thus:

A 38—45   The Elect One
B 46—8   The Son of man
C 49—62.1   The Elect One
D 62.2—71   The Son of man

There are two possible explanations of this significant division. One is that Charles is right in his general assumption that two main sources underlie the Parables—though not necessarily right in his detailed analysis. The other is that the author of the Parables deliberately used the titles in this way for some special purpose. A closer examination of the material may suggest which of these explanations is the more likely.

---

[1] G. Beer, in E. Kautzsch, *Die Apokryphen und Pseudepigraphen des Alten Testaments*, 1900, pp. 227f.
[2] R. H. Charles, *The Book of Enoch*, 1912, pp. 64f.
[3] Loc. cit.

ANALYSIS OF 1 ENOCH 38—71

(a) The First Parable 38—44

ELECT ONE

38   *The subject* of the first parable: the righteous and the Righteous One to appear; the wicked to be judged and driven from the earth.

39   *The vision* begins. Enoch sees the dwelling-place of the righteous, and the Elect One with them.

40   He sees four angels standing before the Lord of Spirits.

41   He sees the judgement of men, followed by astronomical secrets.

42   Wisdom is extolled.

43—44   More astronomical secrets are revealed.

(b) The Second Parable 45—57

ELECT ONE

45   *The subject* of the second parable: the destruction of sinners, judged by the Elect One, who will be enthroned and who will dwell with the elect in a transformed heaven and earth.

SON OF MAN

46   *The vision* begins. Enoch sees the Head of Days and the Son of man who is righteous and who has been chosen; he is to uproot the mighty and the sinners.

47   The prayer of the righteous is heard. Enoch sees the Head of Days enthroned; the books are opened.

48   The Son of man (already named before creation) is named. He is the stay of the righteous. The fate of the wicked described.

ELECT ONE

49   Wisdom dwells in the Elect One.

50   The future victory of the righteous and punishment of the wicked.

51   The resurrection of the dead, at the appearance of the Elect One, who is to sit on God's throne: joy on the earth.

52   The mountains of metal will melt before the Elect One.

53   Preparations for the destruction of sinners.

54   Chains prepared for Azazel.

54.7—
55.2   Fragment about Noah.

55   The mighty will have to behold the Elect One enthroned.
56   The angels of punishment. Final cataclysm.
57   Enoch sees men coming from all quarters.

(c) The Third Parable 58—69

ELECT ONE

58   *The subject* of the third parable: the glorious lot of the righteous.
59   Secrets of thunder and lightning.
60   Fragment from Noah.[1]
61   *The vision* begins. Enoch sees angels measuring. The elect will be safe. The Lord of Spirits places the Elect One on the throne of glory, where he acts as judge. Exultation in heaven.
62   The kings are told to look at the Elect One and see if they recognize him.

SON OF MAN

They are seized with terror when they see the Son of man enthroned in glory. They will worship him, but will be delivered up to punishment, while the righteous rejoice and live with the Son of man.
63   The kings will repent, but they will be driven from the presence of the Son of man.
64   Enoch sees the fallen angels.
65.1—
  69.25 Fragment from Noah.
69.26– Joy because the name of the Son of man has been revealed. He
  29   has appeared and been enthroned as judge.

(d) The Epilogue 70—1

SON OF MAN

70   Enoch is raised to heaven.
71   Enoch is greeted by angels and told that he is the Son of man.

2. REVELATION OF ENOCH

While it is true that we cannot expect apocalyptic thought to present a systematic theology, or to fit neatly into a logical pattern, the

---

[1] This section contains the phrase "son of man" in 60.10, but it is used there in an entirely "non-technical" sense; the seer himself is addressed as "son of man", as in Ezekiel and Dan. 8.17.

analysis above suggests that Enoch is not so completely without form and void of profound thought as some scholars have maintained. Thus we see that each "parable" follows the simple but consistent plan of an introductory chapter which states in broad outline the theme of the whole,[1] followed by the vision, to which explanations are added where necessary.

After the general introduction in chapter 37, the first parable begins in the following chapter with a statement of its theme, which is the quite general one of the appearing of the righteous—together with the "Righteous One"—and the subsequent judgement of the wicked, who are to be driven from the face of the earth. This theme is developed in the vision which follows, in which Enoch sees the resting place of the righteous and the judgement of sinners, who are dragged off for punishment. The "Elect One" is mentioned only twice (39.6; 40.5), and on both occasions it is in association with the "elect"; the same association is found in the prologue to the parable in 38, but the terms used there are the "Righteous One" and the "righteous". Although the titles used are different, it is clear that the same being is meant.[2] Nowhere in this parable does this figure exercise any particular function: he merely "appears".

When we come to the second parable, we find that the subject is more specific. As stated in the prologue in chapter 45, it is the destruction of sinners, who are to be judged by the enthroned Elect One, who is to dwell with the elect ones in a transformed heaven and earth. The first and last elements here are repeated from the first parable; it is the positive rôle of the Elect One as judge which is new and significant.

Having stated what is to be the subject of his second parable, the author now describes the vision itself. At first sight it might appear that he has broken off from his original purpose and has introduced a different theme, but closer examination shows that he has been faithful to his subject. The vision in fact begins with an elaborated version of Dan. 7.9–14 and an explanation of it.

---

[1] Charles, *Enoch*, p. 83, says that "It is idle to expect an accurate description of the contents of the Parable from the opening verse or superscription". He has not looked far enough, however: it is the whole chapter which must be taken into account, and not merely the introductory phrase "concerning the . . ." (which is, in any case, not used in 38). There is no break after 38.2 or 58.2, and no reason, therefore, why we should confine our attention, as Charles does, to the first two verses of these chapters.

[2] Even Charles does not distinguish here.

Enoch sees a figure like a man, and it is explained to him that this is the Son of man who has righteousness, who reveals what is hidden, who has been chosen by the Lord of Spirits and is pre-eminent before him, and who is to uproot the mighty from their places and bring them to punishment. In case Enoch still has any doubt as to who this Son of man is, all is made plain in chapter 48. There he is named in the presence of the Lord of Spirits (v. 2) as the one named by him before the creation (v. 3); he is revealed as the one who has been chosen (v. 6), and whom all men will worship (v. 5). Hitherto he has been hidden (v. 6), but he is revealed to the righteous, who are saved by him (v. 7, cf. v. 4); the mighty, on the other hand, to whom he has not been revealed, will be punished (vv. 8,9), because "they have denied the Lord of Spirits and His Anointed" (v. 10). All doubt in the readers' minds as to who this Son of man is should by now have been dispelled. The Son of man of Enoch's vision is the one who is "chosen" and "anointed", who is closely associated both with the righteous and with the punishment of the wicked. In other words, he is the "Elect One", who was stated in chapter 45 to be the subject of this parable; now that he has been revealed for what he is, the author can refer to him by his proper title, and in the rest of the parable he is spoken of again as the "Elect One". The remaining chapters elaborate the same theme; as in the first parable, the blessedness of the elect and the overthrow of the mighty are described, but the Elect One is the central figure throughout.

The theme of the third parable, as stated in 58, is said to be the glorious lot of the righteous. In fact, although much of what follows is concerned with this theme, the reverse side of the picture—the dismay and destruction of the wicked at the revelation of the Son of man—is equally important. It is possible that part of the prologue has been lost through the additions of the fragments about Noah.

The vision itself begins in 61, where the Elect One is enthroned and is entrusted with judgement. In the following chapter the "mighty" of the earth are commanded to look at him and see if they recognize him. This they do, and they are immediately seized with terror and confusion "when they see that Son of man sitting on the throne of his glory". Once again we have an abrupt change in names, in the middle of a parable, and from now till the end of chapter 71 the author continues to speak of the Son of man,

4—S.O.M.

not the Elect One. The point at which this is done is of great significance: the phrase "Son of man" is reintroduced immediately
after the enthronement of the Elect One and his manifestation to
the kings and the mighty. When they see the Elect One enthroned
they are overcome with pain and terror because they recognize
him to be "that Son of man". The next verses tell us how the Son
of man was hidden from the beginning but was revealed to the
elect; they will dwell with him for ever, but the kings and the
mighty will be punished. The whole passage is very similar to that
in chapter 48, which occurs immediately after the naming of the
Son of man in the second parable.

The final verses of this parable sum up its theme, and so com-
pensate for any inadequacy in the prologue. A brief description is
given of the joy of the elect because the name of the Son of man
had been revealed to them,[1] and of his manifestation, enthronement, and judgement.

The pattern of this parable thus closely follows that of the
second, and yet is at the same time the reverse of it. In the second
parable we have a vision of the enthronement of the Son of man,
followed by the question "Who is he?" and the revelation that he
is the Elect One. Here, we have a vision of the enthronement of the
Elect One, followed by the question to the kings "Who is he?" and
the realization that he is the Son of man. Thus we are presented
with two propositions which, while certainly compatible, do not
seem to lead to any profound conclusion:

(a) The Son of man is the Elect One

(b) The Elect One is the Son of man

At first sight the author of Enoch seems to be leading us in a
circle. Moreover, if we begin with the preconceived theory that
"Son of man" was in any case a recognized title of the Elect One
at that time, then we may well reach the conclusion that what
Enoch has to reveal is worthless and takes us nowhere at all—not
even in a circular argument—since he merely tells us twice over
what we already know. The final chapters, in which Enoch him-

---

[1] Charles (*Enoch*, p. 140) describes this clause as "obscure". Its meaning becomes clear when considered in relation to the interpretation of the parables which
we have given. The name of the Son of man has been revealed to the elect (cf.
48.7 and 62.7), and since it is those who know him who will be saved when he
appears they have good cause to rejoice.

self is declared to be the Son of man, then merely add to the confusion.

The distribution of the titles, however, suggests, as we have seen, that the author, at least, was under the impression that he was saying something of significance when he identified the Son of man with the Elect One. We must ask, therefore, why it was that he thought it necessary to say the same thing twice, working in opposite directions. Was he trying to emphasize his point, or simply indulging his flight of fancy? These motives may have contributed to the reduplication, but a more significant reason is discovered when we examine the setting of the two disclosures.

In the second parable, Enoch sees the Son of man in heaven with the Head of Days; his name is named before the Lord of Spirits, and is revealed to the righteous and elect. Although the Son of man is revealed as the Elect One, Enoch does not yet see him enthroned, and his judgement of men and the punishment of sinners are still spoken of as future events. In the third parable, however, the Elect One is actually enthroned.[1] This time the revelation is not made before the throne of God in heaven, but to "those who dwell on the earth".[2] In the second parable, the identification is made known in heaven, and is passed on to the righteous and elect, who are privileged to share in the secrets of heaven. In the third, however, the time for the general unveiling has arrived, and the secret which has sustained the elect is now made known to others, to whom it can bring only discomfiture. Now, too, we see the reason for the reversal in the form of the revelation. For in the second parable we are shown the Son of man, whose revelation to the righteous as the Elect One brings them hope. In the last parable, on the other hand, we begin with the Day of the Elect One and his enthronement. The figure is recognizable as the Elect One from the start, but it is only on closer examination that those brought to judgement before him discover that he is in fact the Son of man.

At this stage, with the identification made doubly plain, there is only one question left unanswered: who *is* this Son of man, known to the righteous to be the Elect One? His name, we are told, has been revealed to the elect, and his identity is the secret which has been entrusted to them. Do they, then, know merely that "this Son of man" is the Elect One—is the "name" revealed to them

---

[1] 61.8; 62.2,5. [2] 62.1.

simply "Elect One", or do they in fact know him by a personal name?

The answer is given in chapter 71, which forms the climax and logical conclusion of the whole section. This final chapter provides a third proposition, and so supplies the solution to the problem of the Parables. The secret which is known now to the elect[1]— which is, indeed, being made known by means of this book—is that the Son of man who will one day be manifested to all as the Elect One of righteousness and faith is Enoch himself.

To many scholars, the epilogue has proved, not the key to the riddle, but a stumbling-block. How, it is asked, can Enoch be identified with a heavenly pre-existent being?[2] It is no answer either to "amend" the text, as was done by Charles,[3] or to dismiss the final chapters as a later addition;[4] to do so is merely to push the problem one stage further on, and to leave unexplained how an editor or translator was able to make the identification. The most probable answer to the problem is that it is one which never existed for the author; his main concern is not with metaphysical speculations, but with the "disclosure" of a secret truth: already in heaven God has revealed the name of his Elect One, who is shortly to preside at the final judgement. This Son of man is the Righteous One *par excellence*, who will preserve the righteous from the final cataclysm which will descend upon the wicked. His name is now revealed to the elect as Enoch, the man who according to Genesis "walked with God", and whose "ascension" was regarded as the result of his righteousness.

It is not, indeed, certain whether the author did in fact regard the Son of man as "pre-existent".[5] The basis for the belief is the statement in 48.3 that the Son of man was named before the creation, together with those which speak of his being chosen and hidden from the beginning (48.6; 62.7). Since the Son of man is

---

[1] Cf. S. Mowinckel, *He That Cometh*, pp. 386f.

[2] Cf. E. Sjöberg, op. cit., pp. 147–89.

[3] *Enoch*, pp. 144f.

[4] G. Beer, op. cit., p. 228. By contrast, M. Black, in "The Eschatology of the Similitudes of Enoch", *J.T.S.*, new series, 3, 1952, pp. 1–10, argues that chapters 70—1 represent an earlier tradition than 37—69.

[5] Sjöberg argues that the Son of man is pre-existent, op. cit., pp. 83–101. So, too, S. Mowinckel, *He That Cometh*, pp. 370–3. For the opposite view, see M. Black, "Unsolved New Testament Problems: The 'Son of Man' in the old Biblical Literature", *E.T.*, 60, 1949, pp. 11–15; S.-B., *Kommentar*, II, p. 334; T. W. Manson, "The Son of Man in Daniel, Enoch and the Gospels", *B.J.R.L.*, 32, 1950, pp. 180–8.

also named in 48.2, in the course of one of the visions, it is difficult to maintain that the naming in the next verse must be meant in
the sense of "creating".[1] Nor is the idea of pre-existence necessarily implied in the statement that the Son of man was chosen and
hidden by God before the creation:[2] rather the idea is of the Son
of man as part of the eternal purposes of God, hitherto hidden but
now about to be revealed. It may well be that in expressing this
idea the author has done so in terms borrowed from the "Man" of
eastern mythology; in so doing he has led himself into inconsistency.[3] It is doubtful, however, whether this inconsistency would
have been either obvious or perplexing to the author and his
readers. For apocalyptic by its very nature held together what was
at once present and future, that which was already in existence,
but yet still had to take place. If future earthly events exist already
as heavenly realities,[4] then there is no great inconsistency in the
author's identification of Enoch with the Elect One.

3. THE TERM "SON OF MAN"

We must now consider briefly the much-debated question whether
or not the author was using an established title when he spoke of
the "Son of man". If our interpretation is correct, then it is clear
that the phrase cannot be a mere synonym for the "Elect One". If
"Son of man" is a recognized title, then it must refer to some
heavenly "Man" who had not, hitherto, been identified with the
Elect One, but who was well known in Judaism; we must believe
that the author of the Parables identified these two figures—and
thought, moreover, that in doing so he was doing something significant—and that he then went on to identify both with the man
Enoch. The alternative is to suppose that "Son of man" was *not*
a recognized title and that what the author did was to identify a
"Son of man" (whose name he later reveals) with the figure of the

[1] T. W. Manson, op. cit., p. 182, suggests that the most likely explanation of
the naming is to be found in instances where it means "the designation . . . to
some high destiny".
[2] T. W. Manson, op. cit., pp. 183–5.
[3] A similar inconsistency is found in 2 Esdras 13, where the heavenly man
comes up from the sea; here, too, the inconsistency probably results from the use
of a feature from mythology. Cf. S. Mowinckel, op. cit., pp. 390f.
[4] Cf. C. K. Barrett, "New Testament Eschatology", *S.J.T.*, 6, 1953, pp.
138f.

Elect One. The interpretation which we have given of the Parables suggests that what is being portrayed here is not, in fact, the identification of one heavenly being with another, and then the identification of both with Enoch. Rather it is the revelation of the identity of the Elect One; the man who is God's Elect One is, in fact, named in chapter 48, but the author does not allow his readers to overhear it: like a writer of good detective fiction, he keeps them in suspense until the last page.

Several other factors also tell in favour of this second, simpler, solution. First, we may note that the Ethiopic translator has used three different phrases to translate "Son of man". This, of course, is only secondary evidence, but it suggests that to the translator, at least, the Son of man was not a recognizable figure whose identification with the Elect One would be of significance.[1] More important, the phrase is used almost always with the demonstrative pronoun. While it is possible that the demonstrative may merely represent the Greek definite article,[2] it seems unlikely that this is a sufficient explanation here. Not only does the "this" refer back to the one "whose countenance had the appearance of a man", but its use is in striking contrast to the absence of any comparable demonstrative with "Elect One".[3]

The author first introduces the Son of man with a reference to Daniel's vision, and if we are to understand his meaning, then our interpretation must also begin there. The Son of man is not introduced as a well-known, recognizable figure, but as an enigmatic one which needs explanation: the explanation which follows is certainly an interpretation—or reinterpretation—of Daniel, and the author possibly intended it to be regarded as such by his readers. In chapters 46 and 48 the phrase "Son of man" appears consistently with the demonstrative. Sjöberg, who believes that "Son of man" is a recognizable title of a Redeemer figure, nevertheless agrees that the phrase is not used in these chapters as a title, but in every case points back to the figure in the vision of

---

[1] The variation can scarcely be explained by the theory that different translators have been at work. The phrase *walda sab'ĕ* is used consistently in chapters 46 and 48, but *walda bĕ'ĕsî* is found in 62.5; 69.29 (bis); 71.14; with *walda 'ĕguâla 'ĕmahĕyâw* in 62.7,9,14; 63.11; 69.26,27; 70.1; 71.17.

[2] As maintained by Charles, *Enoch*, pp. 86f. Sjöberg agrees, but maintains that this can only remain a *possibility*, and cannot be proved, op. cit., pp. 43–8.

[3] T. W. Manson, op. cit., p. 178. Manson points out that the Ethiopic gospels do not use a demonstrative with "Son of man", which is there a recognized title.

46.1.[1] He regards the phrase in vv. 2 and 4 of that chapter as a definite reference to the figure which Enoch has seen in v. 1, while the demonstrative in 48.2, occurring after the noun, strongly suggests an underlying Greek demonstrative. Sjöberg writes of 46.3 (where the demonstrative is a copula) that: "Sprachlich kann man ebenso gut 'Dieser ist Der Menschensohn—dem Gerechtigkeit gehört' als 'Dieser ist der Mensch, dem Gerechtigkeit gehört' übersetzen."[2] He maintains, however, on the basis of his interpretation of the Son of man elsewhere in the Similitudes as a "ganz besondere himmlische Mensch", that in either case the phrase has a special association, and cannot be translated simply as "Dieser Mensch (den du gesehen hast) ist der, dem Gerechtigkeit gehört".[3] Working back from this interpretation, he concludes that the same association must be recognized in the other verses, and that the phrase in these chapters points not merely to the vision, but also to the heavenly reality behind it. Such an interpretation, however, is based upon the assumption that the reality was known and accepted. If there is no other evidence to support the contention that the figure of the "Son of man" was already known to the readers—and the way in which the phrase is introduced and explained suggests that it was not—then it cannot be maintained that any special significance attaches itself to the phrase here. Sjöberg agrees that the connection between the Son of man and the vision of 46.1 is still implicit in later passages, even in those cases where the reference is not expressed by means of a demonstrative.[4]

When Sjöberg comes to 71.14, where a statement similar to 46.3 is found, he argues that the relative clause, although parallel to that in the earlier verse, is not to be understood as a closer definition of the Man, but as a reference to the earthly Enoch.[5] Sjöberg is forced to maintain this because for him the Son of man is a heavenly figure, of whom it cannot be said that he is born. If, however, the Son of man is not in himself a recognizable figure, but is simply, in this context, the Son of man who has been revealed to the righteous as the Elect One, then the relative clause can be understood in both verses as an identification. The author is then not merely saying in 46.3 that the figure whom Enoch has

---

[1] E. Sjöberg, *Der Menschensohn im Äthiopischen Henochbuch*, pp. 48–54.
[2] Ibid., p. 50.   [3] Ibid., p. 51.   [4] Enoch 62.7; 69.29. Op. cit., p. 57.
[5] Ibid., p. 56.

seen is the Son of man, and adding the information that righteousness belongs to him; nor is he saying, in 71.14, that Enoch, who is
born to righteousness, is the Son of man. In both cases he is saying
that this figure (or Enoch) is *that Son of man who is born unto
righteousness*—in other words, the Righteous One.

In making righteousness the fundamental characteristic of the
Son of man, the author of the Similitudes has been faithful to the
Danielic vision, where it is the saints of the Most High who are
the Son of man: as we have already seen, the faithful Remnant are
Son of man by virtue of their election by God and their obedience
to his will; in Enoch, we find that the Son of man's other titles are
"The Righteous One" and "The Elect One". But in another respect, also, the author of the Similitudes has to a large extent been
faithful to his source: for it is not only the Son of man who is
described in Enoch as "Righteous" and "Elect"; these titles are
given also to the community which dwells with him. Although the
Son of man himself is an individual, he is nevertheless closely
associated with the community of the righteous of which he is the
head; this is demonstrated by the way in which the terms "The
Righteous One" and "The Elect One" are almost invariably[1]
linked in the text with the plural expressions, "the righteous ones"
and "the elect ones". This link with the corporate nature of
Daniel's figure has been stressed by N. Messel[2] and by T. W.
Manson;[3] the former, indeed, maintained that the Son of man is a
corporate figure in Enoch as in Daniel, but he could do this only
by omitting a great many of the relevant passages as later additions.
Manson preferred to speak of an oscillation between the individual
and the corporate, such as we meet with elsewhere: we may perhaps agree that there is truth in this view, noting that whereas in
Daniel the one like a Son of man is a corporate figure with individual traits, in Enoch he has become an individual with corporate
characteristics; in spite of the shift of emphasis, there is no great
gulf fixed between the interpretations of Daniel and Enoch, for in
the former he is the elect community (which undoubtedly has a
leader at its head) and in the latter he is the leader of the same elect
community. The fortunes of the Son of man are to a large extent

---

[1] The exceptions are 52.6,9; 55.4 and 62.1; in these passages, however, the
context is the Son of man's rôle as judge of the kings and mighty.
[2] *Der Menschensohn in den Bilderreden des Henoch*, 1922.
[3] "The Son of Man in Daniel, Enoch and the Gospels", *B.J.R.L.*, 32, 1950,
pp. 171–93.

bound up with those of the righteous community;[1] Enoch's interpretation would seem to be a natural development from Daniel's own.

In one respect, however, the later reinterpretation would seem to be a wild departure from the sober terms of Daniel's expectation, and this is in the Similitudes' final revelation of Enoch himself as the Son of man. Once again, however, it is possible that this feature also is at least a logical development from Daniel: for once the one like a Son of man has been interpreted as an individual, then there is no more likely or worthy candidate than Enoch, the man who "walked with God" in righteousness. Moreover, it is possible that the author was helped to this interpretation by his reading of the text of Daniel. We have already noticed[2] that in Dan. 8.17 Daniel himself is addressed as "son of man": is it possible that the author of the Similitudes, reading that passage, understood Daniel, the narrator of the visions, to be revealed here as himself the one like a Son of man whom he had seen in his previous vision?[3] If so, then it is understandable that he identifies his own visionary, Enoch, with the same glorious human figure whom his hero had seen in heaven.[4]

4. DATE

One final problem which must be mentioned is the question of the dating of the Similitudes, a subject which has received a great deal of attention, and widely differing solutions. Broadly speaking, scholars fall into four different groups: (*a*) those who uphold an early Maccabean dating, about the middle of the second century B.C.;[5] (*b*) those who place the book later in the Maccabean period, at the beginning of the first century B.C.;[6] (*c*) those who believe

---

[1] E.g. in chapters 45—50.

[2] Above, p. 31.

[3] I owe this suggestion to Professor C. K. Barrett.

[4] If this is a correct interpretation of the author's reasoning, then the use of the phrase "son of man" for Enoch in 60.10 may be a deliberate echo of Dan. 8.17 by the final redactor and intended as a clue to the mystery of the Son of man.

[5] E.g. J. B. Frey, "Apocryphes de l'Ancien Testament", *Dictionnaire de la Bible*, Supplement vol. I, 1928, ed. L. Pirot, cols. 360–4.

[6] E.g. R. H. Charles, *Enoch*, pp. liv, 72f; G. Beer, in E. Kautzsch, *Die Apokryphen und Pseudepigraphen des Alten Testaments*, p. 231.

it to have been written during the Roman period;[1] (d) those who regard it as Christian or post-Christian in origin.[2] The suggestion that the work is Christian is without foundation; there is no hint that the picture of the Son of man owes anything to Christian theology, for while there are similarities between 1 Enoch and the eschatological "Son of man" sayings in the gospels, the distinctively Christian interpretation of the Son of man is absent from the former. This does not, of course, rule out the possibility that the Similitudes are a late Jewish (i.e., post-Christian) work, but the negative evidence of the Qumran scrolls cannot be regarded as in any sense decisive.[3] The evidence of the Similitudes themselves suggests that they should probably be dated during the Roman period, some time between 63 B.C. and A.D. 70,[4] but a more precise dating within these limits is difficult.

While it is not impossible, therefore, that Otto may have been right in his belief that the Similitudes were known to Jesus, it is by no means certain that they were in fact written before or during his lifetime, or that, if they were written, they were widely known. Their importance lies rather in the fact that they are roughly contemporaneous with Jesus, and show us the way in which at least one Jew of this period interpreted Dan. 7. This was not necessarily the only way in which Daniel's vision was interpreted, however: we have no right to assume, simply on the basis of the evidence of 1 Enoch, that during the first half of the first century A.D., the "one like a Son of man" in Dan. 7 was universally interpreted by the Jews as an individual eschatological and glorious judge.

[1] E.g. it has been placed between 64 and 37 B.C. by W. Bousset, *Die Religion des Judentums im späthellenistischen Zeitalter*, 3rd edn, revised by H. Gressmann, 1926, p. 13; E. Sjöberg, *Der Menschensohn im Äthiopischen Henochbuch*, pp. 35–9, suggests the reign of Herod; N. Messel, op. cit., pp. 78–85, places it in the time of the Roman procuratorship.

[2] E.g. J. T. Milik, *Dix ans de Decouvertes dans le Desert de Juda*, 1957, p. 31. Milik modified his views slightly in the English edition of his book, *Ten Years of Discovery in the Wilderness of Judaea*, 1959, p. 33, where he attributed the Similitudes to "a Jew or a Jewish Christian of the first or second century A.D.".

[3] Cf. A. Dupont-Somer, *The Essene Writings from Qumran*, E.Tr. 1961, pp. 298–300; G. H. P. Thompson, "The Son of Man: The Evidence of the Dead Sea Scrolls", *E.T.*, 72, 1961, p. 125.

[4] See N. Messell, loc. cit.

4

Son of Man and Related Concepts in the Apocrypha and Pseudepigrapha

1. 2 ESDRAS

The man-like figure of Dan. 7.13 reappears in 2 Esdras 13. Here, in the non-Latin versions, we read of one who has as it were the form of a man, emerging from the wind-stirred seas. Much of the imagery of this chapter is reminiscent of Daniel's language,[1] and the vision seems to have been constructed from traditional motifs.[2] In the preceding two chapters we find a reinterpretation of the fourth beast of Dan. 7.7,[3] and the "Man" of chapter 13, who flies with the clouds of heaven, appears to be taken from Dan. 7 too. Once again, however, the one like a son of man is interpreted as an individual. Unlike Daniel's figure, Ezra's "Man" plays a very active part in the events described, and this activity possibly reflects a growing influence by the Anthropos tradition.

Other sections of this book are perhaps of even greater importance for our subject. Of particular interest is the passage in

[1] Cf. the wind(s) stirring up the sea—13.2, Dan. 7.2; the four winds of heaven —13.5, Dan. 7.2; the mountain cut out from an unknown place—13.6f, Dan. 2.34f; fire, flame and sparks—13.10, Dan. 7.9f; enemy destroyed by fire—13.11, Dan. 7.11; only dust left—13.11, Dan. 2.35.

[2] G. H. Box, *The Ezra-Apocalypse*, 1912, pp. 280–6, considers that the incongruities between the vision and the interpretation later in the chapter are due to the author having utilized an already constructed vision, the details of which he did not understand. They may equally well have resulted, however, from the author's own attempt to construct a vision out of mythological material which he did not fully comprehend but wished to employ; cf. W. O. E. Oesterley, 2 *Esdras*, 1933, p. 155. The fact that the "vision" appears to be a conflation of Dan. 2 and 7 supports the latter interpretation.

[3] Ezra admits his dependence in 12.11f. Daniel's unspecified beast has been changed to an eagle in order that it may symbolize Rome.

6.53–9, which occurs at the end of the author's detailed description of the creation. It reads:

> On the sixth day thou didst command the earth to bring forth before thee cattle, beasts, and creeping things; and over these thou didst place Adam, as ruler over all the works which thou hadst made; and from him we have all come, the people whom thou hast chosen. All this I have spoken before thee, O Lord, because thou hast said that it was for us that thou didst create this world. As for the other nations, which have descended from Adam, thou hast said that they are nothing, and that they are like spittle, and thou hast compared their abundance to a drop from a bucket. And now, O Lord, behold, these nations, which are reputed as nothing, domineer over us and devour us. But we thy people, whom thou hast called thy first-born, only begotten, zealous for thee, and most dear, have been given into their hands. If the world has indeed been created for us, why do we not possess our world as an inheritance? How long will this be so?

Here we find clearly stated the author's belief that the people of Israel alone are the true heirs of Adam: it was for their sake that the world was created, and the world is thus their rightful inheritance. The natural question as to the position of the other nations is raised only to be dismissed: technically they may indeed be descended from Adam, but God has declared them to be as nothing before him, and has named Israel as his "first-born, only begotten, ... and most dear". The real problem which faces the author is not why Israel should be chosen and the other nations rejected, but is one which arises from this assumption of Israel's election: it is the permanent problem of all Jewish thinkers at that time—why should the other nations, whose claim to Adam's inheritance God does not recognize, nevertheless "domineer over ... and devour" the chosen people? Why, asks Ezra, are the people of Israel not allowed to take possession of their inheritance, and rule over the world? The ideas used here are exactly those which we found in Dan. 7. In both passages the conviction that Israel ought to rule the world is based on a belief regarding man's true position in the scheme of creation; in both, the proper order of things has been reversed, and the rightful ruler is in fact under the domination of others. But whereas Daniel's vision expresses his confidence that the correct relationships will soon be re-established, Ezra's prayer is one of complaint that the existing order continues so long.

Similar ideas are found elsewhere in 2 Esdras. Thus in 7.1of the statement made in 6.59 that the world was created for Israel's sake is repeated in the angel's reply to Ezra's complaint; the same idea reappears in 9.13, but here it is referred more exactly to the righteous in Israel. In the former passage an attempt is made to offer an explanation for Israel's suffering: the way to the nation's inheritance is likened to the narrow and dangerous entrances to a broad sea or a good city, and the reason for the narrowness and danger in this case is traced to Adam's failure to obey God's commands.

A similar connection between Adam's sin and Israel's suffering is made in chapter 3. Here, in v. 7, we read:

> And thou didst lay upon [Adam] one commandment of thine; but he transgressed it, and immediately thou didst appoint death for him and for his descendants. From him there sprang nations and tribes, peoples and clans, without number.

The author then goes on to say that "every nation walked after its own will and did ungodly things", since all had inherited an evil heart from Adam; even Israel, chosen by God and given the Law, was no better than other nations. But, argues the author, Israel was also no worse than the others! Why, then, he pleads, should Zion be given into the hands of God's enemies, while they, flagrant evildoers, receive no punishment? Here Ezra is not on very firm ground, since he has already acknowledged that the people of Israel had followed Adam in his sin and that their punishment was just. The only reason he is able to give why they should now receive "reward" is that they alone have known God and believed his covenants: the distinction between Israel and the other nations lies not in the people's own righteousness, but solely in their election by God to be his people and the recipient of his Law. The author thus uses here the same ideas regarding the election of Israel and the people's relation to their enemies which we noted in 6.54ff, and his argument begins in both passages with a statement regarding the descendants of Adam. Yet his use of this theme in the two passages appears to be almost completely contradictory, since his argument in chapter 3 is based on the statement that all men are descended from Adam, while in chapter 6 he declares that Israelites alone are Adam's true descendants. The difference is explained when we realize that in the first passage Ezra is concerned with an inheritance of evil, and in the second with one which is good. As far as sin and death are concerned, the author has no reason to deny that all men have inherited these tendencies from Adam. His attitude regarding the privileges and position of Adam is, however, different: these are the true possession of Israel alone, since the other nations have been rejected by God.[1] The two passages are thus complementary rather than contradictory: Ezra admits in 6.54 that the other nations are descended from Adam— but he can dismiss them from consideration as far as the rights of inheritance are concerned, since he has already discussed in chapter 3 God's choice of Israel through Abraham, Isaac, and Jacob, and his rejection of Esau.[2]

Another passage of great interest is found in chapter 8, which continues Ezra's supplication for his nation; with the rest of mankind he is not concerned, and declares that he is content to leave them to God, acknowledging that in this matter he knows best; concerning the Jews, however, he is not so confident about the Almighty's wisdom.[3] The prayer which follows suggests that the author felt that Israel as a whole should be saved because of the virtues of the righteous: he asks God to regard the latter, and not the sins of the impious. The divine reply indicates that God will indeed do just that—but not in the way which Ezra hopes: the righteous will receive their reward, but the wicked will be destroyed. The contrast between the two groups is drawn in 8.26–30, which reads:

> O look not upon the sins of thy people,
> but at those who have served thee in truth.
> Regard not the endeavors of those who act wickedly,
> but the endeavors of those who have kept thy covenants amid
> afflictions.
> Think not on those who have lived wickedly in thy sight;
> but remember those who have willingly acknowledged that thou
> art to be feared.

---

[1] It is interesting to note that J. Jervell, who discusses the interpretation of man as Israel, *Imago Dei*, 1960, pp. 33–7, connects this identification with the Gottebenbildlichkeit, and thus with the idea of privilege. The beneficial aspect is undoubtedly the central one, but the idea does, as we shall see, extend beyond this.

[2] Similar ideas regarding the choice of Israel are expressed in 9.17–25. See especially v. 21, where the nation is saved by God as "one grape out of a cluster, and one plant out of a great forest".

[3] 2 Esdras 8.15f.

Let it not be thy will to destroy those who have had the ways of
cattle;
but regard those who have gloriously taught thy law.
Be not angry with those who are deemed worse than beasts;
but love those who have always put their trust in thy glory.

The last two verses are of particular significance, because we find
once again the idea which we have already discovered in Daniel and
the Psalms, that "beastliness" is typical of those who rebel against
God—in this case of those whose behaviour is like that of non-Jews.

A further point of interest appears in v. 44 of this chapter. Un-
fortunately the text of the existing versions is not certain,[1] but the
general meaning of the passage is clear: the author expresses indignation at the idea that the fate of mankind should be like that of
seed, a vast proportion of which is doomed to perish. The following verse, however, shows that it is not man in general who is in
mind here, but the chosen people, Israel: the Son of man, or man,
"who has been formed by thy hands and is called thy own image
because he is made like thee, and for whose sake thou hast formed
all things" is in fact "thy people and . . . inheritance".

In the light of this passage it seems very likely that we should
understand an earlier reference to man in this chapter in the same
way. In 8.6, the author prays for "every mortal who bears the
likeness of a human being".[2] Oesterley describes this as a prayer
"for humanity in general, a universalistic note which is by no
means always found in our book".[3] The note of universalism has,
indeed, already disappeared by vv. 15–16, where, as we have seen,
the author expresses unconcern about the fate of other nations.
Even before this, however, it is clear that he is thinking primarily
of the chosen nation, since he writes: "Thou hast brought him up
in thy righteousness, and instructed him in thy law, and reproved
him in thy wisdom",[4] words which could be applied only to an
Israelite. This suggests that v. 6 may not be quite as universalistic
as at first appears, and does not contradict the thought of v. 15 as
sharply as is supposed. If this is so, then "every mortal who bears
the likeness of a human being" in v. 6 cannot equal "all mankind"

---

[1] Most Latin MSS. read *hic pater et filius*, though one has *sic pat et filius*.
Editors restore either *hic perit* or *sic patitur*.

[2] The Latin has *locum hominis*, but this is evidently due to a confusion between
τόπον and τύπον: the Syriac understood the latter.

[3] Op. cit., in loc.

[4] V. 12.

in v. 15.[1] We have already seen, in 6.56, that the author dismisses non-Israelites as "nothing" and "spittle", so that there is a strong likelihood that in 8.6 he is automatically thinking of Israel. But we can perhaps go further than this. The fact that "omnis corruptus" needs further definition while "omni homine" does not could be due to the fact that "corruptus" can include more than just mankind; but the idea of corruptibility, taken with the reference to creation in the following verse, and the rather strange phrase about bearing the likeness of a man, suggests that the author may have intended a reference to Adam.[2]

Another reference in this chapter to ideas connected with Adam occurs in the description in vv. 51–4 of the glory which is to be enjoyed by Ezra and those who, like him, are righteous. Their final blessedness is portrayed very largely as a return of those things which Adam once enjoyed but lost: for them paradise is to be opened, where the tree of life is planted; sin, illness, sorrow and death will all be banished, and immortality itself will at last be enjoyed.[3]

The connection between Israel and Adam is found also in the section of chapter 7 which is omitted from the majority of Latin MSS., but which is an integral part of the book. This connection is usually overlooked, however, since the author speaks here in general terms of mankind; thus when he asks, in v. 46, "who among the living is there that has not sinned, or who among men that has not transgressed thy covenant?" he does not limit his enquiry to Israel. But the context shows that he is, in fact, thinking of Israel in particular—and that for the natural reason that any exceptions to the general rule of condemnation could occur only in Israel. In fact, after expressing despair regarding the small number who may be expected to enjoy the world to come, he goes on immediately in the first person to speak of the evil heart which "has grown up in us, and which has alienated us from God, and has brought us into corruption and the ways of death, and has shown us the paths of perdition and removed us far from life—and that not just a few of us but almost all who have been created!"

[1] The difference in the author's attitude to man in v. 6 and to mankind in general in v. 15 appears to be overlooked by J. Jervell, op. cit., pp. 33f, who argues in a footnote that 2 Esdras 8.6–13 refers to man in general, and that it is only with vv. 15ff that the author turns to Israel in particular.

[2] The double reference would, of course, have been obvious if 2 Esdras was originally written in Hebrew, as is maintained by G. H. Box, op. cit., pp. xiii–xx.

[3] Cf. the reference to the renewal of creation in 7.75.

Here the author takes up the ideas which he has already discussed in 7.10f, of the connection between sin and sorrow, and of Israel's inheritance of "this world" and "the greater world". That the "living" of v. 46 are, as in v. 14, to all intents and purposes synonymous with "the children of Israel", is confirmed when we consider the words which introduce his appeal: "But what of those for whom I prayed?" It is the chosen nation, the subject of his prayer in 6.55-9, that still occupies his mind in this passage; other men are of no account.[1]

It is in the light of the author's concern for his people that the remaining references to mankind in this chapter must be interpreted. Ezra is pleading, not for mankind in general, but for his own race. It is not the fate of the Gentiles which calls forth his words in v. 65, where he pictures the reversal of Gen. 1.26f, with the human race lamenting and the beasts of the field rejoicing. Nor is he concerned with the punishment of non-Israelites in vv. 70-4, when he speaks of those who did not keep the commandments. This passage is usually interpreted as evidence that the author thought that the Gentiles had been offered the Law but had rejected it.[2] Certainly he refers to "Adam and all who have come from him", but the description of those who "had understanding . . . received the commandments . . . and . . . obtained the law" scarcely fits Gentiles who rejected these things. Once again, although the author is speaking in general terms, he appears to be thinking automatically of Israel.

This process is clearly seen in a later section of this chapter, in vv. 118-26, which opens with the despairing words:

> O Adam, what have you done? For though it was you who sinned, the fall was not yours alone, but ours also who are your descendants.

[1] Cf. also 8.15.

[2] See G. H. Box, op. cit., p. 139. 2 Esdras 7.20ff is similarly interpreted—ibid, pp. 105f; W. O. E. Oesterley, 2 Esdras, p. xxx. Vv. 20-4 are closely parallel to vv. 70-2, and speak in similar terms of those who have despised the law and covenants, the commandments and statutes of God. Oesterley admits (pp. 67f) that v. 20 refers primarily to the Jews, but maintains that vv. 22 and 23 speak of "humanity in general" (p. xxx); he appears to base this judgement on the reference to Adam in v. 11—but overlooks the fact that the context of that verse speaks of Israel; moreover, v. 17 introduces this section with a reference to God's provision in his Law "that the righteous shall inherit these things, but that the ungodly should perish"—a provision which applies to those who have accepted the Law and covenant, not to those outside it, who automatically perish. Oesterley's whole argument in this section of his preface (pp. xxviii–xxx) on the author's universalism and sympathy for men of all races (contrast his remark on 8.6 quoted above, p. 53) overlooks the references to Israel with which the author defines his understanding of Adam and humanity.

Here we might expect, as in 3.7, that there would be no reason to limit Adam's descendants to Israel alone. The following verses, however, go on to explain who the speakers in v. 118 are: they are those to whom "an eternal age has been promised . . . and . . . an everlasting hope" and those for whom "safe and healthful habitations have been reserved"—in other words, Israel; but, because of their sin, these same speakers will be prevented from entering paradise and enjoying its fruits. Once again, therefore, the universal truth is applied by the author to the individual nation: the fall—like the sin in v. 46 and the judgement in v. 70—refers to all men, but the author's concern is with Israel alone.

We find, therefore, that the author's references to man reflect the attitude which he expresses in 6.56: all men are indeed descended from Adam, but, since the other nations have been dismissed as "nothing" and "spittle", the terms which are in fact applicable to all men can be used to refer primarily to Israel. This particular application of universal truth can be used in speaking of both good and evil attributes of humanity, the only difference being that the author would deny the general validity of the former, and not that of the latter.

Thus the book of 2 Esdras as a whole offers us a strange anomaly in its use of Daniel's imagery. How far it is indebted to the book of Daniel is not clear, but some dependence, at least, is acknowledged in 12.11f. The later chapters reinterpret motifs from Dan. 7: the fourth beast is reinterpreted because it does not fit the Roman Empire as pointedly as the author wished it to do; the one like a Son of man is reinterpreted and individualized, perhaps under the influence of an Anthropos tradition, perhaps because the author failed to understand it. Yet in the earlier chapters of the book we find the ideas which underlie Daniel's human figure perfectly understood and applied to Israel. The connection between Israel's final victory and Adam's lordship which we assumed to exist in Daniel is here clearly stated. The theme of the "beastliness" of other nations also reappears. Now, also, is found some attempt to explain the "manhood" of Israel, on the basis of divine election and the bestowal of the Law, and to find a reason for the nation's sufferings in the sin of Adam.

2. ECCLESIASTICUS

2 Esdras is a comparatively late book, dating from the first or second century A.D.[1] Its importance for our study lies, not in any possible influence on the New Testament, but in the evidence which it offers of contemporary thought and interpretation. When we turn to other apocryphal and pseudepigraphal writings of this period we find that the ideas which we have examined reappear elsewhere. In the apocrypha itself, the narrative books naturally offer less opportunity for such speculations, but points of contact with the ideas which we have found in 2 Esdras are to be seen in the two books of wisdom. Thus in Ecclesiasticus, we find emphasis on the fact that man, through Adam, is created from the ground.[2] In two passages it is stated that God created man and that he "showed [men] good and evil", giving them the ability to choose between the two.[3] In every case the reference is to man in general, not to Israel, but the knowledge of good and evil is here naturally connected with ὁ νόμος and αἱ ἐντολαί. Thus the first passage appears in chapter 15, which is concerned with "the man who fears the Lord ... and [the man] who holds to the law"; the author goes on to tell the reader that "if you will, you can keep the commandments".[4] The other, in chapter 17, emphasizes the authority which was given to man at the creation:[5]

> [The Lord] granted them authority over the things upon the earth.
> He endowed them with strength like his own,
> and made them in his own image.
> He placed the fear of them in all living beings,
> and granted them dominion over beasts.

After speaking of man's knowledge of good and evil, the author continues:[6]

> He bestowed knowledge upon them,
> and allotted to them the law of life.
> He established with them an eternal covenant,
> and showed them his judgments.

---

[1] Cf. G. H. Box, op. cit., pp. xxviii–xxxiii; W. O. E. Oesterley, *2 Esdras*, pp. xliv–xlv; C. C. Torrey, *The Apocryphal Literature*, 1945, pp. 119ff.

[2] Ecclus. 17.1; 33.10; 40.1.

[3] Ecclus. 15.14–17; 17.1–7. The author appears to ignore the fact that this knowledge, according to Gen. 3.22, was not given by God but acquired through the Fall. A similar outlook is found in other writings, e.g. 2 Enoch 30.15.

[4] Ecclus. 15.1,15.   [5] Ecclus. 17.2–4.   [6] Ecclus. 17.11–14.

Their eyes saw his glorious majesty,
and their ears heard the glory of his voice.
And he said to them, "Beware of all unrighteousness."
And he gave commandment to each of them concerning his
neighbor.

Here we have moved once again from a reference to the creation
of man to speaking of God's Law and the covenant which he made
with Israel. It might perhaps be maintained that these words could
be applied to the covenant made with Noah, and that the author
is thus still thinking of mankind in general; the description of a
theophany in v. 13, however, is clearly a reference to the revelation
at Sinai, and the summary of the commandments in the next verse
as being concerned with conduct to one's neighbour confirms that
it is the Mosaic Law which the author has in mind.[1] The position
of other nations is not here discussed, but a differentiation is made
between them and Israel in v. 17, where it is stated that:

> He appointed a ruler for every nation,
> but Israel is the Lord's own portion.

Commentators find difficulty in this verse in its present position,
since it breaks the logical sequence between verses 15 and 19,
which, in the normally accepted text, it joins. Its relevance to vv.
11–14 is, however, clear, and Ryssel[2] transposes it to follow that
section. Such a transposition would leave vv. 15, 19, 20, 22–4 as a
general description of God's attitude to man's behaviour, without
any particular reference to Israel. Whatever the intention of the
original author, however, it is clear from the text found in the two
Greek MSS. 70 and 248, that at a very early stage it was interpreted
in terms of Israel.[3] According to these MSS. vv. 15–21 should
read:[4]

Their ways are always before him,
they will not be hid from his eyes.

[1] Cf. J. Jervell, *Imago Dei*, pp. 31f.
[2] In E. Kautzsch, *Die Apokryphen und Pseudepigraphen des Alten Testaments*,
1900, vol. I. Cf. also G. H. Box and W. O. E. Oesterley in R. H. Charles, *The
Apocrypha and Pseudepigrapha of the Old Testament*, 1913, vol. I.
[3] There is no need to discuss here the critical questions involved, since these
do not affect the fundamental fact that this interpretation was current in some
circles at least. Box and Oesterley discuss the problem (op. cit., pp. 280–8), and
consider that the two types of text "existed at a very early period, probably as
early as the last century B.C." The longer form of the text is generally attributed
to Pharisaic circles; see also J. H. A. Hart, *Ecclesiasticus*, 1909, pp. 272–320.
[4] The translation given here departs at some points from that of the R.S.V.

Their ways from youth tend towards evil,
and they are unable to make their hearts of flesh instead of stone.
For in the division of the nations of the whole earth, he
appointed a ruler for every nation;
and Israel is the Lord's portion,
whom, being his first-born, he brings up with discipline,
and allotting to him the light of his love, does not forsake him.
All their works are as the sun before him,
and his eyes are continually upon their ways.
Their iniquities are not hidden from him,
and all their sins are before the Lord.
But the Lord, being merciful and knowing his creation,
neither forsook nor abandoned them, but spared them.

Thus the idea of God's election of Israel and the designation of the nation as his first-born are connected with a further final reference to creation in the words τὸ πλάσμα αὐτοῦ.

This same combination of ideas appears once again in a later passage of the book, in chapter 36, a prayer to God for the destruction of Israel's enemies which echoes the language of creation mythology.[1] Here the author prays:[2]

Have mercy, O Lord, upon the people called by thy name,
upon Israel, whom thou hast likened to a first-born son. . . .
Bear witness to those whom thou didst create in the beginning,
and fulfil the prophecies spoken in thy name.

Once again, those whom God created (τοῖς ἐν ἀρχῇ κτίσμασίν σου) are regarded as being, to all intents and purposes, the children of Israel.[3]

---

[1] Note, e.g., the references to signs, wonders, and mighty deeds, wrought by God's hand and right arm (vv. 6, 8), and to crushing the heads of the enemy (v. 10). There is very close similarity in thought, extending at some points to language, between this chapter and Ps. 74 (Greek 73). Cf. σημεῖα in v. 6 (Greek 5) here with σημεῖα in Ps. 74 (73).9; the Hebrew in both cases is אות. The χεῖρα καὶ βραχίονα δεξιόν of the same verse echoes χεῖρά σου καὶ τὴν δεξιάν σου of Ps. 74(73).11; here the Hebrew is even closer, Ecclesiasticus reading יד . . . וימין and the Psalm ידך וימינך. In both passages there are references to the beginning —Ecclus. 36.11 (10) ἀπ ἀρχῆς–קדם; 15 (14) ἐν ἀρχῇ–מעשיך; Ps. 74 (73).2 ἀπ ἀρχῆς–קדם; 12 πρὸ αἰῶνος–מקדם. The references are to Rahlfs' edition of the Septuagint.
[2] Ecclus. 36.12,15 (Greek 11,14).
[3] There is again a close parallel between these words and Ps. 74 (73) where, in v. 2, the psalmist prays: "Remember thy congregation, which thou hast gotten of old." The idea of creation is used here instead of begetting. Cf. also the opening phrases of the two verses in Hebrew:

זכר עדתך (Ps. 74.2)

תן עדות (Ecclus. 36.15)

The idea that the righteous will rule the nations appears in chapter 4, though it is not connected with the rule of Adam. Here, in the eulogy of wisdom—which the author identifies with the Torah—it is said that "He who obeys her will judge the nations".[1] Commentators have maintained that this sentence "is quite out of harmony with the rest of the passage, and, indeed, with the general tone of the book, which is not concerned with those outside of Israel".[2] It is thus frequently emended, on the basis that the Greek translator has misunderstood the Hebrew.[3] Even if this correction is justified, however, the Greek alone provides sufficient evidence to show that to the translator, at least, righteousness was associated with judging the nations. This exalted position is reached only after hardship, however, since[4]

> At first she will walk with him on tortuous paths, she will bring
>   fear and cowardice upon him,
> and will torment him by her discipline until she trust him,
> and she will test him with her ordinances.

Finally, we may note briefly the use of two ideas relevant to our theme: first in Ecclus. 49.14–16, Adam, Seth, Enoch and Shem are included in the catalogue of famous men as though they, like all the others, had been Israelites;[5] second, in two passages—4.30[6] and 25.15–17[7]—wild beasts form the natural metaphor for evil behaviour.

There are other parallels between these two passages: Ps. 74 (73).2 continues: "which thou hast redeemed to be the tribe of thy heritage! Remember Mount Zion, where thou hast dwelt"; the following verse mentions the sanctuary. In Ecclus. 36.11,13f (10,12f) we find mention of the tribes of Jacob as an inheritance, of the sanctuary and of Zion. The Greek does not give an exact parallelism, although the Greek κατακληρονόμησον αὐτούς in Ecclus. 36.11 (10) is closer to Ps. 74(73).2 than the Hebrew וְיִתְנַחֲלוּ; the correspondence between the Hebrew roots, however, is exact (שׁבט; נחל; ציון; קדשׁ).

[1] Ecclus. 4.15.
[2] W. O. E. Oesterley, *The Wisdom of Jesus the Son of Sirach or Ecclesiasticus*, 1912, in loc.
[3] The Hebrew has אמת, which the Greek understood as אֱמֹת but which Oesterley and others read as אֱמֶת.
[4] Ecclus. 4.17.
[5] Cf. J. Jervell, *Imago Dei*.
[6] The Greek reads "lion" and the Syriac "dog"; each is supported by a Hebrew MS.
[7] Codex B and the Syriac read "like sackcloth" in v. 17, but all other Greek MSS. and the Hebrew (v. 16) read "like a bear". In the following chapter, 70 and 248 add a passage which mentions in v. 25 a woman "regarded as a dog".

3. THE WISDOM OF SOLOMON

Turning to the book of Wisdom, we find again the thought that man is descended from Adam, and thus formed from the earth.[1] In 10.1f it is said that Wisdom gave Adam "strength to rule over all things", an ability which he possessed even after the Fall.[2] In the preceding chapter, the same idea is made the basis of Solomon's prayer for wisdom in ruling his people:[3]

> O God of my fathers and Lord of mercy,
> who hast made all things by thy word,
> and by thy wisdom hast formed man,
> to have dominion over the creatures thou hast made,
> and rule the world in holiness and righteousness,
> and pronounce judgment in uprightness of soul,
> give me the wisdom that sits by thy throne,
> and do not reject me from among thy servants.

This passage is of particular interest, since it shows how the idea of Adam's position of authority in creation could be transferred to the sphere of human relationships, and be applied to the rule of human subjects: man's rule of the animals is paralleled by Solomon's rule of men.

God's purpose in creation is discussed in an earlier part of the book and occurs in the section in chapters 2—5 which deals with the persecution of the righteous man and his final vindication. In 2.23 it is said that[4]

> God created man for incorruption,
> and made him in the image of his own eternity.

Although, in keeping with the author's custom of avoiding all proper names, Adam is not here mentioned, the reference to Gen. 1.26f is clear. In the following verse, the author tells how God's intention was thwarted, when death entered the world through the devil. In chapter 3, however, he goes on to explain that the souls of the righteous, who seemed to have died, are nevertheless at peace in the hand of God. What appeared to men as punishment

---

[1] Wisd. 7.1; 15.8.
[2] According to Gen. 9.2, also, this ability was renewed after the Fall.
[3] Wisd. 9.1-4.
[4] MSS. 248 and 253, followed by most patristic writers, read ἀϊδιότητος. ℵ, A, and B have ἰδιότητος.

was in fact the small chastening by which God tried them and found them worthy of himself. At the time of their visitation they will be glorified, and[1]

> They will govern nations and rule over peoples,
> and the Lord will reign over them for ever.

Here we find once again the idea expressed in Dan. 7, that the righteous will, under God, rule and judge the rest of mankind; as in Ecclus. 17.17, their king is no human figure, but God himself. Once again, too, the idea arises from a description of Adam: he was created in God's image and intended for immortality—an immortality which, in a spiritual sense, the righteous enjoy. The connection between Adam and the righteous is clear, even though the author moves from physical incorruption and death to spiritual immortality; in describing the final triumph of the righteous, however, the author returns to this-worldly terms, and portrays it as world rulership.

4. JUBILEES

We turn next to the book of Jubilees, which provides valuable evidence for the relationship which a writer at the end of the second century B.C.[2] understood to exist between Adam and Israel. This is expressed as early as 2.23, where it is said:[3]

> There [were] two and twenty heads of mankind from Adam to Jacob, and two and twenty kinds of work were made until the seventh day; this is blessed and holy; and the former also is blessed and holy; and this one serves with that one for sanctification and blessing.

Jacob is here linked with both Adam and the sabbath; with the former, because man was the twenty-second work of God and Jacob was the twenty-second "head" of mankind after Adam; with the sabbath, because both he and it (as number 23) were blessed and sanctified. In heaven, the privilege of keeping the

---

[1] Wisd. 3.8.
[2] R. H. Charles, *The Book of Jubilees*, 1902, pp. lviii–lxvi, dates the book between 135 and 105 B.C.; in *The Apocrypha and Pseudepigrapha*, II, 1913, he defines the date even more closely as being between 109 and 105 B.C. H. H. Rowley, *The Relevance of Apocalyptic*, 1944, pp. 81–5, also supports the end of the second century B.C. C. C. Torrey, *The Apocryphal Literature*, 1945, pp. 127f, argues for a later date, in the second half of the last century B.C.
[3] Translations are from R. H. Charles, *Jubilees*.

sabbath with God was limited to the two chief orders of angels, while on earth it was to be kept by the children of Jacob alone;[1] in this respect, therefore, Israel enjoyed a privilege not given to Adam, although associated with him in the story of creation.

The command to circumcise in chapter 15 is linked, not with Adam, but with the angels of the presence and the angels of sanctification, who were created circumcised.[2] There is no suggestion in Jubilees of the later tradition that Adam also was created circumcised.[3]

In the case of these two fundamental commands of Judaism, therefore, the author emphasizes the difference between Israel and the Gentiles by a reference to the divine election of this one nation to share the privileges of the higher orders of angels. Elsewhere, however, the commands which differentiate Israel from the neighbouring nations are linked with Adam and the other patriarchs. Of particular interest is a passage which occurs in chapter 3. Here the author is protesting against the way in which some Jews adopted the Greek custom of stripping for athletic sport. He is able to introduce his protest at this juncture by a reference to the clothes which God made for Adam and his wife. The significant point, and the one on which the author bases his argument, is that it was to Adam alone that God gave garments "to cover his shame, of all the beasts and cattle. On this account, it is prescribed on the heavenly tables as touching all those who know the judgement of the law, that they should cover their shame, and should not uncover themselves as the Gentiles uncover themselves."[4] Thus the ground of the author's demand for a distinction between "those who know the judgement of the law" and the Gentiles is a distinction which was originally made between Adam and "the beasts and cattle".

In a similar fashion, the author refers various commands of the Mosaic Law back either to Adam or to another of the patriarchs. Thus the laws regarding purification after childbirth are traced back to the creation of Adam and Eve,[5] and Adam himself is said to have made the first incense-offering;[6] many other commandments of the law are traced to Enoch, Cain, Noah, Abraham, and Jacob.[7]

---

[1] Jub. 2.17–31.   [2] Jub. 15.27.
[3] Midrash Tehillim, Ps. 9.7. 'Abot de-Rabbi Natan, 2.
[4] Jub. 3.30f.   [5] Jub. 3.8–14.   [6] Jub. 3.27.
[7] For a full list, see R. H. Charles, *Jubilees*, pp. lii–liii.

By connecting these commands with Adam and his early descendants, the author emphasizes the link between them and Israel. A similar connection is made in 12.25–7, where it is recorded that Hebrew was revealed to Abraham; Hebrew is not only the language in which God communicates with Abraham, but is "the tongue of the creation" in which the first men had spoken and written until it was forgotten at the time of the overthrow of Babel. The link between Adam and Israel is expressed clearly in 2.23, which we have already noted, and again in 19.24,27, where Abraham's blessing of Jacob is traced back through the patriarchs to Adam. Similarly Isaac, in 22.11–13, asks that Jacob may inherit the blessings which were given to him, to Noah and to Adam. In this passage we find the hope of national domination expressed, most notably in the words:

> May nations serve thee,
> And all the nations bow themselves before thy seed.
> Be strong in the presence of men,
> And exercise authority over all the seed of Seth.

Associated with this nationalistic hope, however, is an emphasis on the need for righteousness, upon which it is dependent:[1]

> May he cleanse thee from all unrighteousness and impurity,
> That thou mayest be forgiven all [thy] transgressions, [and] thy
> sins of ignorance.
> And may he strengthen thee
> And bless thee.
> And mayest thou inherit the whole earth.

As we have seen, these ideas are linked here with "the blessings . . . wherewith [God] blessed Noah and Adam", to both of whom, as the author records,[2] God gave dominion and authority over the earth and all creatures on it.

Finally we may note two passages in the book of Jubilees which suggest a return to the condition which pertained at the beginning. The first is in 16.26, where it is said that Abraham knew "that from him would arise the plant of righteousness for the eternal generations, and from him a holy seed, so that it should become like him who made all things". Here we find that righteousness and holiness are the prerequisites of becoming like the Creator—a phrase which

---

[1] Jub. 22.14. Cf. the whole prayer.   [2] Jub. 2.14; 6.5f.

echoes the thought of Gen. 1.26f. The author of Jubilees, like many other Jewish writers, does not mention the *imago dei* when discussing Adam's creation,[1] but in 6.8 he follows Gen. 9.6 in saying that God made man in his own image. A parallel idea is reflected in 23.26f; here it is said that when the children of Israel

> begin to study the laws
> And to seek the commandments
> And to return to the path of righteousness
> [Then] the days will begin to grow many and increase amongst those children of men,
> Till their days draw nigh to one thousand years,
> And to a greater number of years than [before] was the number of the days.

The return to righteousness thus brings with it a return to the longevity enjoyed by the patriarchs. Earlier in this chapter,[2] the author has discussed this question of the disparity in length between the lives of the patriarchs and those of his contemporaries, and has noted that whereas, before the Flood, the patriarchs had lived for nineteen jubilees, "after the Flood they began to grow less than nineteen jubilees, and to decrease in jubilees, and to grow old quickly. . . . And all the generations which will arise from this time until the day of the great judgement will grow old quickly, before they complete two jubilees." The nineteen jubilees mentioned here agree with the statement in 4.29f that Adam died in the last but one year of the nineteenth jubilee, at the age of 930, and in that passage it is explained that his death before he had reached his thousandth year fulfilled the words of Gen. 2.17, since "one thousand years are as one day in the testimony of the heavens". Noah is said to have lived to be 950, which was slightly more than the nineteen jubilees;[3] the death of the patriarchs between Adam and Noah is not mentioned. The author explained in chapter 23 that the general decrease in the length of men's lives is due to wickedness, and since he is here describing the death of Abraham, he is careful to state that, since Abraham himself was "perfect", his early death was due to the wickedness prevailing among men. Abraham, however, lived to be 175, or more than three and a half jubilees, which, according to the standards of later times was a considerable age: in the author's time, "a jubilee and a half of

---

[1] Cf. J. Jervell, *Imago Dei*, 1960, pp. 15–51.
[2] Jub. 23.9–11.   [3] Jub. 10.16.

years" was considered too long, accompanied as they were by "pain and sorrow and tribulation".[1] Still worse, however, was to come, for by the time of the final cataclysm[2] "the heads of the children will be white with grey hair, and a child of three weeks will appear old like a man of one hundred years." Thus when the author continues, in vv. 26f, by saying that a spread of righteousness will lead to a gradual lengthening of life until men live almost to a thousand years, it is clear that in this return to antediluvian longevity he envisages a reversal of the decrease in life which he has already described and attributed to men's wickedness.[3]

5. THE TESTAMENTS
OF THE TWELVE PATRIARCHS

Several passages relevant to our theme occur in the Testaments of the Twelve Patriarchs, a work dating from the same period as Jubilees.[4] Here again we find the idea that the children of Israel will rule over the wild beasts, but always these latter are linked with the evil spirits of Beliar. If men live virtuously, then the spirits will flee from them, and the wild beasts will fear them;[5] the opposite is also variously expressed, and it is said that the wicked will be ruled, or the righteous will not be ruled, by devils and beasts.[6] The subjection of evil spirits is also spoken of alone, without the parallel reference to wild beasts, but once again in connection with righteousness;[7] this idea appears in some passages linked with another concept which is associated elsewhere with man's lordship, namely the thought of a return to paradise—most notably in Test. Levi 18, where it is said that the Messiah, after the cessation of sin in the world,[8]

> shall open the gates of paradise,
> And shall remove the threatening sword against Adam.

---

[1] V. 12; cf. v. 15 and Ps. 90.10.   [2] V. 25.   [3] Cf. vv. 14–17.
[4] See R. H. Charles, *The Testaments of the Twelve Patriarchs*, 1908, pp. i–liii; also *The Greek Versions of the Testaments of the Twelve Patriarchs*, 1908, pp. xlii–xliii. Cf. F. C. Burkitt's review of the latter in *J.T.S.*, 10, 1909, pp. 135ff. C. C. Torrey, op. cit., p. 131, again argues for a later date.
[5] Test. Iss. 7.7; Test. Naph. 8.4; Test. Ben. 5.1–3.
[6] Test. Naph. 8.6; Test. Ben. 3.3–5.
[7] Test. Sim, 6.2,6; Test. Zeb. 9.7f; Test. Dan. 5.1.
[8] Test. Levi 18.10–12, translation of R. H. Charles; cf. Test. Dan. 5.10–12.

And he shall give to the saints to eat from the tree of life,
And the spirit of holiness shall be on them.
And Beliar shall be bound by him,
And he shall give power to his children to tread upon the evil
  spirits.

In the Testaments we may notice also echoes of the old mythology in references to the dragon, whose head will finally be
broken,[1] and to the destruction of Beliar by fire.[2] Of interest also
is the use of the imagery of wild beasts to describe the attitude of
his brothers to Joseph.[3]

6. 1 ENOCH

We have already examined the figure of the Son of man in 1
Enoch; there are, however, other features in this book which recall
the ideas associated with Daniel's imagery. Thus the idea found in
the Parables that the kings and mighty will be delivered into the
hands of God's elect,[4] and that dominion will thus pass from the
sinners to the righteous, appears also in the final section of 1
Enoch.[5] In the Parables the kings are condemned for their wrong
attitude to God, "because they do not extol and praise him, nor
humbly acknowledge whence the kingdom was bestowed upon
them";[6] they are also likened to lions rushing from their lairs and
to hungry wolves causing havoc in the flock, who "go up and tread
under foot the land of his elect ones".[7] The characterization of
Israel's enemies as wild beasts is developed in the section of
"Dream Visions" in 1 Enoch, where animals are substituted for
the names of people and nations. Adam and his immediate descendants are represented as bulls, Cain and his children being black,
and Seth and his children being white, while the "giants" of Gen.
6 appear as elephants, camels, and asses.[8] Israel is descended from
the line of white bulls, of whom Adam, Seth, Noah, Shem, Abraham, and Isaac are specified; the line of inheritance is narrowed
by the exclusion of Noah's other sons, who are red and black

---

[1] Test. Ash. 7.3.
[2] Test. Jud. 25.3; cf. Dan. 7.11.
[3] Test. Dan. 1.8; Test. Gad. 2.2.
[4] See especially 1 Enoch 38.5; 48.8f.
[5] 1 Enoch 91.12; 95.3; 96.1; 98.12.
[6] 1 Enoch 46.5. Cf. Dan. 4; Wisd. 6.1–6.
[7] 1 Enoch 56.5f. Cf. Dan. 7.7.
[8] 1 Enoch 85—6.

bulls, of Ishmael, a wild ass, and of Esau, a black wild boar.[1]
Jacob himself is not a bull but a white sheep, and his descendants
are uniformly depicted as sheep, who are continually being attacked
and destroyed by the wild beasts—by succession wolves, dogs, lions,
and tigers, followed by birds of prey;[2] finally[3]

> a great sword was given to the sheep, and the sheep proceeded against
> all the beasts of the field to slay them, and all the beasts and the birds
> of the heaven fled before their face.

At this stage in the vision the Lord of the sheep arrives and the
final judgement takes place; the familiar reversal of status is made
and the writer sees[4]

> all the beasts of the earth, and all the birds of the heaven, falling
> down and doing homage to those sheep and making petition to and
> obeying them in every thing.

The final scene is the birth of the Messiah, depicted by a white bull,
and the transformation of all other animals into white oxen; the
original order of things is thus restored.[5] We have here the traditional images of the Lord's flock and the wild beasts: the latter image

---

[1] See 1 Enoch 89.9–12.
[2] The wolves represent the Egyptians, 1 Enoch 89.13–27; the dogs are
Philistines, and foxes and wild boars are associated with them, 89.42–8; lions
and tigers represent the Assyrians and Babylonians, 89.55–8, 66; the eagles are
the Greeks, 90.2–4, and the ravens the Syrians, 90.8–12.
[3] 90.19.   [4] 90.30.
[5] 1 Enoch 90.37f. At this point, according to Charles, the chief white bull
becomes a lamb, an idea which is quite out of harmony with the rest of the
passage. He bases this interpretation on the suggestion originally made by
Goldschmidt (Das Buch Henoch, p. 91) that the Ethiopic text, which here reads
nagar = word, is a corruption due to a confusion between מִלָּה = word and an
original טָלֶה = lamb; Charles supports this by appealing to Test. Jos. 19.3f,
where twelve harts become twelve sheep, and to v. 8 of the same chapter where,
on the basis that the bull calf of the previous verse is to be identified with the
lamb mentioned here, he alters the text to mean that the former turned into the
latter; this emendation is entirely speculative, however, and cannot fairly be
referred to in support of yet another speculative emendation in 1 Enoch. The
emendation suggested by Dillmann (Das Buch Henoch übersetzt und erklärt,
1853) that an original רְאֵם = buffalo was transliterated into Greek as ρημ and
understood by the Ethiopic translator as ῥῆμα is even less convincing. There is
no suggestion in the text as it stands that the bull turned into another kind of
animal; rather we may suppose from the context that the Messiah is distinguished from the other bulls by his size and position, for he "became a great
animal and had great black horns". The present Ethiopic text appears to be
corrupt, but in place of "word" we expect a reference, not to another animal, but
to the Messiah's authority; this suggests that the corruption might have originated in a confusion between מָשַׁל ruler, and מָשָׁל, byword, saying.

has been developed to include not only Israel's enemies but all the nations of the earth, and those which have not been in conflict with Israel are seen as comparatively harmless species of animals. Combined with this we have also the idea that Israel is the true heir of Adam and will, under the Messiah, regain what he enjoyed: this idea is expressed, however, not in terms of man, but in accordance with the apocalyptic imagery which depicted all men as animals, by speaking of Adam and the long-lived patriarchs as white bulls, white representing righteousness, and the bull perhaps representing the power and authority of the head of the herd.

The idea of restoration appears also in the first section of 1 Enoch. In 10.17–22 the restoration of righteousness is associated with a life long enough to "beget thousands of children" and with the renewed fruitfulness of the earth, no longer cursed but "full of blessing". In 24.4f the author describes the tree of life, and in the following chapter it is said that "no mortal is permitted to touch it till the great judgement. . . . It shall then be given to the righteous and holy." As a result the righteous "shall live a long life on earth, such as thy fathers lived", and all forms of unhappiness will be banished.[1] It is interesting to note that in the Parables, the righteous and elect are pictured as already living in the "Garden of the Righteous";[2] we have already noted the equation in this section between present heavenly realities and future earthly events;[3] here, too, however, there is mention of a future transformation of the earth.[4]

7. OTHER WRITINGS

The idea of Paradise as the place prepared for the righteous appears also in 2 Enoch. The author places the garden with the tree of life in the third heaven, and says that it is reserved as an eternal inheritance for those "who walk without fault before the face of the Lord".[5] Other passages in this book speak of the lordship of Adam on earth, without connecting this specifically with Israel.[6]

The Adam books naturally contain material relevant to our study. In both the Apocalypse of Moses and the Life of Adam and

---

[1] 1 Enoch 25.4, 6.   [2] 1 Enoch 61.12; 60.8,23; cf. 70.2–4.
[3] See above, p. 43.   [4] 1 Enoch 45.5.
[5] 2 Enoch 8—9.   [6] 2 Enoch 31.3; 58.1–3.

Eve we find an account of an attack by a wild beast on Seth;[1] Eve
reproves the beast, asking how it dares to fight with the image of
God and reminding it (in the Apocalypse) that it had long ago been
made subject to the image; in reply, the beast declares that it is
from Eve herself, and on account of her sin, that the rule of the
beasts has arisen, and their nature been transformed. The same
idea is expressed later in the Apocalypse of Moses, when Eve recalls God's words to Adam:[2] "The beasts, over whom thou didst
rule, shall rise up in rebellion against thee, for thou hast not kept
my commandment." At his death, however, Adam is promised
final restoration, and God says to him:[3] "I will transform thee to
thy former glory, and set thee on the throne of thy deceiver."
Similarly, Apoc. Moses 13.3–5 promises a return of "the delights
of paradise", God living in the midst of the people, who sin no
longer; this follows a resurrection of "all flesh . . . from Adam till
that great day—all that shall be of the holy people"; the qualification appears to reflect once again a particularist interpretation of
Adam's descendants.

This appears also in the Assumption of Moses, where we find
the familiar statement that God created the world for his people,
in a context which contrasts the conviction of the Gentiles.[4]

The author of 2 Baruch makes repeated use of the same idea.
In 14.17–19 he describes the creation of the world, and of

> man as the administrator of thy works, that it might be known that
> he was by no means made on account of the world, but the world on
> account of him. And now I see that as for the world which was made
> on account of us, lo! it abides, but we, on account of whom it was
> made, depart.

The context makes it clear that the first person plural here refers
to the righteous in Israel, so that once again we have a particularist
interpretation of Adam and his position of authority; this is taken
up a few verses later, where it is stated that not only has this world
come on account of the righteous, but "so also again shall that,
which is to come, come on their account".[5] The idea is introduced again in 21.24, where Abraham, Isaac, Jacob, and "all those

---

[1] Apoc. Moses 10—11; Life of Adam and Eve, 37—8.   [2] Apoc. Moses 24.4.
[3] Apoc. Moses 39.2. Cf. Life of Adam and Eve, 48.2f.   [4] Ass. Moses 1.12.
[5] 2 Baruch 15.7. Cf. 2 Baruch 44.15, where it is said that the righteous "shall
be given the world to come, but the dwelling of the rest who are many shall be
in the fire".

who are like them" are described as those "on whose account thou didst say that thou hadst created the world".

Daniel's scheme of four kingdoms is taken up in 2 Baruch, but apart from a reference to sinners as fleeing like evil beasts to a forest, there is no contact with the imagery of Dan. 7. The idea of restoration appears at the end of the Apocalypse, in chapters 73—4, where we find the familiar ideas of long and untroubled life, the subjection of the animals, and the reversal of the punishment imposed on Adam and Eve:[1]

> And wild beasts shall come from the forest and minister unto men,
> And asps and dragons shall come forth from their holes to submit
>   themselves to a little child.
> And women shall no longer have pain when they bear,
> Nor shall they suffer torment when they yield the fruit of the
>   womb.
> And it shall come to pass in those days that the reapers shall not
>   grow weary,
> Nor those that build be toilworn.

8. SUMMARY

In this inter-testamental literature, therefore, we find that the ideas used in Dan. 7 continue to play an important part in apocalyptic thought. The idea that Israel was the chosen nation, and thus the people in whom God's purpose in creation was to be fulfilled, was expressed in terms of Israel as the true descendant of Adam, and led to the equation of Israel with man. As such, the nation was destined to inherit the dominion which Adam had lost by his disobedience—but only through the people's obedience to the Law and covenant. The final kingdom, or the world to come, is to be possessed only by the righteous in Israel, who, by their righteousness, bring about a restoration to original conditions such as is already pictured in the Old Testament.[2] In this restoration Israel and man are again identified; the nation's earthly enemies are destroyed by fire, while devils, like the beasts, are subjected to man's control. It is significant that these same ideas—man's dominion over the world, his obedience to the Law, and the eschatological

---

[1] 2 Baruch 73.6—74.2. Cf. 32.6, which speaks of the renewal of the creation.
[2] E.g. Isa. 11.6–9; 51.3; 55.12f; 65.17, 20; Amos 9.13f.

6—S.O.M.

hope—and their confinement to Israel, are precisely those which J. Jervell, in his recent study *Imago Dei*, discusses in connection with the interpretation of Gen. 1.26f in the apocryphal writings.[1] These same ideas are found again in 1 Enoch in association with the Son of man and the righteous and elect who are joined to him. We find, therefore, that there is a very close connection between the figures of Adam and the Son of man—a connection whose cause, however, appears to lie in Hebrew ideas regarding creation, election and corporate personality, rather than in foreign speculations about a primal or heavenly man.[2] The latter may have influenced the development of the two as distinct figures, but the idea which gave rise to the emergence of the Son of man—that Israel was Adam's true heir—lives on, both in connection with the thought of the Son of man, and outside it.[3]

9. APPENDED NOTE I:
THE DEAD SEA SCROLLS

There is very little material in the documents from Qumran which throws any light on the ideas discussed in this chapter. There are a few examples of the phrase "son of man" or "sons of men" being used as a poetic synonym for "man" or "men".[4] Of more particular interest, however, is a passage in the Manual of Discipline which is reminiscent of the ideas we have been examining. In 1 QS III 17f, we find the statement that man was created to rule the earth. This is followed by a discussion of the two spirits allotted to man, the spirit of truth and the spirit of falsehood, which have dominion over the sons of light and the sons of darkness respectively; a description of the characteristics of each spirit and the respective "rewards" which will be given to those who walk according to each of them leads up to an account of the struggle

---

[1] Pp. 24–46.

[2] See S. Mowinckel, *He That Cometh*, pp. 420–37.

[3] We may perhaps refer at this point to a passage in Philo which is relevant to our study. In a list of the various names of the Logos in *Conf. Ling.* 146, Philo includes both a reference to Gen. 1.26 and the term "Israel": καὶ γὰρ ἀρχὴ καὶ ὄνομα θεοῦ καὶ λόγος καὶ ὁ κατ᾽ εἰκόνα ἄνθρωπος καὶ ὁ ὁρῶν, Ἰσραήλ, προσαγορεύεται. The context is a discussion of the term "sons of God"; Philo declares that those who are unworthy of this term may nevertheless be sons of his image, i.e. the Logos.

[4] E.g. 1 QH IV 30, 32; V 15.

between them and a declaration that finally God will destroy the spirit of evil, so that truth will be triumphant. The righteous will then be purified and given understanding, "for God has chosen them for an everlasting covenant, and all the glory of Adam shall be theirs".[1] Once again, therefore, we find the idea that the righteous in Israel (presumably in this case the Qumran community) are to inherit the authority and splendour of Adam.

10. APPENDED NOTE II:
THE RABBINIC WRITINGS

In the rabbinic writings there are a few references to the phrase "Son of man" which are relevant to our study. One is the well-known passage in the Babylonian Talmud, Sanh. 98a, where R. Alexandri reports R. Joshua's words on the manner of the Messiah's coming, which is said to depend upon the behaviour of the Jews: "If they are meritorious, *with the clouds of heaven* (Dan. 7.13); if not, *lowly and riding upon an ass* (Zech. 9.9)." This comparison has been variously interpreted—in literal terms, or as an indication of the speed or the slowness of the Messiah's arrival, or as symbolic of the comparative glory or lowliness of the Messiah.[2] Dating from c. A.D. 250, this saying cannot be regarded as proof of a messianic interpretation of Dan. 7 at the time of Jesus, though it demonstrates the kind of way in which the text might have been applied then.

In the Palestinian Talmud, a reference to the Son of man is found in Taᶜanith II 1, where, in a discussion of Num. 23.19, we find the comment: "If a man says 'I am God' he lies; if he says 'I am the Son of man' he will regret it." This is apparently a piece of anti-Christian propaganda, and is of no help to our enquiry.

More important is the comment on Ps. 2.7 in Midrash Tehillim, where we read: "The Children of Israel are declared to be sons in the decree of the Law, in the decree of the Prophets, and in the decree of the Writings." In support of this statement the following texts are cited: Ex. 4.22, Isa. 52.13 and 42.1, Ps. 110.1, and Dan.

---

[1] 1 QS IV 22f (translation by G. Vermes, *The Dead Sea Scrolls in English*, 1962).
[2] See T. F. Glasson, *The Second Advent*, 2nd edn, 1947, pp. 229f.

7.13f. It is interesting to find all these passages being interpreted here of Israel as a whole, rather than of an individual.

Another reference in Midrash Tehillim is found in the comment on Ps. 8.5(4)ff. Here each phrase of the psalm is interpreted of a different character in Jewish history: "man" is identified as Abraham, and "son of man" as Isaac; "made little less than God" is applied to Jacob, and "crowned with glory and honour" to Moses; Joshua is the one who has been "given dominion over the works of thy hands", and David the one of whom it is said "Thou hast put all things under his feet"; "all sheep and oxen" are subject to Solomon, "the beasts of the field" to Samson, "the birds of the air" to Elijah, and "the fish of the sea" to Jonah; those who "pass along the paths of the sea" are the children of Israel at the Exodus. This ingenious exposition ends with an interpretation of the final verse, "O Lord, our Lord, how majestic is thy name in all the earth!"—"Thy glory is to sojourn with thy people and with thy children". Although the actual phrase "son of man" is interpreted of Isaac, therefore, the psalm's whole description of the glory and dominion given to man is understood of the position of Israel, through the nation's various leaders. Once again, it is the children of Israel to whom God has given honour and dominion over the earth.

There is also evidence in the rabbinic writings of a similar interpretation of the term "man". Ezek. 34.31, where the "sheep" of Israel are described as "man" in contrast to other nations, is several times used as a proof that various other texts which refer to man apply to Israelites only, and not to members of other nations.[1] We also find the idea that the world was created for the sake of Israel,[2] but this special rôle of Israel is conditional on the people's obedience to God: so we find it said that the fate of creation depended upon Israel's acceptance of the Torah;[3] similarly, the dominion given to man in Gen. 1.26f is dependent upon his (Israel's) worthiness.[4] As in the other literature which we have examined, the rôle of Israel as God's chosen people is expressed in terms of God's purposes for "man" and the obedience which is required of those whom he has chosen.[5]

---

[1] E.g. B. Ker. 6b; B. Baba M. 114b; B. Yeb. 61a; Ex. R. 40.1.
[2] E.g. Ex. R. 38.4; Lev. R. 36.4.   [3] B. Shab. 88a.   [4] Gen. R. 8.12.
[5] See the full discussion of this subject in J. Jervell, *Imago Dei*, pp. 78–84. Cf. also H.-M. Schenke, *Der Gott "Mensch" in der Gnosis*, 1962, pp. 126–34.

PART TWO

ST MARK

5

Method of Investigation

When we turn to a consideration of the term "Son of man" in the gospels we find ourselves immediately confronted by a considerable difficulty, since its use there is not determined solely by contemporary thought and exegesis, but is linked both with the so-called "messianic consciousness" of Jesus and with the Christology of the early Church. In spite of the recent attempt by Vielhauer to eliminate every occurrence of the phrase from the words of Jesus,[1] the evidence that the term was used by Jesus himself seems overwhelming: there is no other reasonable explanation of the manner of its distribution in the New Testament.[2] It is also clear that the evangelists at least, and presumably the early Church also, understood Jesus to be referring to himself in his use of the phrase.

Our method of investigation here is of vital importance. We could take as our starting-point a discussion of Jesus' "messianic consciousness",[3] and examine the traditional view that Jesus believed himself to be "the Son of man" and deliberately modelled

---

[1] P. Vielhauer, "Gottesreich und Menschensohn in der Verkündigung Jesu", *Festschrift für Günther Dehn*, ed. W. Schneemelcher, 1957, pp. 51–79. Cf. also B. H. Branscomb, *The Gospel of Mark*, 1937, pp. 146–9, 156–9; E. Käsemann, *Essays on New Testament Themes*, 1964, pp. 43f (translation of an essay first given in 1953, and published originally in *Z.Th.K.*, 51, 1954); H. Conzelmann, "Gegenwart und Zukunft in der synoptischen Tradition", *Z.Th.K.*, 54, 1957, pp. 277–96. For a criticism of Vielhauer's position, see H. E. Tödt, *Der Menschensohn in der synoptischen Überlieferung*, 2nd edn, 1963, Excursus VI, pp. 298–316, E.Tr. pp. 329–47; also E. Schweizer, "Der Menschensohn", *Z.N.T.W.*, 50, 1959, pp. 185–209, and "The Son of Man", *J.B.L.*, 79, 1960, pp. 119–29. Vielhauer has defended his position in "Jesus und der Menschensohn", *Z.Th.K.*, 60, 1963, pp. 133–77.

[2] See the discussion by J. Drummond, "The Use and Meaning of the Phrase 'The Son of Man' in the Synoptic Gospels", *J.T.S.*, 2, 1901, pp. 546–56; also E. Schweizer, op. cit.

[3] As, e.g., J. W. Bowman, *The Intention of Jesus*, 1945; T. W. Manson, *The Servant Messiah*, 1953; L. Paul, *Son of Man*, 1961, pp. 191–201.

his behaviour and actions in accordance with what he read of this figure in the Old Testament. Such an approach, however, could produce only conjectures whose validity cannot, in the nature of the case, be proved; moreover, it would distort the evidence by placing the emphasis where Jesus himself did not place it. Even the negative approach of John Knox to this question, with its dismissal of categories which are—to him—psychologically incredible, is open to the same hazards of subjectivity.[1] To begin with the question, "Did Jesus identify himself with the Son of man?" is to approach the problem from the wrong end: such a method begs the question by assuming that the figure of the Son of man is one with which "identification" is possible; it may be, however, that the Son of man was not in any sense an expected "messianic" figure, and that the choice of the term by Jesus (or the Church) is due, not to any identification between Jesus and this Son of man, but rather to the fact that this term seemed the most adequate and appropriate one to express his person and destiny: in this case, the often-asked question regarding Jesus' self-identification with the Son of man could be misleading.

Alternatively, we could begin with a consideration of the relation of the term "Son of man" to contemporary Messianism, and an examination of the philological problems involved. Previous discussion of these subjects has shown, however, that our evidence is insufficient to give us any firm conclusions on these points.[2] To attempt to define the nature and scope of the phrase in the light of our insufficient knowledge of it, and then to apply this definition to the New Testament evidence, is likely to lead, once again, to a distortion of the evidence. Too many commentators have approached the Synoptic material with fixed ideas about the meaning of the phrase, and about where and how it could be used—ideas which have not only coloured their interpretation of the passages concerned, but distorted their judgement as to the genuineness of

---

[1] J. Knox, *The Death of Christ*, 1959, ch. 3, "The Psychological Question", pp. 52–77. A similar argument is put forward by F. C. Grant, *The Gospel of the Kingdom*, 1940, pp. 151–63.

[2] See the discussion by H. Lietzmann, *Der Menschensohn*, 1896, and G. Dalman, *The Words of Jesus*, 1909, pp. 234–67. Cf. also P. Kahle, *The Cairo Geniza*, 1947, pp. 129–31; J. Bowman, "The Background of the Term 'Son of Man'," *E.T.*, 59, 1948, pp. 283–8; J. Jeremias, "Die aramäische Vorgeschichte unserer Evangelien", *Theologische Literaturzeitung*, 74, 1949, pp. 527–32; M. Black, *An Aramaic Approach to the Gospels and Acts*, 2nd edn, 1954, pp. 235f and 246f.

the various sayings, leading to the rejection of any which did not conform to the accepted pattern.

A third method of approach would be to consider the authenticity of each saying in turn, and to dismiss from the discussion every saying whose genuineness or whose original reference to Jesus seems doubtful.[1] Yet this approach too has its dangers. It is comparatively easy to argue against the authenticity of any one particular saying considered in isolation;[2] the arguments look less convincing when they are weighed against the total evidence of all the Son of man sayings, for, as Aesop long since demonstrated, "union is strength". Moreover, as we have already maintained, it is certainly hazardous to leave aside those sayings where a decision regarding authenticity is nicely balanced, and to rely solely on those which can be ascribed to Jesus with something approaching certainty: to discard the "possible" and use only the "probable" in making a decision regarding the meaning of "Son of man" is to distort the evidence by ignoring some of it. Indeed, it may be that the question of a saying's "authenticity" often distorts the picture rather than clarifying it, and that it would be better left unanswered, if the only answer it provides is to divide the material into rigid categories. It is commonly argued that some of the "Son of man" sayings reflect the early Church's misunderstanding of the term: but this does not mean that we can safely ignore them, and concern ourselves only with other sayings which are deemed more reliable; for it may be that these other sayings, too, reflect to some extent the early Church's misunderstanding of the term.[3] It may well be, in fact, that *all* our "Son of man" sayings are, to a lesser or greater degree, distorted; and that, conversely, all together are needed to contain the whole truth about the Son of man.

It has long been accepted that our only knowledge of the words and deeds of Jesus is mediated via the evangelists' understanding of those words and deeds, and the "Son of man" sayings are no exception: this being so, we must accept the difficulty of unravelling the words and thoughts of Jesus from the interpretation of the evangelists, and approach the problem by way of their interpretation

---

[1] This is the method adopted by A. J. B. Higgins in *Jesus and the Son of Man*, 1964.

[2] This is demonstrated supremely by the method of P. Vielhauer, loc. cit.

[3] This is, ironically, recognized most clearly by those scholars (e.g. Bultmann) who do confine their attention to a limited number of sayings.

of the material. If it is impossible to distil the words of Jesus from the gospel tradition with anything resembling certainty, then one method would seem to be to examine the total picture presented by one or more of the evangelists, and to consider what light, if any, this evidence can throw on the question of Jesus' own understanding of the phrase. It is for this reason and from this standpoint that we have chosen to examine the Marcan material. Although we must inevitably consider the question of the sayings' "authenticity", we shall not be concerned to make any final judgement on this point, for the reasons already stated. At this stage of the investigation, moreover, it seems inadvisable to divide the sayings, as is so often done, into various categories, since any such classification must to some extent impose a predetermined pattern upon the material;[1] although it is possible to divide the "Son of man" sayings into groups, and although the majority of them fit into these broad divisions, there remain some which do not belong to any one category,[2] and it therefore seems better to examine the sayings in the Marcan order, and allow them to fall into their own pattern.

[1] Although most scholars divide the sayings into three groups (a plan which is followed, e.g., by H. Tödt), other classifications are possible; W. Manson, e.g., "The Son of Man and History", *S.J.T.*, 5, 1952, pp. 113–22, divides them into two groups.

[2] E.g. Mark 10.45. This difficulty is especially apparent in dealing with the "Son of man" sayings in St John's Gospel.

6

Survey of the Material: A

1. MARK 2.10

"But that you may know that the Son of man has authority
on earth to forgive sins"—he said to the paralytic—

Cf. Matthew 9.6; Luke 5.24

The reference to the Son of man in this passage is regarded by the
great majority of critics as an addition of the early Church. In
many cases the basic reason for this judgement has been the
difficulty of fitting this early use of the term "Son of man" into
any of the accepted theories regarding its meaning, though this has
been rationalized by an appeal to form-critical methods, and justified on the basis of the difficult structure of the paragraph. Of those
who retain the words, the majority interpret them as a reference to
man, although the only reason for doing so is once again the difficulty of reconciling any other interpretation of the phrase with its
use later in the gospels.[1] Here, at the beginning of our investigation, we find an example of the way in which the evidence has been
distorted by attempts to explain away those passages which apparently do not fit into the general scheme of "Son of man" sayings.
The significant distribution of the term "Son of man" in the
gospels has led many critics to regard a saying's position relative
to Peter's declaration at Caesarea Philippi as the chief criterion of
its authenticity. A further qualification for acceptance as genuine
is that it should fall into one of the two chief "classifications" of
sayings. On both these counts Mark 2.10 falls down; it is placed in
all three synoptics long before the events at Caesarea Philippi, and

---

[1] Cf. the judgement of G. Dalman, *The Words of Jesus*, p. 261: "This mode of
interpretation would hardly have arisen unless there had been reasons independent of the passages themselves for desiring to supersede the title 'Son of
man' as a title."

it apparently bears no relationship—apart from the use of the central term—to those passages which speak either of suffering or of eschatological glory.

Those who regard the term "Son of man" as a self-evident messianic title must inevitably consider its use here to be "unhistorical and anachronistic";[1] this judgement is shared by many scholars who do not consider it to be an accepted messianic term. Various explanations of this "anachronism" have been offered. The first sees the debate about forgiveness as an expansion of an original healing miracle, perhaps reflecting a controversy between the early Church and the Jewish authorities; in this saying, it is suggested, the Christian leaders expressed their belief about the authority given to Jesus, and sought to justify their own claim to forgive sins in the name of their master.[2] This interpretation fails to explain, however, why the disciples should have assumed authority to do something which Jesus himself had never claimed to do, or why the expansion should have been made in the case of this story in particular[3]—unless, with Dibelius,[4] we hold that the declaration of forgiveness is original, but that the ensuing conversation in vv. 6–10 is fictitious, inserted by the Christian preacher to bring out what he understood to be the point of the encounter; in that case, however, we must ask whether the word of forgiveness would indeed have passed unchallenged, and whether we should not in fact expect some such argument as Mark has supplied.[5] A further question which arises when we throw responsibility for the saying onto the early Church is why the phrase "Son of man" should have been introduced here and so rarely elsewhere—especially since the title is nowhere else associated with the forgiveness of sins.[6] This same difficulty applies to a second explanation which traces the phrase

---

[1] B. W. Bacon, in "The 'Son of Man' in the Usage of Jesus", *J.B.L.*, 41, 1922, pp. 154f. Cf. R. Otto, *The Kingdom of God and the Son of Man*, 1938, pp. 165ff.

[2] So R. Bultmann, *Die Geschichte der synoptischen Tradition*, 1931, pp. 12–14, E.Tr. pp. 14–16; H. E. Tödt, *Menschensohn*, pp. 117–21, E.Tr. pp. 126–30; E. Lohmeyer, *Das Evangelium des Markus*, 11th edn, 1951, in loc. Cf. A. E. J. Rawlinson, *St Mark*, 3rd edn, 1931, in loc.; A. Loisy, *Les Évangiles Synoptiques*, I, 1907, pp. 470–81; C. J. Cadoux, *The Historical Mission of Jesus*, 1941, p. 75; W. Manson, *Jesus the Messiah*, 1943, pp. 40–2; A. J. B. Higgins, *Son of Man*, pp. 26–8.

[3] Cf. B. H. Branscomb, *Mark*, pp. 44f; J. Schniewind, *Das Evangelium nach Markus*, 5th edn, 1949, p. 60.

[4] *From Tradition to Gospel*, 1934, pp. 66f. So too W. Manson, loc. cit.

[5] Dibelius himself admits that the story never existed without this element. If this is so, however, there is no basis or justification for its omission from the events which the story records.

[6] E. Lohmeyer, *Markus*, in loc. But cf. H. E. Tödt, loc. cit.

to the early Church, in this case by supposing that the words of Jesus have been incorrectly recorded, and that the reference to the Son of man replaces an original personal pronoun.[1] A third explanation is to take the whole sentence as "Mark's own comment addressed to the readers of the gospel".[2] The difficulty here is that we then have a reference to Jesus as the Son of man by someone else. This is very unlikely, although, as Acts 7.56 shows, it is possible; the somewhat unusual associations of the phrase in this case make it less probable, not more, since if Mark had himself introduced the term we should have expected him to use it in connection with one of the two themes—suffering and vindication—which were familiar to him from his own account of their use elsewhere.

Any attempt to dismiss this saying, either in part or *in toto*, as a creation of the early Church, can, unless it looks beyond this passage, be criticized for failing to take account of all the facts. For the absence of the phrase "Son of man" in other passages where it might well have been introduced by those who did not grasp its meaning is quite as significant as its isolated appearances in Mark 2. Equally important is the proximity of the two references in that chapter. Any satisfactory solution of the phrase's appearance in Mark 2 must seek an explanation of these facts, either in Mark's own interpretation of his narrative, or in his use of different sources, or in the fundamental historical tradition which underlies his sources.

An alternative method of interpretation accepts the saying as a genuine utterance of Jesus, but regards the phrase "the Son of man" as a mistranslation by Mark of an original reference to man. This solution has been supported by a surprising number of commentators,[3] but once again the real reason for its acceptance has been the impossibility of fitting this passage into the critics' categories. Moreover, this interpretation raises more difficulties than it attempts to solve. As R. H. Fuller remarks,[4] it "reduces the

---

[1] R. Otto, op. cit., pp. 232f.

[2] C. E. B. Cranfield, *The Gospel According to St Mark*, 1959, in loc.

[3] Originally by J. Wellhausen, *Das Evangelium Marci*, 1903, pp. 17f. Also F. Jackson and K. Lake, *Beginnings*, I, pp. 375f; T. W. Manson, *The Sayings of Jesus*, 2nd edn, 1935, p. 214; E. Klostermann, *Das Markusevangelium*, 2nd edn, 1926, in loc. J. Héring, *Le Royaume de Dieu et Sa Venue*, 1937, p. 109. J. Drummond, in *J.T.S.*, 2, 1901, pp. 568–71, and G. S. Duncan, *Jesus, Son of man*, 1948, pp. 149f, take the phrase to mean man in an ideal sense.

[4] *Mission and Achievement*, p. 99. Cf. M.-J. Lagrange, *Évangile selon Saint Mark*, 4th edn, 1947, in loc.; H. E. W. Turner, *Jesus, Master and Lord*, 2nd edn, 1954, pp. 198f.

saying to bathos, and indeed to blasphemy, as the opponents of Jesus rightly perceive"; the scribes are right in saying that God alone has power to forgive sins. If Jesus claims authority to do so, then it is because he—and he alone—shares the divine prerogative. It is significant that, if we are to trust the synoptic account, he claims this authority for himself as the Son of man, and not for himself *per se*.

The various attempts to explain the use of the term "Son of man" here are thus seen to be unsatisfactory. If we are to understand the saying, however, we must first examine the difficult structure of the sentence. As it stands, the important ἵνα clause of v. 10 does not depend on any main verb, and it is usually found necessary to treat the words which follow, λέγει τῷ παραλυτικῷ, as an awkward parenthesis, in order to make sense of the paragraph. Many commentators have regarded this apparent break in construction occurring between vv. 10 and 11 as an indication that the narrative has been patched up by Mark, and that the words about the Son of man are an addition to the original tradition. Although the modern reader may find the paragraph awkward, however, it is significant that Matthew and Luke, while making minor alterations to the construction, nevertheless took over this major anacoluthon; it would be surprising to find that the editors who normally rectified Mark's grammatical slips and inconsistencies accepted this sentence, if it were quite as difficult as modern scholarship has sometimes maintained. Either we must suppose that the construction, though clumsy, is the most natural way to convey the fact which the evangelists wish to record—namely that Jesus, while addressing the scribes, broke off to speak to the paralytic, and yet in doing so completed his words to the scribes; or we must conclude that the sentence is not quite as clumsy as it appears, and that we are dealing with an elliptical construction. It has been suggested that the ἵνα here is imperatival, and that the words of Jesus should be interpreted as a command to the scribes to recognize his authority.[1] Alternatively, we may suppose that the construction is parallel to that found in Mark 14.49, where we read

---

[1] The suggestion was made by D. S. Sharp in *E.T.*, 38, 1927, pp. 428ff. See also the discussion on "The Imperatival Use of ἵνα in the New Testament" by C. J. Cadoux, *J.T.S.*, 42, 1941, pp. 165–73; H. G. Meecham, *J.T.S.*, 43, 1942, pp. 179f; A. R. George, *J.T.S.*, 45, 1944, pp. 56–60; and the summary by C. F. D. Moule, *An Idiom-Book of New Testament Greek*, 2nd edn, 1959, pp. 144f. Examples of the imperatival ἵνα are given in Liddell and Scott and in Moulton and Milligan.

ἀλλ'ἵνα πληρωθῶσιν αἱ γραφαί. In that passage, Matthew has added the phrase upon which ἵνα depends, and has written: τοῦτο δὲ ὅλον γέγονεν ἵνα πληρωθῶσιν αἱ γραφαὶ τῶν προφητῶν. This example of an elliptical construction with ἵνα is of particular interest for our purpose since it follows a statement of two possible courses of action: Jesus remarks that his captors have come out to seize him as though he were a thief; yet he had sat among them daily in the temple and they had not touched him; his enemies have rejected one method and employed the other, and this whole course of events has taken place in order that the scriptures might be fulfilled. At this point we may compare also John 9.2f, where an elliptical construction with ἵνα is found in a context similar to Mark 2—namely a discussion between Jesus and his disciples on the relationship between sin and disease. Here, again, two alternatives are put forward—but this time they are possible explanations of the situation offered by the disciples, and both are rejected by Jesus. The reason for the man's blindness is given by Jesus in terms of purpose, not of cause; the whole series of events, involving not only the man's birth, but also his subsequent meeting with Jesus, has taken place in order that God's works might be made manifest in him—ἵνα φανερωθῇ τὰ ἔργα τοῦ Θεοῦ ἐν αὐτῷ.

Turning now to Mark 2.9f, we find a presentation of alternatives very similar to that made in Mark 14.48f: Jesus might have told the paralytic to get up and go home; instead he spoke the word of forgiveness: in v. 10 we may expect to be told why Jesus behaved as he did—why he spoke the one word before the other, and why this whole chain of events, of forgiveness followed by healing, is taking place. This, in fact, is what we have if we interpret the ἵνα here as Matthew interprets it in Mark 14.49 and as John uses it in 9.3: if we understand here an elided γέγονεν, then v. 10 offers us, not an extraneous saying which has been clumsily grafted onto the original story, but an explanation of Jesus' actions which is an essential and integral part of the original events: these things are being enacted as they are in order that men may know that the Son of man has authority on earth to forgive sins.[1]

An examination of the structure of this story as Mark gives it shows that, though it may defy the rules of form-criticism as to the form which is proper for it, it nevertheless possesses a very definite and logical pattern of its own. Although it falls into two sections

[1] On ἵνα δὲ here as an elliptical construction, cf. Blass-Debrunner, section 470.

it cannot be split into two as the form-critics demand, because its two themes are intertwined, and the whole point of the story is that we find forgiveness where we expect healing and vice versa. The faith of the paralytic's four friends, and the words spoken to him by Jesus in response to that faith, stand in contrast to the disbelief of the scribes, and the words of Jesus to the paralytic which are occasioned by that disbelief. If we accept this double-barrelled story as in any sense an accurate account of an incident in the life of Jesus, then we must ask why he gave this man an assurance of forgiveness, rather than the healing which his friends expected.

The ultimate reason is, as we have seen, given by Jesus in v. 10. But there must also be some particular reason which made the demonstration possible in this instance. At this point we are warned by Loisy against the danger of attempting to explain the story by supplying imaginary psychological details in a case about which we know so little.[1] If Jesus did in fact speak these words, however, we may suppose that it was because he realized that they would meet the sufferer's most urgent need. There is no need for us to speculate here about the previous moral behaviour of the paralytic, or about what relationship Jesus understood to exist between sin and disease: it is sufficient that popular opinion at that time did consider physical misfortune to be the direct result of sin,[2] and that the paralytic would undoubtedly have had ample time in which to reflect upon this fact. A remark in the Talmud,[3] that "No-one gets up from his sick-bed until all his sins are forgiven" is relevant here, not only as an indication of Jewish teaching on this subject, but also as a psychological insight into the situation: it may well be that the man's conviction of his own sin was sufficient to maintain his state of paralysis, and that he was physically incapable of responding to a bodily cure until his mind had been put at rest.

Jesus' words arouse in the scribes the natural reaction: to them they appear as blasphemy. There is no need for them to voice their opposition, for Jesus must realize what they are thinking: indeed, their reaction is justifiable, since as yet Jesus has offered no credentials for such an action. In spite of this, Dibelius would omit vv. 6–10 from the narrative on the basis that the scribes are introduced suddenly and—as he maintains—artificially into the narrative.[4]

[1] A. Loisy, *Synoptiques*, I, pp. 475f.   [2] Cf. again John 9.1–3.
[3] B. Ned. 41a.   [4] *From Tradition to Gospel*, pp. 66f.

It is possible that he is right in regarding these verses as an insertion, but if so they are not necessarily to be dismissed as the invention of the early Church; it is at least as likely that they record an incident which took place immediately after this episode, when the scribes were told of Jesus' claim to forgive sins, and that St Mark has inserted this at the relevant point in his narrative. The genuineness of these verses is supported, not only by the fact that we expect some such reaction as that of the scribes to be recorded, but by the nature of Jesus' reply, which has an authentic ring.[1] The riddle which he poses is similar to that with which he answers the authorities in Mark 11.27-33. These two passages are in fact closely parallel: both are concerned with the problem of Jesus' authority, and in both the criticism of the officials—voiced or unvoiced—is met by Jesus with a question which proves impossible to answer. There is also a somewhat similar situation in the account given by Matthew and Luke of the reply given by Jesus to the messengers sent by John;[2] the fact that in this last case the questioners are friendly may account for the fact that Jesus does not there use a "riddle". Yet once again he does not give a direct answer: his command to them to use their eyes and ears and to draw their own conclusions about his person from his activities is closely related to the questions about his authority which are raised in men's minds by his actions.

What is the meaning of Jesus' question, and what answer did he expect? All possible explanations have been offered: it has been said that healing is easier than forgiveness;[3] that it is easier to say "Be forgiven" than "Be healed" because the second demands visible proof, and the first does not;[4] that both are equally easy for Jesus.[5] But the situation, and the analogy with the puzzle which he poses in Mark 11, suggest that this, too, is a "trick question".[6] The question is not whether it is easier to heal or to forgive—the answer to which is self-evident if, with the scribes, one regards the latter, but not the former, as a divine act—but whether the word

[1] Cf. J. Schniewind, *Markus*, in loc.
[2] Matt. 11.2-6; Luke 7.18-23.
[3] So W. Bousset, *Kyrios Christos*, 3rd edn, 1926, pp. 39f, who amends the story accordingly and omits vv. 7b and 10.
[4] E.g. E. Klostermann, *Markus*, in loc.
[5] So A. Loisy, *Synoptiques*, I, p. 478.
[6] A similar comparison is made by T. A. Burkill, *Mysterious Revelation*, 1963, p. 131.

of healing or the word of forgiveness is the easier to speak. This form is surely deliberate: Jesus is here adopting the terminology of his critics who are, in effect, accusing him of speaking without acting. If the witnesses of this incident recognize its true significance they will understand that for Jesus, as for God, to speak *is* to act: for him neither "word" is easy, since each is an act of restoration. The ultimate answer to the question is perhaps that neither is easier than the other, since in the ministry of Jesus healing is as much a divine act and a sign of God's kingdom as forgiveness. The scribes may have formulated a similar answer in their minds, but if so it will be for a very different reason; since they consider Jesus' words to be blasphemy it is clear that they regard him as speaking empty—and therefore "easy"—words, and if Jesus is unable to heal the man, then the word of healing is equally empty and "easy". The purpose of Jesus' question becomes clear in his next action, for whatever answer the scribes make his authority will be established. Obviously they would not be likely to suggest that the word of healing was easier, for that would be to acknowledge that Jesus had already done the more difficult thing; if they consider both to be easy then Jesus will demonstrate that his words are far from being easy or empty. Similarly, if they regard his first command as the easier, then he will do the more difficult thing—speak the word of healing, the validity of which can be immediately proved—the very form of which, indeed, demands immediate action and proof. The resultant cure demonstrates not only his power to heal but also his authority to forgive, since it would be incredible that a man with blasphemy on his lips should be able to effect such a miracle. Thus the thing which is perhaps outwardly the more difficult is, to those who will accept it, the sign that another fundamental but invisible action has also been performed.

The relevance of Jesus' question to the unspoken charge of blasphemy is now clear;[1] so, too, is the reason why the charge is never in fact made, for Jesus' logic is compelling; by his cure of the paralytic he has demonstrated that his word of forgiveness was not "easy" or empty—that, in fact, he has authority on earth to forgive sins. The scribes may not accept this demonstration or

---

[1] V. Taylor, *The Gospel according to St Mark*, 1957, p. 197, is wrong in saying that the doctrinal question is ignored; as usual, Jesus translates it into practical terms. Cf. his treatment of the question about tribute money in Mark 12.13–17.

recognize his authority, but for the moment they are unable to re-
fute the force of his argument.

According to the synoptic account, the miracle of healing is performed as a sign to onlookers that the Son of man has the authority
to forgive sins. This demonstration is totally different, however,
from the kind of proof which the Pharisees were later to demand
from Jesus. As we have already noted, the reaction of the scribes
was the natural one and would be precisely what Jesus expected.
According to Mark's chronology, this is the first occasion in his
ministry on which Jesus claimed, by either word or action, to be
or to do more than the prophets who had preceded him: if now,
for the first time, he steps beyond those limits, he may be expected
to give some sign which will demonstrate, to those who have the
faith to understand, that his words are not blasphemous, but are
spoken with divine authority. But the miracle is far from being a
"proof" that Jesus is the Messiah: rather it is, as Jesus explicitly
states, a demonstration of the authority of the Son of man, which
is a very different thing. This is a legitimate use of a sign, and like
all Jesus' signs it requires an answering faith which can recognize
the significance of his actions, and see in them the activity of one
whose authority is not from men but from God. Moreover, forgiveness and healing are not here two distinct acts, but are different
aspects of one thing—the total restoration of the paralysed man.[1]
The one guarantees the other, not because it is a miraculous
"proof", but because they belong together. The use which Jesus
makes here of the sign of healing is thus far from being out of
character, as some scholars have maintained;[2] on the contrary, it
is completely in keeping with the rest of his ministry.

It is, then, possible to find a setting for this saying within the
ministry of Jesus himself. If we consider it within this setting,
what information can it offer regarding the term "Son of man"?

1. It is clear that for the evangelists Jesus and the Son of man are
in some way identifiable, for Jesus could have said "But that you
may know that I have authority on earth to forgive sins . . ." The
fact that he speaks here, according to the united synoptic

---

[1] Cf. the words of Jesus in John 5.14, which suggest that he has dealt with the
sins, as well as the paralysis, of the man whom he has healed; see the comment of
C. K. Barrett, *The Gospel according to St John*, 1955, in loc.
[2] E.g. A. E. J. Rawlinson, *Mark*, p. 24.

testimony, of the Son of man, suggests that he considered the act
of forgiveness to be an appropriate function of the Son of man.

2. If form-criticism is correct in stressing that this story had importance for the early Church as a basis for the claim to forgive
sins in the name of Christ, then it would seem that the term "Son
of man" here is to some extent linked with the community: the
authority of Jesus as Son of man is extended to his followers.

3. We may note that the Son of man is one who possesses authority;
moreover, it is an authority which goes beyond anything which
other men possess, for it is the authority to forgive sins, and that
is a divine prerogative; there is no indication in Jewish thought
that even the Messiah was ever credited with such authority.[1] In
this respect at least, therefore, the Son of man has been invested
with the authority of God himself, and he acts as God's representative and with his power. This divine activity is an inbreaking of
God's kingdom into his world, an overthrow of evil by good and a
restoration of man—in other words it is, like healing, one of the
signs of the New Age, and an eschatological event.

4. The sphere of this activity is defined as being $\epsilon\pi\grave{\iota}\ \tau\hat{\eta}s\ \gamma\hat{\eta}s$. There
is some textual uncertainty about the position of these words in the
Marcan text, and in some manuscripts they appear before the
words $\dot{\alpha}\phi\iota\acute{\epsilon}\nu\alpha\iota\ \dot{\alpha}\mu\alpha\rho\tau\acute{\iota}\alpha s$ (following the order in Matthew and Luke)
or between them, or they are even omitted altogether. This un-
certainty could be taken as evidence that the words are a later
addition, reflecting the Church's extension of the authority of the
Son of man from heaven to earth. It is more probable, however,
that the textual variants reflect assimilation to the text of Matthew
and Luke. The precise significance of the phrase in Mark is not
immediately clear. It is possible that the words qualify the noun
$\dot{\alpha}\mu\alpha\rho\tau\acute{\iota}\alpha s$,[2] which immediately precedes them in the probable text,
but if so they seem a little pointless and add nothing to the mean-
ing; obviously sins are committed on earth. More probably the
phrase may be intended as a contrast to the heavenly sphere, in
which case there are two possible interpretations: the authority of
the Son of man on earth may be contrasted either with that which
he may be expected to exercise in heaven at a later date, or with the

[1] Cf. S.-B., *Kommentar*, I, p. 495.   [2] C. E. B. Cranfield, *Mark*, in loc.

authority of God himself. Matthew, who puts the words immediately after the phrase "Son of man", appears to have interpreted them in the former way: his order reflects later Christian belief about the exalted Son of man. If Jesus himself spoke these words, such a contrast would have been of no significance to his hearers, who knew nothing of any authority to forgive sins given to the Son of man (whatever they might understand Jesus to mean by that term). A comparison (if we may term it such) with the authority of God, however, would be logical; indeed, the fact that we have just been explicitly told in v. 7 of the scribes' belief that only God could forgive sins seems to demand some such explanation. On this interpretation, then, it is the *authority* of the Son of man which is defined by these words. Now it is precisely on earth that, according to the biblical view, we should expect to find the Son of man exercising his authority: for if we turn to Gen. 1.26–30 we find that man is created to have dominion over the earth and its creatures and is commanded to subdue the earth and to "have dominion ... over every living thing that moves upon the earth"; in the LXX the phrase ἐπὶ τῆς γῆς occurs three times in these verses—and the word γῆ itself many more times. Moreover, this idea of man's dominion on earth is directly linked with his creation in the image and likeness of God: his authority on earth is dependent upon his likeness to God, who possesses the ultimate authority. The claim of Jesus that the Son of man has the authority on earth to exercise a divine function suggests, therefore, a total fulfilment of God's intention as expressed in Gen 1.26: the Son of man acts now as Adam was intended to act, as the representative of God on earth, and his authority there is a reflection of the authority of God in the universe; but man's likeness to God in the exercise of authority is, as we have seen, closely connected with his likeness to God in matters of obedience and righteousness,[1] and the authority of the Son of man to act as God's vicegerent on earth must be dependent upon a relationship between himself and God which fulfils the original words of the Creator: "Let us make man in our image, after our likeness."

5. The authority of the Son of man is exercised over the power of evil and profoundly influences the lives of men.

---

[1] Above, chapters 2 and 4.

6. There is nothing in this passage to suggest that "the Son of
man" was a "messianic" term.

According to the synoptic account, the words of Jesus evoked
no surprise among the spectators. True, we are told that "they
were all amazed and glorified God, saying, 'We never saw anything like this!'" but the amazement is said to spring from what
they had seen, not from what they had heard. Matthew, indeed,
associated their emotion specifically with the authority given by
God to men, but this may well represent his own interpretation of
their reaction; it is not clear, moreover, whether it is the authority
to forgive or to heal which he has in mind. The record of the
amazement of the crowd is, perhaps, nothing more than the
reference to the impression on the bystanders which, as the form-
critics have shown, usually concludes a miracle story; on the other
hand it may include astonishment at the unseen act of forgiveness
as well as at the visible act of healing. The synoptic setting suggests
the latter explanation, since the remark of the crowd in Capernaum,
where numerous miracles had already taken place, seems unduly
extravagant unless the healing were regarded either as particularly difficult or as significant of something else. In neither case,
however, is the amazement directed at Jesus' use of the term "Son
of man". This, of course, may be due to the influence of later
familiarity with the term, but the synoptic evidence is unanimous
in this point: nowhere does Jesus' use of the term "Son of man"
produce in itself any surprise among his hearers. The only suggestions of surprise or enquiry as to the Son of man's identity occur
in John.[1] Moreover, the form of Jesus' statement, as it appears in
Mark 2.10 and parallels, confirms that it is not the use of that
phrase which introduces the element of surprise: Jesus does not
say "I am the Son of man", or even "that you may know that I am
the Son of man"; on the contrary, he *begins* with the Son of man.
The fact that "the Son of man" is the subject of Jesus' statement,
together with the absence of any surprise on the part of his
hearers, can be interpreted as betraying the late origin of the
narrative: we must then understand the saying about the Son of
man as a dogmatic statement of the early Church, placed in an
artificial setting. On the other hand, there are two possible explanations of the words of Jesus as they stand. Either "the Son of

---

[1] John 9.35f (according to א, B, D); 12.34.

man" was an accepted title for a well-known figure who might properly be taken as the subject of a pronouncement by Jesus; in this case neither the use of the term itself nor the statement that he had the authority to forgive sins would necessarily occasion surprise unless it was clear from the context that Jesus and the Son of man are to be identified. According to the synoptic account, however, this was precisely the situation; on this interpretation, therefore, Jesus would in fact be making the statement "I am the Son of man", an identification which might be expected to produce an immediate and amazed response from his hearers. The alternative explanation is that the phrase "the Son of man" was, though distinctive, not particularly startling or puzzling to its original hearers; it would in itself convey nothing more than its obvious superficial meaning, and thus in this context its reference to Jesus would be clear, and it would not introduce a further "unknown quantity" into the saying. The emphasis would thus be thrown onto the point in dispute—namely the authority to forgive sins.

This would not, of course, mean that "the Son of man" was a colourless phrase: there are good reasons why Jesus should have used it at this point. Its relevance to the present context has been noted already in discussing the words ἐπὶ τῆς γῆς. As we have seen in previous sections, the Son of man in Daniel and Enoch is also given authority "on the earth"; so too, in the apocryphal literature, is Israel, as the inheritor of the promises made to Adam. True, the forgiveness of sins is nowhere mentioned (and therefore calls for demonstration); but it is an activity which we might well have expected from the Son of man—not only because he is given authority from God, but because forgiveness is at once the destruction of evil and the expression of a relationship existing between the Son of man and other men; both these ideas are prominent in Enoch and are implied in Daniel, in so far as the Son of man there is both a corporate and an individual figure.

2. MARK 2.28

So the Son of man is lord even of the sabbath.

Cf. Matthew 12.8; Luke 6.5

This saying, too, is dismissed as irrelevant to our enquiry by the great majority of scholars in much the same way and for much the same reasons as the last. Once again, its position in the synoptic narrative, the use of the term "Son of man" in conversation with Jesus' opponents, and the absence of any reference to suffering or to eschatological glory lead many to regard the saying as a development within the early Church.

The most commonly held view is perhaps that the phrase here is the result of a mistranslation, and that the title has been inserted in place of an original Aramaic phrase meaning "man". The verse is thus no more than the logical continuation of the preceding sentence, and the change from "man" to "Son of man" reflects Mark's misunderstanding of what was, in the original, merely synonymous parallelism.[1] There are less difficulties in accepting this interpretation here than there were in Mark 2.10, but it is nevertheless improbable that Jesus would have declared that mankind in general could dispense as they wished with the Mosaic Law.[2] An alternative interpretation sees this verse as an early addition to an original genuine saying of Jesus recorded in Mark 2.27 to the effect that the Sabbath was made for the benefit of man and not vice versa;[3] this addition reflects the desire of the Church to stress the personal lordship of Jesus over the Sabbath—an idea which is considered unlikely from Jesus himself. On this view, we are left with a saying which is little more than a general application of the principle given in the Midrash: "The Sabbath is delivered unto you, and ye are not delivered to the Sabbath."[4]

The crux of the problem is the relationship between these two verses in Mark. The complete absence of the first verse from both Luke and Matthew suggests that these were originally two separate sayings—and this, if substantiated, would completely undermine the explanation of "Son of man" in v. 28 as a mistranslation of

[1] So the original opinion of T. W. Manson, *The Teaching of Jesus*, p. 214; also J. Drummond, pp. 549f in *J.T.S.*, 2, 1901; G. S. Duncan, *Jesus Son of Man*, pp. 147f; C. J. Cadoux, *The Historic Mission of Jesus*, pp. 75f; J. M. Creed, *The Gospel According to St Luke*, 1930, pp. 84f; F. Jackson and K. Lake, *Beginnings*, I, pp. 375–9; B. S. Easton, *Christ in the Gospels*, 1930, pp. 116f.

[2] So A. E. J. Rawlinson, *Mark*, in loc., followed by V. Taylor, *Mark*, in loc., and C. E. B. Cranfield, *Mark*, in loc.; also R. H. Fuller, *Mission and Achievement*, p. 100. F. W. Beare, "The Sabbath was made for Man?", *J.B.L.*, 79, 1960, pp. 130–6, describes the saying in Mark 2.27 as "wholly inconceivable in any Jewish teacher including Jesus".

[3] So A. E. J. Rawlinson, loc. cit.; V. Taylor, loc. cit.; C. E. B. Cranfield, loc. cit.; W. Manson, *Jesus the Messiah*, p. 116; E. Lohmeyer, *Markus*, in loc.; H. E. Tödt, *Menschensohn*, pp. 121–3, E.Tr. pp. 130–2; M. Dibelius, *From Tradition to Gospel*, pp. 64f; A. J. B. Higgins, *Son of Man*, pp. 28–30.

[4] Mekilta 109b on Ex. 31.14. This is given as the opinion of Rabbi Simeon b. Menssya (c. A.D. 180) but probably represents earlier tradition.

"man". It is, however, significant that Matthew and Luke retain the very verse which, it is suggested, is a Christian comment, and jettison the saying which is considered by many to be an authentic word of Jesus: their evidence, in fact, supports precisely the opposite process to that which is being argued. The problem which confronts us is thus why Matthew and Luke omitted Mark 2.27, rather than why Mark added v. 28.

Another explanation of the relationship between the two Marcan verses was given by T. W. Manson;[1] reversing his original view that "Son of man" in v. 28 was a misunderstanding for man in general, he suggested that "man" in v. 27 was a misunderstanding for "Son of man". In support of this, Manson pointed out that the Sabbath was not, in fact, made for man in general, but was peculiar to the Jews: the comment in the Midrash on Ex. 31.14, quoted above, clearly refers to the Jewish nation; commenting on a similar passage in Ex. 16.29, the rabbis stated plainly that the Sabbath had been given to Israel alone, and that the Gentiles had no right to keep it.[2] Thus Manson, beginning from his assumption that the Son of man was a corporate figure including both Jesus and those who followed him, argued that Jesus spoke in terms of the Son of man—the new Israel—in v. 27, and that v. 28 was the logical conclusion from this principle.

This evidence is relevant to our enquiry, quite apart from the particular interpretation which Manson gives to the term "Son of man", and his suggestion that it should be read in v. 27. In saying that the Sabbath was made for man, Jesus was following the tradition which we have already examined, which spoke of Israel as man; its application in a saying about the Sabbath is of particular interest, since the Sabbath was not celebrated by Adam, and was unknown among men until Moses. This interpretation of the Sabbath is completely in accord with the viewpoint of the author of the book of Jubilees. As we have seen,[3] the keeping of the Sabbath is described in detail in Jubilees 2, immediately after the creation of man, when the first Sabbath was celebrated in heaven. The author stresses that the keeping of the Sabbath was not at this

---

[1] "Mark ii 27f", *Coniectanea Neotestamentica XI in honorem Antonii Fridrichsen*, 1947, pp. 138–46. This explanation—but not Manson's interpretation—is accepted by F. W. Beare, loc. cit. Beare traces both verses to the early Christian community.

[2] Ex. R. 25.11; Deut. R. 1. 21; cf. Midr. Teh. on Ps. 92.2.

[3] Above, pp. 62f.

stage known on earth:[1] it was a privilege reserved for Israel. Nevertheless, the discussion is introduced at this point because the author wishes to make clear the link between Adam and Jacob, and the relationship between the latter and the Sabbath: in the first part of this chapter he has given a description of the various works of creation, and has noted the number completed on each day, amounting together to a total of twenty-two; when these twenty-two works were finished, the Sabbath was kept: now we are told that there were "two and twenty heads of mankind from Adam to Jacob, and two and twenty kinds of work were made until the seventh day; this is blessed and holy; and the former also is blessed and holy; and this one serves with that one for sanctification and blessing."[2] So the Sabbath and Jacob occupy the same numerical position in creation: as the former followed twenty-two works, so the latter followed twenty-two "heads of mankind", the generations from Adam to Isaac; as the Sabbath marked the completion of creation, so Jacob marked the "completion" of mankind, and fulfilled God's original intention in creating Adam. A further point of interest in the narrative of Jubilees is that the keeping of the Sabbath is clearly portrayed as a privilege. God "did not sanctify all peoples and nations to keep Sabbath thereon, but Israel alone: them alone he permitted to eat and drink and to keep Sabbath thereon on the earth".[3] There is no suggestion here of the Sabbath as an oppressive institution hedged round with petty rules and regulations: it is true that Israel is commanded to do no work, but this is pictured as a blessing, rather than a burden; the Sabbath is a joyful occasion, shared with God and the angels, and associated with eating and drinking.[4] The author of Jubilees might well have summarized this section in the words of Jesus: "The Sabbath was made for man, not man for the Sabbath."

If this is the background against which we should understand Mark 2.27, the relevance of the saying to the context in which Mark has set it is clear; the Sabbath was made for man—that is Israel—and not vice versa; the attitude of the Pharisees, which treats the Sabbath as a troublesome duty and not as a privilege, is thus directly opposed to God's intention in creating the Sabbath as a blessing for his people.

What, then, is the relationship between this saying and that about

---

[1] Jub. 2.30.   [2] Jub. 2.23.   [3] Jub. 2.31.
[4] With Jub. 2.31 cf. also 2.21; 50.9–12.

the Son of man? Are those scholars right who maintain that the term in both verses should be the same? This seems unlikely: in spite of the reality of corporate personality, it is difficult to see how the nation as a whole could be regarded as lord of the Sabbath; Jesus' words do not mean that every individual Jew is free to use the Sabbath as he sees fit, or to ignore the Sabbath regulations. The principle of Sabbath observance stands—but the principle is demonstrated as resting on privilege, and not upon the letter of the law.[1]

At this stage we must ask what connection there is between Mark 2.27-8 and the argument which immediately precedes it, about David's unlawful eating of the shewbread. At first sight there would seem to be none—apart from the central theme of the setting-aside of regulations. Again, there seems to be little connection between vv. 25-6 and the original dispute; David broke regulations concerned with the shewbread, not with the Sabbath: the superficial similarity which exists in the connection of both cases with food breaks down when we remember that the disciples were rebuked for plucking and rubbing the corn, and not for eating it; the suggestion that the need of the disciples for food was in any way parallel to the desperate hunger of David and his men is scarcely convincing.[2] Closer investigation, however, suggests that there is a real parallel between these incidents, and one which we are in danger of overlooking if we seek out incidental parallels in the details of the stories.[3] Jesus' words about David relate how

---

[1] This appears to be the meaning of the incident recorded by Codex D at this stage of the narrative in Luke 6.5; it is the man's attitude to the Sabbath which determines the nature of his action: if he regards the Sabbath as a blessing then he, too, is blessed; if he is simply disregarding the regulations he is a transgressor.

[2] See A. Loisy, *Synoptiques*, I, pp. 505-13. T. W. Manson, *The Sayings of Jesus*, 1949, thinks that Jesus and his disciples were on a missionary journey, and that the corn was plucked to satisfy real hunger. R. H. Fuller, *Mission and Achievement*, p. 100, suggests that "the situation in which Jesus and his disciples find themselves, namely, in urgent expectation of the coming Kingdom, which is already breaking in, is an emergency situation comparable to that in which David took the shewbread". The existence of a general state of "emergency", however, is scarcely relevant to the present situation, unless Fuller means that the disciples were hungry and could obtain no other food.

[3] It is possible that the incident recorded in 1 Sam. 21.1-6 took place on the Sabbath, since the loaves which the priest had to hand were "removed from before the Lord, to be replaced by hot bread, on the day it is taken away", and this was done, according to Lev. 24.5-9, on the Sabbath; the Midrash on 1 Sam. 21 takes this view; this point is irrelevant to the comparison in Mark, however, since the day of the week is incidental to the infringement of the regulations by David and his men.

regulations which were made to safeguard something which is holy were set aside for David, who enjoyed a special position, and for "those who were with him"; he and they were allowed to eat what was normally permitted only to the priests. So now, in the case of Jesus and his disciples, the regulations which were made to safe-guard something which is holy—in this case the Sabbath—are again set aside for one who is in a special position and for those who are with him. In this case, however, the reason is not any pressing need, but the fact that the Son of man is the lord of the Sabbath.

This section in Mark appears, after all, to possess a certain unity and the final words of Jesus are of direct relevance to the situation. Nevertheless, the somewhat tortuous nature of the argument, to-gether with the comparison which is implied between David and Jesus, suggests that Mark (or a predecessor) may be responsible for this homogeneity. Moreover, the introductory formula καὶ ἔλεγεν αὐτοῖς in v. 27 indicates that the last two verses are a separate saying which has been added to round off the argument. However, these facts can tell us nothing about the origin of these two verses, which indeed have a better claim to being regarded as words of Jesus than the possibly intrusive section about David in vv. 25f. The Son of man's claim to authority is not dependent upon the implied comparison with David, but upon his relationship to Israel, the "man" for whom the Sabbath was made. The declara-tion in v. 28 is deduced from and dependent on v. 27; why, then, have Matthew and Luke omitted an important part of the saying? The answer is perhaps that they failed to see its importance. For them, "the Son of man" was an accepted title, whose meaning and reference to Jesus was plain; moreover, the authority of the Son of man and its origin were to them clear, and they needed no explana-tion about the relationship between man and the Sabbath to justify his claim to Lordship: this would thus seem to them un-necessary. Furthermore, in their judgement it was perhaps not merely unnecessary but liable to distract from what they regarded as being the central point of the incident: without it, Luke's account underlies the comparison and contrast between David and the Son of man, while Matthew substitutes for Mark's words other sayings, demonstrating that the authority of the Son of man is greater than that of David, of the priests, and even of the temple; after this list, a reference to man would seem an anti-climax.

If we accept Mark's version of the saying, then we may make the following observations about the Son of man in this passage:

1. The identification between Jesus and the Son of man is here by no means clearly made; it is, however, implied, since Jesus is questioned about the conduct of his disciples —who are thus regarded as being under his authority—and his reply appeals to the authority of the Son of man.

2. The context, which relates this saying to the behaviour of the disciples, suggests either that the Son of man is a corporate term, or that there is a very close relationship between the Son of man and his followers.

3. The Son of man is again portrayed as one who possesses authority—an authority which goes beyond that exercised by any ordinary individual.

4. The sphere of his authority is the Sabbath, and the ideas associated with the Sabbath take us back once more to the fulfilment of God's purpose in creating man: in the presence of the Son of man the blessing which was offered to Jacob/Israel is renewed.

There is some evidence to suggest that the Sabbath itself was associated with this theme of restoration. Certainly the idea of rest was a synonym for the enjoyment of the Promised Land,[1] and when both rest and land were lost, the future restoration was portrayed in terms of return and rest.[2] It is possible that this rest was linked with the idea of the Sabbath,[3] and the connection would appear to be an obvious one: according to the explanation of Deut. 5.14f, indeed, the Sabbath was kept as a memorial of God's deliverance of his people from Egypt, the saving act which brought them to the enjoyment of the rest of the Promised Land. A passage in 2 Esdras which we have already examined is of

---

[1] See, e.g., Deut. 3.20; 12.9; Josh. 1.13–15; Ps. 95.11.
[2] E.g. Isa. 14.3; Jer. 30.10; 2 Esdras 8.52. Cf. the picture of Israel as a flock of sheep resting in good pasture in Ezek. 34.
[3] E. C. Hoskyns, in his essay, "Jesus the Messiah", *Mysterium Christi*, 1930, ed. G. K. A. Bell and A. Deissmann, pp. 67–89, argued that this link is suggested by the use of ἀνάπαυσις–ἀναπαύειν and κατάπαυσις–καταπαύειν to translate both שבת and such words as נוח and רבץ.

interest here:[1] in 6.35–59 the author describes in detail the six
days of the creation, but the seventh day is missing; instead, we
have a complaint that God's chosen people, for whose sake the
world was made, have not entered into their inheritance—the purpose of creation is not yet fulfilled, for Israel does not rule the
earth but is oppressed and devoured by the other nations; it is possible that the author sees the inheritance and peace which Israel
does not yet enjoy as the Sabbath rest which will come only when
God's command to Adam to rule the other works of creation is
fulfilled. This idea is closely parallel to that of the millennium,
which is based on the interpretation of one day as a thousand
years,[2] and expects world history to follow the pattern of the week
of creation, lasting in all seven thousand years; evidence for this
idea in Judaism is, however, both late and scanty, and the relationship between the final thousand years and the Sabbath is by no
means clear.[3] Further hints of this idea are found in rabbinical
sayings which depict the Sabbath as a foretaste of the future,
though once again the evidence is late.[4]

The idea reappears in the New Testament, most notably in Heb.
3.7—4.13, which expounds Ps. 95.11 in terms of Christian salvation: the Jews, because of their disobedience, never entered into
God's rest, and so it is given to others to enter it: "There remains

---

[1] Above, pp. 49f.

[2] See Jub. 4.30; cf. Ps. 90.4.

[3] R. H. Charles, *Apocrypha and Pseudepigrapha of the Old Testament*, II,
p. 451, claims to find the idea of 6,000 years followed by 1,000 years of rest in
2 Enoch 32—3. Certainly this passage speaks of the seven days of creation followed
by 7,000 years of world history, but although the Sabbath is mentioned in 32.2
the parallel between this and the final thousand years is not drawn; the emphasis
is on the beginning of the eighth "day", when time will cease and there will be
desolation. Cf. 1 Enoch 93.1–10, where the righteous are rewarded after the end of
the seventh week. The plan of 6,000 + 1,000 years is found in rabbinical literature,
e.g. B. Sanh. 97a, B. Rosh Hashana 31a, but the thousand years is again desolation
rather than rest; moreover, the rabbis are disagreed in their arithmetic, some
expecting a sequence of 5,000 + 2,000, on the basis of Hos. 6.2. Cf. S.-B.,
Kommentar, III, p. 687.

[4] In Gen. R. 17.5 and again in 44.17, we find the judgement of R. Hanina b.
Isaac that there are three incomplete phenomena: sleep is the incomplete form
of death; a dream, of prophecy; the Sabbath, of the world to come. B. Berakoth 57b
speaks of the Sabbath as a foretaste of the world to come, one Sabbath being a
sixtieth part of the future world. B. Rosh Hashana 31a lists the psalms sung by the
Levites on different days of the week and says that on the Sabbath they sing Ps.
92 "for the day which will be all Sabbath"; this is interpreted by Rashi as
meaning the time "when God shall be alone, between the end of the world and
the resurrection of the dead." Ruth R. 3.3 compares this world and the next to
the eve of and day of the Sabbath, but this is probably intended only as a comparison, the point being that preparation must be made in time, because there
is no return.

a sabbath rest for the people of God; for whoever enters God's rest also ceases from his labours as God did from his." In Matthew, we find that the incident in the cornfields follows immediately after a passage in which Jesus specifically offers rest to his followers in words closely related to Ecclus. 51;[1] his easy yoke and light burden, through which this rest is achieved, stand in contrast to the regulations of the Pharisees, which defeat their own purpose of safeguarding the Sabbath rest. Many of the healings recorded in the gospels are said to have taken place on the Sabbath;[2] it is possible that Jesus even regarded the Sabbath as a particularly appropriate day for the work of restoration.[3]

The significance of these Sabbath healings is discussed in John 5.16–18, where Jesus justifies his action in healing on the Sabbath with the words: "My Father is working still, and I am working." The whole section John 5.1–18 is of particular interest for our discussion here, since it has points of contact with both the passages in Mark 2 with which we are concerned. The healing of the paralytic, the words with which the cure is effected, and the reference to sin, all find parallels in the story related in Mark 2.1–12; the complaint of the Jews that the man—on the authority of Jesus— is breaking the Sabbath regulations is very similar to the situation in Mark 2.23–8. In John 5.16 the controversy switches from the action of the ex-paralytic to that of Jesus himself: in his reply, Jesus claims that his activity parallels that of his Father—words which express, in Johannine language, an idea very close to that which we have examined in Mark 2.1–12. In relation to the Sabbath, this means that for Jesus, as for God, there is in fact no Sabbath, since the creative activity of both still continues;[4] there can therefore be no rest until the work of restoration is completed.

---

[1] Matt. 11.28–30.

[2] Mark 1.21–7; 1.29–31; 3.1–5; Luke 13.10–16; John 5.2–16; 9.13f.

[3] C. F. Evans, in the article on "Sabbath", *A Theological Word Book of the Bible*, ed. A. Richardson, 1950, p. 205, suggests that Jesus "went out of his way to heal on the Sabbath". Cf. also E. C. Hoskyns, op. cit., pp. 74–8, who argues that Jesus understood the Sabbath "as a ritual anticipation of the advent of the Messianic age", and that his action in healing on the Sabbath exhibited the presence of the Messiah; in view of the late nature of the Jewish evidence, he considers this to be an original thought of Jesus—though his meaning would have been clear to the Pharisees. A. G. Hebert, *The Throne of David*, 1941, pp. 143–63, discusses Jesus' use of the Sabbath and reaches very similar conclusions.

[4] For Jewish references to the idea of God as eternally creative, see C. K. Barrett, *John*, p. 213.

It would not be legitimate to conclude, on the basis of a Johannine passage, that the authority of the Son of man in Mark 2.28 is presented as an extension of that exercised by God. Nevertheless, the Johannine interpretation is perhaps only a clear expression of an idea that is implicit in Jesus' words: for if the Son of man is lord of the Sabbath—and is therefore entitled to abrogate the regulations concerning it if he wishes—then he possesses an authority which is at least equal to that of the Mosaic Law, a law which was not of human origin, but was given by God himself. Once again, therefore, the authority of the Son of man goes beyond any merely human authority: his lordship of the Sabbath is another element of the New Age, a part of man's restoration and of God's activity ἐπὶ τῆς γῆς.

5. There is some vital connection between man and the Son of man: his lordship of the Sabbath is linked with, and is dependent upon, man's possession of the Sabbath. Since "man" stands here for Israel, the connection is with Israel in particular. This relationship is in some sense reciprocal: those men who follow the Son of man enjoy the privileges of the Sabbath because he is the lord of the Sabbath; he is its lord because it was made for them to enjoy.

6. There is no evidence in the saying itself that "the Son of man" was a messianic term. The parallel with David might suggest a messianic interpretation, but the point of the comparison is different: the Son of man is not portrayed as David's successor, but as exercising a similar sort of authority in a different sphere. Moreover, as we have seen, this comparison with David may well be later than the saying about the Son of man.

7

Survey of the Material: B

1. MARK 8.31

And he began to teach them that the Son of man must suffer
many things, and be rejected by the elders and the chief priests
and the scribes, and be killed, and after three days rise again.

Cf. Matthew 16.21; Luke 9.22

This saying, the first major prediction of the passion, is more
generally accepted as a genuine word of Jesus than those which we
have examined in Mark 2, though it is, of course, rejected by those
scholars who regard all references to the passion as *vaticinia ex
eventu*. Bultmann,[1] for example, dismisses it on two grounds: (*a*)
Jesus could not have foretold his passion; (*b*) only sayings about
the "coming" Son of man are genuine. The first of these bases
is against not only the gospel evidence, but also reason, since Jesus
must have been aware of the official opposition to him and realized
where this, taken with his own refusal to allow his followers to
fight for him, was likely to lead.[2] The second basis begs the question; it is the judgement of one who has already decided the meaning of the term "Son of man" before approaching the gospel
evidence.

The context of this saying is of the greatest importance. According to all three evangelists, it was spoken immediately after Peter's
confession at Caesarea Philippi, and before the teaching of Jesus

---

[1] *Theology of the New Testament*, I, 1952, pp. 29ff; he is followed by A. J. B.
Higgins, *Son of Man*, pp. 30–3.
[2] Cf. the comment of C. H. Dodd in *The Parables of the Kingdom*, 2nd edn,
1936, p. 57: "It needed not supernatural prescience, but the ordinary insight of
an intelligent person, to see whither things were tending, at least during the later
stages of the ministry." See also C. J. Cadoux, *The Historic Mission of Jesus*,
1941, pp. 249ff.

8—S.O.M.

on the conditions of discipleship. This whole incident is interpreted by Bultmann and others as a "Glaubenslegende", which carries back into the life of Jesus the early Church's confession of him as Messiah.[1] This simple explanation raises more problems than it solves;[2] in particular, if Jesus' rebuke of Peter is not historical, then we must imagine a controversy within the early Church of sufficient bitterness to have caused its invention. Although the narrative will undoubtedly have been influenced by the later knowledge and faith of the Church, it is highly probable that it embodies early tradition, and it is therefore valid to consider whether the Marcan account can be understood within the context of Jesus' ministry.

It should be observed that the initiative throughout these verses is taken by Jesus.[3] The confession of faith is made by Peter, but it is made in response to a question put by Jesus himself; similarly, Peter's protest is called forth by Jesus' teaching. By his question Jesus encourages his disciples to declare their faith in him as Messiah. Yet, according to both Mark and Luke, he gives no indication that he has accepted the title. One reason for this "omission" —as it seems to us to-day—is undoubtedly that it would not have occurred to either evangelist that any of their readers could ever suppose that Jesus had not believed himself to be the Messiah: it did not seem necessary to make clear (as Matthew has, perhaps incidentally, done) that Jesus accepted and approved Peter's confession. Have the evangelists, however—or have others before them—misinterpreted the tradition? Is the absence from the Marcan tradition of a statement like that given by Matthew in 16.17 significant? Many scholars consider that it is: according to their interpretation, Jesus apparently led his disciples to confess him as Messiah merely in order to shatter their belief[4] or to re-

---

[1] R. Bultmann, *Geschichte*, pp. 275–8, E.Tr. pp. 257–9.

[2] See the discussion by V. Taylor, *Mark*, pp. 374f.

[3] This in itself is regarded by Bultmann as a mark of secondary material—see *Geschichte*, loc. cit. and p. 70, E.Tr. p. 66. This is a singularly unconvincing argument. It may be true, as Bultmann points out, that one mark of the lateness of St John's Gospel is that there "all that Jesus does springs from his own initiative", but we are surely not, on that account, to deny *all* initiative to the historical Jesus.

[4] Thus J. Héring, *Le Royaume de Dieu et Sa Venue*, 1937, pp. 122–7, maintains that Jesus rejected both of Peter's declarations. So, too, J. Knox, *The Death of Christ*, pp. 78–80.

interpret it out of all recognition.[1] If Jesus had not wished them to think of him as Messiah, however, he would scarcely have given them this open invitation to declare their belief, unless he had followed it immediately with a strong denial: of such a denial there is no trace. It has, indeed, been suggested that the intention of the words recorded in Mark 8.30 has been misunderstood: Jesus' command to silence was imposed, it is argued, not because he wished his Messiahship to remain temporarily secret, but because the idea itself was false.[2] It is incredible, however, that an emphatic denial should have been misinterpreted in this way, or, indeed, that the incident would have been remembered, far less regarded erroneously as a landmark, if Jesus had indeed denied that he was the Messiah.[3]

The words of Jesus in 8.30 are not a rebuke, but a command to keep silent;[4] the disciples are to keep silent, not because their information is false, but because it is secret.[5] This command to secrecy underlies a contrast which is found throughout the whole of this passage—namely the distinction between "men" in general and the disciples. The distinction has been made already in the questions which Jesus put, asking the disciples first for the opinion of others, and then for their own; the form of this second question, with its emphatic ὑμεῖς, shows that the contrast is deliberate, and not merely a way of leading up gently to the central question. By the answer of Peter, the disciples are confirmed in their separation from other men, for they alone know who Jesus really is;[6] but now that they have entered into his secret they must keep both it and their separation from those who do not

---

[1] E.g. O. Cullmann, *The Christology of the New Testament*, 1959, pp. 122–7.

[2] J. Héring, loc. cit.; J. Knox, op. cit., p. 80. Cf. R. H. Fuller, *The Foundations of New Testament Christology*, p. 109.

[3] Cf. B. H. Branscomb, *Mark*, p. 153.

[4] The word ἐπιτιμάω means not only to "rebuke, reprove, censure", but also to "speak seriously, warn in order to prevent an action or bring one to an end"; it is "followed by ἵνα or ἵνα μή to introduce that which the censure or warning is to bring about or prevent", Arndt-Gringrich, *Lexicon*, in loc.

[5] There is a close parallel to this command of Jesus in Matt. 12.16, where he imposes a similar condition of secrecy on those whom he has healed: καὶ ἐπετίμησεν αὐτοῖς, ἵνα μὴ φανερὸν αὐτὸν ποιήσωσιν. Mark 3.12 directs the same command to the unclean spirits; here, and in Mark 10.48 and parallels, ἐπιτιμάω is used with reference to an activity which is already in progress.

[6] R. H. Lightfoot, *The Gospel Message of St Mark*, 1950, pp. 33f, suggests that the real significance of Mark's account of this event is to be found in this "contrast between those who perceive and confess the divine nature and office of the Lord, however and whenever they may have gained this knowledge, and those who in St Paul's words still only know him after the flesh".

understand, for the secret cannot yet be shared with all men. Why this secret? Mark offers no explanation. One was supplied by Wrede, however,[1] who regarded the command to secrecy as part of the artificial "messianic secret" imposed by Mark upon his material. It is more than likely that Wrede is at least partially correct in attributing this motif of secrecy to the activity of the early Church; the fact that what was so obvious to them had remained hidden from Jesus' contemporaries must have seemed to them explicable only on the assumption of a deliberate concealment. This does not mean, however, that the idea of a hidden Messiahship is necessarily totally foreign to the original tradition,[2] nor that the recognition of Jesus' Messiahship is not to be traced back into his lifetime; on the contrary, the evidence that Jesus was charged at his trial with being a messianic pretender (but one who had made no open claim) seems reliable. If it is correct to suppose that Jesus was recognized as more than a rabbi by his disciples during his ministry, however, then some such event as Mark describes here seems to be almost necessary.[3] The best indication as to whether or not Mark's narrative has any foundation within the life of Jesus is to be found in its inner consistency or lack of it.

The need for secrecy in the situation which is depicted by Mark is plain: Peter has summed up in a few words all the hopes and beliefs of the disciples about their master, a declaration which would inevitably have been a moment of emotion and elation, however long these ideas had been in their minds; their natural reaction, once they felt that they were sure who Jesus was, would be to rush off and tell everyone they met about him. This is precisely the situation which Jesus apparently wished to avoid—perhaps the reason why he chose the region of Caesarea Philippi for this discussion—and so the words of Peter are immediately followed by the strict order to refrain from doing what they would so much like to do. Clearly, this secrecy could not continue

---

[1] W. Wrede, *Das Messiasgeheimnis in den Evangelien*, 3rd edn, 1963, pp. 237–9.

[2] E. Sjöberg, *Der Verborgene Menschensohn in den Evangelien*, 1955, pp. 218f, argues that secrecy is a necessary element in the belief in Jesus' Messiahship, whether this is primary or secondary in the tradition.

[3] Cf. E. Schweizer, "The Son of Man", in *J.B.L.*, 79, 1960, p. 121, who believes that there are too many difficulties in attributing the narrative about Caesarea Philippi solely to the faith of the early Church. Cf. also E. Sjöberg, op. cit., pp. 103–8.

indefinitely, for a permanently hidden Messiah (however that word might be interpreted) would be a contradiction in terms: if Jesus were indeed the Messiah, then this must be revealed one day. Jesus' purpose, however, is not to precipitate a messianic uprising, but to call forth the obedient response of men and women to the claims of God's kingdom.

So far, Mark's narrative is consistent. At this point, however, Jesus begins, somewhat abruptly, to speak of the suffering which lies ahead. It is here, too, that the phrase "Son of man" is suddenly reintroduced: Mark and Luke are agreed in using it, and its absence from Matthew is not significant, since its omission is no doubt due to the author, a stylistic variation compensating for its addition in 16.13. If Mark and Luke are correct, then it is clear that Peter, whatever he may have understood by Jesus' use of the term, did at least realize that he was using it of himself: a corporate significance is not, of course, excluded, but the primary reference must be to Jesus. We must therefore ask whether there could be any reason why Jesus should choose to refer to the Son of man at this point, rather than take up the title which Peter has just given him, or use the pronoun "I", which would be the most natural manner of referring to himself. This last method is, of course, precisely that which many scholars presume Jesus to have employed: the use of the phrase "Son of man" in the passion predictions is explained as due to Mark, who understood it as Jesus' own way of designating himself as Messiah.[1] We must therefore examine the saying more closely and discover whether there is any indication of any other reason for the use of the term in this particular context.

The vital clue to the meaning of this verse is perhaps to be found in the word δεῖ, used by all three evangelists: the sufferings of the Son of man are not merely certain but necessary. Why must the Son of man suffer? The term δεῖ expresses a conviction that his suffering and death are in accordance with the will of God revealed in Scripture.[2] Is this only an expression of the early Church's belief, arising from their attempt to explain the passion, or does it reflect also the interpretation of Jesus himself? It has

---

[1] So J. Knox, op. cit., pp. 102–4.
[2] See E. Fascher, "Theologische Beobachtungen zu δεῖ", *Neutestamentliche Studien für Rudolf Bultmann*, Beihefte zur *Z.N.T.W.*, 21, 1954, pp. 228–54; also H. E. Tödt, *Menschensohn*, pp. 174–8, E.Tr. pp. 188–93.

been maintained that Jesus had drawn the conclusion that he must suffer from the Jewish scriptures, which had convinced him that his death was foreordained by God.[1] This explanation tends, however, to portray Jesus as possessed of a crude literalism, modelling his life and death to conform to certain Old Testament texts.[2] It fails to offer any explanation of the term "Son of man", and it tells us nothing about the meaning and purpose of the Son of man's suffering, the ultimate reason for which is still not clear.

The fault perhaps lies in the form in which the problem is presented. In answering the question "why must the Son of man suffer?" the central term is in fact usually ignored quite as effectively as it is by those scholars who excise the reference to the Son of man from the saying altogether; in practice, the question becomes "why must *Jesus* suffer?" If the use of the term *is* original, however, then there ought to be some connection between it and the necessity expressed in the word $\delta\epsilon\hat{\imath}$: conversely, if we find the idea of the necessity of suffering inherent in the phrase "Son of man", then the case for the use of the term here by Jesus will be considerably strengthened.

The suggestion that the idea of the Son of man necessarily includes that of suffering seems at first absurd: he is a figure naturally associated with glory. It is true that the saints in Dan. 7 suffer, but this suffering is not a necessary part of what being the Son of man should mean—quite the reverse. At this point, however, we may perhaps approach the problem in a different way, and ask, not "Why must the Son of man suffer?" but "How can the Son of man suffer?" This, incidentally, is much more likely to be the question which the disciples asked themselves when faced with the same problem. If we turn again to Daniel, the answer to *this* question is immediately clear: the Son of man can—and will—suffer when his rightful position and God's authority are denied: this is the situation in Dan. 7, where the "beasts" have revolted against God and have crushed Israel who, as Son of man, should be ruling the earth with the authority granted by God. Given this situation of the nations' revolt and their rejection of the claims of

---

[1] E.g. J. W. Bowman, *The Intention of Jesus*, 1945, pp. 128–36; O. Cullmann, op. cit., pp. 60–9.

[2] E.g. E. C. Hoskyns, in *Mysterium Christi*, ed. G. K. A. Bell and A. Deissmann, 1930, p. 87, wrote that Jesus "provoked his death consciously and of set purpose, because its necessity was laid upon him as the Messiah, in order that the Old Testament Scriptures might be fulfilled".

the one who is intended to exercise authority, it is true to say that the Son of man not only can but must suffer. The position in Enoch is similar: the Son of man there has become individualized and we read nothing of his sufferings, but the righteous and elect associated with him are clearly still undergoing persecution; their sufferings will cease when he is recognized by the usurping powers as the elect one of God. In 2 Esdras the people of Israel suffer, although they are Adam's heirs, because the other nations have seized power and denied them the inheritance: "man" will rule—and therefore be released from suffering—only when the nations are subdued and recognize Israel's authority.

If we return now to the saying in Mark 8.31, and ask how the Son of man there can suffer, the answer will be the same: he can—and will—suffer, if men set themselves up against God and reject the claims of the one to whom he has given authority. In this situation the suffering of the Son of man is inevitable, and the suffering will end only when his authority is recognized and accepted. Now if we are to believe Mark, this is precisely the situation which already exists. The rejection of Jesus by the authorities is described here as a future necessity but, in fact, it has already taken place; scribes and Pharisees have already refused to accept his claim to God-given authority; Pharisees and Herodians have already determined to kill him. The authority of the Son of man has been demonstrated and rejected, and unless and until the powers which have set themselves up in opposition to God are overthrown, suffering is inevitable.

The fact that the evangelists link this teaching about the necessity of the Son of man's sufferings with Peter's declaration at Caesarea Philippi, rather than with the rejection recorded in Mark 3.6, does not destroy the connection between the rejection and the suffering, though it has perhaps obscured it for the modern reader. There are several possible explanations of the gap between 3.6 and 8.31: Mark's topical layout of the material may have tended to emphasize the lapse of time between these events. According to Mark's own scheme, it was immediately after his rejection by the authorities in 3.6 that Jesus "withdrew with his disciples" and "appointed twelve, to be with him, and to be sent out to preach and have authority to cast out demons"; the intervening chapters have been largely concerned with this theme, and the events at Caesarea Philippi stand as the climax to this section of the gospel,

before Jesus turns towards Jerusalem. The connection between
8.31 and 2.1—3.6 is brought out by the renewed use of the term
"Son of man", and by the reference to his rejection by the Jewish
leaders.

At this point we must ask, however, whether we are right in interpreting the Jewish leaders as the powers which deny authority
to the Son of man, and set themselves up in opposition to God. It
is obvious that they do refuse to recognize the authority of Jesus,
and that they are instrumental in bringing about his death, but
they are scarcely great enough for the rôle of powers which rule the
world. It may perhaps be that they are only instruments, acting—
unconsciously—as agents of the real power which has seized the
government of the world, and so has defied God and snatched
authority from man, whom he created to control the world. There
are numerous indications in the gospel narratives that Jesus saw
the whole of his life and ministry as a battle against Satan; it
would be surprising if he had not regarded his death also in the
same light. The opposition of the leaders is more than human:
their rejection of Jesus is evil, and to one who regarded evil as a
personal force, their attitude must appear Satanic.[1] Thus the
conflicts in Mark 2.1—3.6 are signs of a deeper opposition and it is
this—the power of Satan over the world, of which the human conflicts are but a part—which makes the Son of man's suffering and
his rejection by the Jewish leaders certain.

Mark appears to have been correct, therefore, in not associating
too closely the beginning of the teaching about the Son of man's
sufferings and the conflicts with the Jewish authorities. The further
question arises, however, whether he was also correct, not only in
placing all the predictions after Caesarea Philippi, but in linking
the first of them with that occasion—an association which is emphasized by the word ἤρξατο. If he is, then there would seem to be
some deep and fundamental connection between Jesus' Messiahship and the teaching about suffering. If we are to understand this,
then we must consider also the relationship between the Messiah
and the Son of man.

It is generally assumed by those who accept the Marcan narrative as historical that Jesus introduced the teaching about the
sufferings of the Son of man at this point as an explanation or

---

[1] Thus even Peter can be addressed as Satan, Mark 8.33.

qualification of the meaning of his Messiahship: his idea of the Messiah did not coincide with theirs, and it was therefore necessary to change their ideas as to what it involved.[1] This explanation is not satisfactory, however: if it had merely been a question of re-educating the disciples in their understanding of Messiahship, we should expect him to begin this much earlier, rather than wait until they had reached a distorted picture of what he was, and then seek to correct it. Mark's narrative suggests that this teaching not only was not but could not be given until after the recognition of Jesus as Messiah: it appears as if the Messiahship of Jesus and the sufferings of the Son of man are so vitally related that the second cannot be understood until the first is acknowledged. The necessity of suffering is indeed spoken of only to the disciples, to those who have acknowledged him as Messiah, and are as a result separated from other men: and yet even they are unable to understand this teaching; they recoil against it, and in doing so they immediately put themselves back into the circle of outsiders, so that their spokesman, Peter, is rebuked for thinking like men and speaking like Satan. We must ask, therefore, why the relationship between the recognition of Jesus as Messiah and the teaching that the Son of man must suffer is so strong that the first must precede the second, and the denial of the second implies the denial of the first.

To answer this question we must return to the explanation which we offered of the necessity for the Son of man's sufferings: this arose, we suggested, from the rejection of his authority, and the opposition of forces hostile to God; paradoxically, the very authority which should give him dominion will lead to suffering if it is denied and opposed. It is this paradox which provides the clue to Jesus' earlier silence about his suffering, for if the necessity for suffering and rejection arises from his authority, then it is clear that they can be explained only to those who recognize that authority. The situation which will lead to suffering has already arisen, but it is only when the disciples have acknowledged the authority of Jesus that they are in a position to understand the consequences of the rejection of that authority by others, and that they can be taught why the Son of man must suffer. The sufferings of the Son

---

[1] See R. H. Fuller, *Mission and Achievement*, pp. 109ff; H. E. W. Turner, *Jesus, Master and Lord*, 1953, p. 112; A. E. J. Rawlinson, *Mark*, in loc.; E. Klostermann, *Markus*, in loc.

of man are thus not a qualification of the idea of Messiahship, but the inevitable consequence of the rejection of the Messiah.

It is necessary here to consider the relationship between the Messiah and the Son of man, since Peter's confession of Jesus' authority is in fact made in terms of the former, not the latter. The change in titles which is made by Jesus can be explained— if we accept the use of the different terms here as original—either as evidence that the two were interchangeable,[1] or as part of the reinterpretation of Messiahship which Jesus found it necessary to make.[2] There is some truth in both these views, but either of them, taken alone, is misleading. The first is correct in its assumption that the phrase "Son of man" could be—and occasionally was —interpreted messianically; but there is scanty evidence to support the idea that it was a recognized messianic "title". The second interpretation is undoubtedly right in suggesting that the disciples' views about Messiahship did not coincide with those of Jesus, since the vision of the former was limited by their ideas of political and temporal power; nevertheless, to stress the contrast in this way is to suggest that there was a rigid concept of the Messiah in existence at this time. In fact, however, as recent studies have emphasized,[3] the idea of the Messiah was an extremely nebulous one, and did not necessarily indicate the Son of David; even to say that there were two views about the Messiah, the one Davidic and the other apocalyptic,[4] perhaps suggests something too akin to established doctrines. It is unfortunate that our use of the Hebrew and Greek words "Messiah" and "Christ" inevitably produces a tendency to think of them merely as titles; to first-century Jews, however, the words would retain their original meaning, even when the special application was made, so that when they spoke of the "Anointed" they were not using a strange technical term, but a word whose fundamental significance would be inescapably present in their minds. There is no need to suppose that Jesus "rejected" or "modified" the term, for it was one which was

---

[1] R. Otto regards the terms as synonyms, see *The Kingdom of God and the Son of Man*, p. 231.

[2] A. Richardson, *An Introduction to the Theology of the New Testament*, 1958, pp. 134f; M.-J. Lagrange, *Marc*, in loc.

[3] See S. Mowinckel, *He That Cometh*, chapter 9; O. Cullmann, op cit., pp. 111–17. Cf. also G. F. Moore, in *Beginnings*, I, pp. 346–62; F. C. Burkitt, *Christian Beginnings*, 1924, pp. 26ff.

[4] S. Mowinckel, op. cit., chapters 9 and 10; cf. J. Kallas, *The Significance of the Synoptic Miracles*, 1961, pp. 14–23.

applicable to a variety of persons—including both the Son of David
and the Son of man: precisely for this reason, however, it demands
definition if its real meaning is to be understood; as an acknowledgement that Jesus stands in a special relationship to both God
and his people, the term "Messiah" is apt, but as an explanation
of the meaning of that relationship, it is inadequate.

Jesus, therefore, might well prefer the term "Son of man" as a
self-designation, not because of any opposition between this and
"Messiah",[1] but because it could define and explain the nature
of his Messiahship. This does not mean, of course, that the two
are synonymous. In Daniel, as we have seen, the Son of man is not
an individual, but stands for Israel as a nation: nevertheless, in so
far as the Son of man tends towards individuality in Daniel—in
the parallelism with the four kings who lead the enemy nations—
then he is the king of the future, glorified, Israel—in other words
he is Messiah. It is, indeed, only as Messiah—i.e. as one who is
leader and representative of his nation—that the one like a Son of
man in Daniel can be interpreted as an individual. Thus, when
Enoch, retaining the Danielic context, regards the Son of man as
an individual, he concludes that he is none other than the Elect
and Anointed One.[2] Later references in the gospel[3] suggest that
Jesus, too, had Daniel 7 in mind, and that the Son of man, if he
is an individual, must therefore also be Messiah. Mark's portrait
of the disciples, therefore, is entirely credible, for though they
would never have replied "You are the Son of man" in response
to Jesus' question, they could nevertheless, believing him to be
Messiah, accept the term as his own self-designation without un-
due surprise.

What the disciples were unable to accept, however, was the
corollary to Jesus' use of the term: namely, that if the authority of
the Son of man is not recognized, suffering must ensue: they have
not yet realized the nature of the opposition, or understood what
its consequences will be. The response of Jesus to their objections
is illuminating: just as the human opposition to Jesus' authority
was, we suggested, part of something which was ultimately of
Satanic origin, so now Peter, who is rebuked for thinking as men
think, is addressed as Satan; those who think like men, instead of
with God, are on the opposite side to God, and align themselves

---

[1] As maintained by O. Cullmann, op. cit., pp. 117–27.
[2] See above, pp. 38–41.   [3] Mark 13.26; 14.62.

with Satan. To deny the necessity of the Son of man's sufferings is in effect to deny the authority of the Son of man which is the cause of that suffering, and Peter is thus putting himself into the enemy camp. The interesting point emerges here, however, that Satan is responsible both for the opposition which defies the authority of the Son of man and makes his sufferings inevitable, and for the temptation to avoid suffering and death: Satan is in fact divided against Satan, and as Jesus has already pointed out in Mark 3.24–6, such a situation means the destruction of Satan and the end of his kingdom.

We have suggested that the saying about the Son of man's sufferings, far from being created *ex eventu*, is an integral part of the narrative, and a necessary corollary to his authority. This does not mean, of course, that all the details mentioned here were necessarily part of the original saying. The particulars given by Mark of what the Son of man must undergo are that he must:

1. Suffer many things.

2. Be rejected by the elders and the chief priests and the scribes.

3. Be killed.

4. After three days rise again.

If we accept the fact that Jesus did speak of his sufferings, then the first item seems unexceptionable: he could scarcely have spoken about suffering in a more general way. The second, the rejection of the Son of man, is, as we have seen, the fundamental cause of his sufferings, and must be original, though the reference to the various Jewish authorities may well be a later amplification. The word ἀποδοκιμασθῆναι itself has been traced by various commentators to Ps. 118 (117).22,[1] a verse quoted elsewhere, according to all the synoptics, by Jesus himself.[2] The verb ἀποδοκιμάζω is used both in the LXX (translating מָאַס) and in the quotation, which follows the LXX exactly; it means a rejection after trial or testing. It is possible that Jesus applied this Old Testament text to himself and he may well have had it in mind at this point, but

---

[1] See H. E. Tödt, *Menschensohn*, pp. 150–7, E.Tr. pp. 161–70; J. Schniewind, *Markus*, in loc.; C. E. B. Cranfield, *Mark*, in loc.

[2] Mark 12.10; Matt. 21.42; Luke 20.17.

this does not mean that he derived the idea of rejection itself from this psalm; this, as we have seen, is found in the "Son of man" concept itself, though the idea would undoubtedly have been strengthened under the influence of other passages of Old Testament scripture.

The third and fourth items must be considered together, since it would be strange if Jesus had spoken of his death without any reference to resurrection: death without restoration would be the defeat of God's purpose for the Son of man, and the end of all hope of his final triumph and vindication; restoration is thus as much a part of the things which are necessary for the Son of man as are suffering and rejection. It is highly probable, however, that the saying was originally far more obscure than it appears to us. One possibility is that Jesus may have spoken simply of rejection and vindication and not of death and resurrection. Against this it can be urged that he must have been increasingly aware that death would be the inevitable outcome of this rejection; moreover, those commentators are perhaps right who argue that Mark's phrase μετὰ τρεῖς ἡμέρας does not suggest a saying composed *ex eventu*,[1] and that if it had indeed originated after the resurrection, then we should expect to find in Mark, as well as in Matthew and Luke, the phrase τῇ τρίτῃ ἡμέρᾳ which the later evangelists have substituted for it in the interests of accuracy. Another possibility is that the prediction was given in less detail than now appears; in fact the only detail given here is this phrase referring to the time of the resurrection, and it is possible that the Marcan form of it was not intended as a precise dating, but was an indefinite expression for a short period of time.[2] Finally, it is possible that it is our interpretation of the saying, as much as its Marcan form, which is distorted by the knowledge of later events. Those who would excise these references to death and resurrection from the narrative point to the disciples' amazement and unpreparedness when these events took place, as an indication that they have been inserted *post eventum*.[3] To us, looking back from an advantageous viewpoint, the meaning of these words is obvious, and we regard them as a "major prediction of the passion"; they must have appeared to

---

[1] E.g. C. E. B. Cranfield, *Mark*, in loc.; J. Schniewind, *Markus*, in loc.; M.-J. Lagrange, *Marc*, in loc.
[2] C. E. B. Cranfield, loc. cit.
[3] *Beginnings*, I, pp. 381f; A. Loisy, *Synoptiques*, II, 1908, pp. 16f.

the evangelists in a somewhat similar light. To the disciples at the time, however, the words would be strange and unexpected, at variance with their hopes, isolated from their experiences, and unconnected in their minds with actual events: it is not surprising if they found them incomprehensible, and failed to relate them adequately with later happenings. The incident recorded in Mark 8.32f, however, indicates that they did follow—even though they did not fully understand—at least the gist of Jesus' meaning, and realized that he was speaking of his own sufferings and rejection, if no more.

2. MARK 8.38

For whoever is ashamed of me and of my words in this adulterous and sinful generation, of him will the Son of man also be ashamed, when he comes in the glory of his Father with the holy angels.

Cf. Matthew 16.27; Luke 9.26

The first reference to the suffering of the Son of man is followed in all three synoptic gospels by a group of sayings about discipleship. Most commentators agree that Mark 8.34a is an editorial link introducing a section which was not originally connected with what precedes;[1] the sudden appearance of a crowd certainly suggests that a join has been made, and Matthew and Luke have both removed this reference in order to make a smoother narrative. The connection may, nevertheless, be a valid one. There is, as we shall discover, a very close relationship between the sufferings of the Son of man and the sufferings which are forecast for those who follow Jesus: they will suffer because he has suffered and because they are his followers. The disciples' sufferings are a corollary to the divine "must" regarding the Son of man, for the rejection of his authority must involve those who accept it in suffering. Thus it is only at this stage that Jesus can begin to teach his disciples what following him really involves.

The climax of this section is the reference to the Son of man in Mark 8.38. The attention of commentators has been concentrated upon the apparent distinction between Jesus and the Son of man, and the question whether or not this is real. Those who think that

---

[1] V. Taylor, *Mark*, in loc.; C. E. B. Cranfield, *Mark*, in loc.

it is, maintain that Jesus did not consider himself to be the Son of man, and that the identification was first made by the early Church.[1] Alternative explanations suggest a distinction between Jesus and "the Elect Community",[2] or between his earthly life and future glory when he will "become" Son of man.[3] Preoccupation with this question has obscured what is perhaps a more fundamental distinction in this passage: for the real contrast is between being ashamed of Jesus and its opposite—namely following him. Even without the similar saying in Q (Luke 12.8f and Matt. 10.32f) for comparison, we expect to find a positive element here, to balance this negative saying: in Q, denying Jesus stands in contrast to confessing him, and in Mark's reference to being ashamed of Jesus there is an implicit contrast to the opposite way, for to be ashamed of Jesus is to refuse to follow him. It has, indeed, been suggested that Mark 8.38 is another version of the Q saying, with the positive element missing.[4] It must not be overlooked, however, that this positive aspect is in fact present in the Marcan context, and is found in verse 34: the contrast is between those who wish to come after him and those who are ashamed of him. Commentators have tended to ignore this contrast because they regard this section as a collection of isolated sayings which owe their association to editorial work:[5] but it must be noted that their connection appears to go back to a very early pre-Marcan stage, for Matthew records the Q version of Mark 8.34–5 and 38 in close proximity.[6] The parallelism between v. 34 and v. 38 is obscured by the fact that the two are cast in different forms. There is, nevertheless, an obvious contrast between the man who wishes to follow Jesus and his counterpart in v. 38: the disciple is in fact one who is *not* ashamed of Jesus—who is prepared to accept the shame of the

---

[1] E.g. R. Bultmann, *Theology of the New Testament*, I, pp. 28–30; J. Knox, *The Death of Christ*, pp. 93–7; G. Bornkamm, *Jesus of Nazareth*, 1960, pp. 175–8, 228–31; B. H. Branscomb, *Mark*, pp. 146–9; A. J. B. Higgins, *Son of Man*, pp. 57–60.

[2] T. W. Manson, *The Sayings of Jesus*, 1949, p. 109; V. Taylor, *Mark*, p. 384.

[3] A. Schweitzer, *The Mystery of the Kingdom of God*, 1914, pp. 190–4; R. H. Fuller, *Mission and Achievement*, pp. 101–3.

[4] A. Loisy, *Synoptiques*, II, p. 25; T. W. Manson, op. cit., pp. 108f; E. Klostermann, *Markus*, in loc.; H. E. Tödt, *Menschensohn*, pp. 37f, E.Tr. pp. 40f. Cf. T. F. Glasson, *The Second Advent*, 1945, pp. 74f.

[5] V. Taylor, *Mark*, in loc.; C. E. B. Cranfield, *Mark*, in loc.; J. Schniewind, *Markus*, in loc.; E. Lohmeyer, *Markus*, in loc.; E. Klostermann, *Markus*, in loc.

[6] Matt. 10.38f, 32f. Luke has them in separate contexts, in 14.27; 12.8f; 17.33.

Cross, and to deny himself rather than Jesus (cf. Matt. 10.33, Luke
12.9).[1] According to the negative form of the saying in Q (Matt.
10.38; Luke 14.27), the man who does not do this is not worthy of
Jesus and cannot be his disciple: a comparison between this and
the Marcan version supports the suggestion that ἀκολουθείτω should
be translated "so let him follow" rather than as a third item in the
conditions of discipleship.[2] This explains why following Jesus is
referred to again—a repetition which otherwise seems like mere
tautology—for the man who wishes to follow Jesus can do so only
as and when he fulfils these conditions: then indeed he may follow
him.

There is apparently nothing in this first saying to balance the
words καὶ ὁ υἱὸς τοῦ ἀνθρώπου ἐπαισχυνθήσεται αὐτόν in v. 38—no
promise to stand over against this threat. Yet the parallelism is perhaps closer than at first appears. To be a disciple of Jesus is not
just a question of accepting shame and death for his sake: it is
also a privilege—something of which one has to be worthy—and
following Jesus is therefore its own reward. Moreover, discipleship
is a reciprocal relationship: it is not enough simply to want to
come after Jesus—the disciple must live his obedience in such a
way that Jesus will not be ashamed of *him*, but will recognize him
as his follower. In v. 38, the situation is expressed in terms of the
present and future; similarly, in v. 34 a continuous tense, depicting
a continuing state which is future as well as present, is used.[3]
There is a real contrast here between those who follow Jesus (and
who will therefore be with him) and those who do not follow
(and whom he will therefore not recognize as belonging to his company). The contrast is brought out clearly in the intervening verses
in terms of losing and saving one's life, which stand in clear
parallelism. It is possible that the antithesis between verses 34 and
38 was originally much clearer, and that the insertion at some
stage of vv. 36f obscured this, and so led to changes in the form of
v. 34; some of the details of v. 38 may also be later additions; the

---

[1] This contrast supports the originality of the verb ἐπαισχύνομαι, as against
the view of Loisy, *Synoptiques*, II, p. 38. The verb is rare in the LXX, but
αἰσχύνειν and καταισχύνειν occur frequently, mostly for בּושׁ. It is often used by
the psalmist of the shame which is to be brought upon his enemies at his vindication, e.g. Ps. 35(34).26.

[2] Cf. C. E. B. Cranfield, *Mark*, in loc.; E. Klostermann, *Markus*, in loc.

[3] The first two imperatives in v. 34 are aorist, but the final one is present.
V. Taylor, *Mark*, p. 381, comments: "Two are decisive acts, and the third is a
continuous relationship." Similarly, C. E. B. Cranfield, *Mark*, in loc.

original logion, therefore, may well have consisted of an earlier version of vv. 34 and 38, with the chiastic saying of v. 35 either in its present position or following it.[1]

There is one important difference between the saying recorded in Mark 8.38 and the form found in Luke 12.8f (cf. Matt. 10.32f), which may well be closer to the original words of Jesus.[2] Whereas here we have a reference to the Son of man coming in the glory of his Father and with the angels, the Q version has none of these features: there the picture is a static one—the Son of man ("Jesus" in Matthew) acknowledges or denies before the angels of God ("his Father" in Matthew) those who have acknowledged or denied Jesus. In both cases the scene is one of judgement and vindication, and in both cases the imagery appears to be derived from Dan. 7. But in Mark 8.38 and parallels we have the Son of man coming with angels—and though this may possibly be no more than an echo of the language found in Dan. 7.13, where the one like a Son of man comes to the Ancient of Days,[3] it is highly probable, in view of Mark 13.26, that Mark interpreted this of the parousia. In either case, the fact that the Son of man "comes" in glory points to the time when judgement is pronounced in his favour and he assumes authority to judge others.

The fact that Jesus refers to himself in the first person in both vv. 34 and 38 need occasion no surprise: he is speaking to those who wish to follow him as they know him in his earthly life. In order to follow him, a man must be prepared to deny himself and carry his own cross to the place of execution—in other words, he must expect to face both shame and death for the sake of his master. Even if Mark is wrong in associating these words so closely

---

[1] We can no longer recover its original form, but it may have run somewhat as follows:

> He who wants to come after me
> Must deny self, pick up his cross, and so follow me.
> He who wants to save his life will lose it,
> He who loses his life for me will save it,
> He who is ashamed of me,
> The Son of man will be ashamed of him.

[2] Cf. T. F. Glasson, *The Second Advent*, p. 75; J. A. T. Robinson, "The Second Coming—Mark xiv. 62", *E.T.*, 67, 1956, pp. 336f; V. Taylor, *Mark*, p. 383. We can perhaps trace the development of the saying from Luke 12.8f, through Mark 8.38, to Matt. 16.27. Cf. E. Schweizer, "Der Menschensohn", *Z.N.T.W.*, 50, 1959, p. 188, who points out that in Luke 12.8f the Son of man acts as witness for or against the accused.

[3] The hosts of heavenly beings are mentioned in Dan. 7.10 and Enoch 61.10.

with those of v. 31, the disciples could scarcely have failed to notice a connection with the strange prediction of Jesus that the Son of man must face both suffering and rejection; to follow Jesus means, in fact, to follow the same path of suffering which is a necessity for the Son of man. But just as v. 31 contains a reference to final restoration, so in these words of Jesus to his would-be followers, there is the promise that those who lose their lives for his sake will in fact be saved, for they are following him.

Those who care for their own safety, on the other hand, will be lost: they are ashamed of Jesus and of his words, and the Son of man will therefore be ashamed of *them*. Is Mark correct in introducing the Son of man at this point, and if so, why did Jesus speak of himself in this way here, instead of using the simple "I"? One solution is, as we have seen, that Jesus did *not* in fact mean himself by this term, and that the Church has misunderstood him: either he thought of the Son of man as a figure quite separate from himself, whose arrival he expected in the near future, or he used the term to denote the Elect Community of which he was to be the head. The former explanation can be maintained only if we reject all the "Son of man" sayings except those which are eschatological; moreover, it leaves unexplained the nature of the relationship between Jesus and the Son of man, and the importance which is attached to one's attitude to Jesus; the parallelism with v. 34 is destroyed, and the figure of the Son of man is introduced at the climax for no obvious reason. The difficulty regarding the alternative explanation, which interprets "Son of man" as a corporate term for Jesus and his followers, is not so great, but there is nothing in this passage itself to support it, unless we accept the alternative reading "mine" for "my words" in v. 38.[1] If, on the other hand, the phrase "Son of man" does refer to Jesus, and to him alone, then we must note the conditions under which it is applicable: it is appropriate at some future point of time when Jesus will recognize publicly those who are his followers, and when non-recognition will apparently be a disaster. This is clearly the moment described in Dan. 7.13f, when the authority of the one like a Son of man is recognized, and the dominion and kingdom are given to him; it is closely parallel to the same moment of consummation as is described in Enoch 62, when the Son of man is

---

[1] The word λόγους is omitted by W, k*, Sa, and Tert. Some MSS. omit the same word from the parallel verse in Luke 9.26.

enthroned, and the "kings and mighty" are overcome with shame and confusion.

If we accept the identification of Jesus with the Son of man, then we may explain the apparent distinction between them which is made in Mark 8.38 in one of two ways. The first is to say, as for example R. H. Fuller originally did,[1] that Jesus will *become* Son of man in the future. There is, however, no indication in this passage (any more than in Daniel or Enoch) of any change in the Son of man himself. Moreover, in order to reconcile this theory with other passages we are forced to talk of the Son of man exercising his authority proleptically, and of Jesus being the Son of man *designatus*.[2] This, however, is not the way in which, according to the gospels, Jesus himself speaks; he does not say, "I must suffer before I become the Son of man", or, "I can forgive sins now by virtue of the authority which I shall have when I am Son of man": he speaks instead of the present authority and sufferings of one who is already the Son of man. The alternative explanation is that Jesus speaks of his future activity in terms of the Son of man because it is then—and only then—that his authority as Son of man will be generally acknowledged. At present, his authority is veiled, but when it is revealed, then the paradox which has brought suffering and shame to both the Son of man and his disciples will cease, and he will be recognized as the rightful ruler.

Although this recognition is future, however, we find Jesus already speaking of the Son of man to whom authority belongs; moreover, according to Mark, this speech was made quite openly to the crowd. It is possible, of course, that Matthew is correct in stating that these words were addressed to the disciples alone,[3] though the basis of his alteration is more likely to have been a desire for good style than a superior tradition; even in Mark, however, Jesus' audience apparently consisted of potential disciples. It is difficult to believe that the use of the term "Son of man" here was either intended by Jesus or understood by the crowd as a direct messianic claim. If it was spoken in their hearing, then we must suppose that the phrase was ambiguous:[4] either those in the

---

[1] *Mission and Achievement*, pp. 101–3.

[2] Ibid., pp. 103–8; cf. A. Schweitzer, *The Mystery of the Kingdom of God*, pp. 192f.

[3] Matt. 16.24. Luke's phrase πρὸς πάντας in 9.23 is closer to Mark than to Matthew.

[4] Cf. E. Sjöberg, *Der Verborgene Menschensohn in den Evangelien*, pp. 236f.

crowd were misled (like some modern commentators!) into thinking that Jesus was speaking of someone else; or they took it to be
an elaborate way of referring to himself. The disciples, on the other
hand, knew that this was Jesus' chosen way of referring to his messianic authority, and they ought, therefore, to have been able to
grasp his meaning.

3. MARK 9.9 AND 9.12

And as they were coming down the mountain, he charged
them to tell no one what they had seen, until the Son of man
should have risen from the dead.

And he said to them, "Elijah does come first to restore
all things; and how is it written of the Son of man, that he
should suffer many things and be treated with contempt?"

Cf. Matthew 17.9,12

These two sayings must be considered together, since in their
present setting both occur in the conversation between Jesus and
his disciples which followed the transfiguration. Interpretations of
the transfiguration itself differ greatly, and the story is variously
treated as a legend based on a mis-placed resurrection story,[1] as
symbolical invention,[2] or as historical narrative.[3] It is, however,
clear that for the evangelists, at least, the story is a confirmation of
the Messiahship of Jesus, and is to be understood in connection
with the events which have been related immediately before, namely
the declaration of Peter at Caesarea Philippi, and Jesus' teaching
about the suffering and exaltation of the Son of man and about
discipleship. There is good reason to believe that this connection

---

[1] E.g. R. Bultmann, *Geschichte*, pp. 278–81, E.Tr. pp. 259–61; E. Kloster-
mann, *Markus*, in loc.; A. Loisy, *Synoptiques*, II, pp. 39f. Against this explanation, see G. H. Boobyer, *St Mark and the Transfiguration Story*, 1942, pp. 11–16;
R. H. Lightfoot, *The Gospel Message of St Mark*, 1950, pp. 43f; C. H. Dodd,
"An Essay in Form Criticism of the Gospels", *Studies in the Gospels*, ed. D. E.
Nineham, 1955, p. 25. Dodd "cannot find a single point of resemblance" between the Transfiguration and Resurrection narratives". Cf. also W. Mundle,
"Die Geschichtlichkeit des messianischen Bewusstseins Jesu", *Z.N.T.W.*, 21,
1922, pp. 305f.
[2] E.g. E. Lohmeyer, "Die Verklärung Jesu nach dem Markus-Evangelium",
Z.N.T.W., 21, 1922, pp. 185–215; *Markus*, in loc. The Jewish background of the
motifs which appear in the transfiguration are examined in detail by H. Riesenfeld, *Jésus Transfiguré*, 1947.
[3] E.g. C. E. B. Cranfield, *Mark*, in loc.; M.-J. Lagrange, *Marc*, in loc.

may in fact be historical. It is, of course, not particularly significant that all three evangelists agree in linking these events together—although it should be noted that Luke's ordering is not necessarily dependent upon Mark's, since he appears to be following a different tradition. What may be more significant, however, is the phrase "after six days" in Mark 9.2 and Matt. 17.2, and "after about eight days" in Luke 9.28. In spite of Luke's cautious ὡσεί, the evangelists are all more precise here than at any other point in their account of the ministry. There are very few references to time in the synoptic gospels—probably because of the fragmentary nature of the tradition.[1] The temporal link at this point is therefore all the more remarkable—especially since it is recorded in two different forms. If Luke had substituted an exact reckoning for a vague one in Mark, we might suppose that he was "correcting" Mark, and providing what he believed to be a more accurate dating; but his more general phrase "about eight days" suggests that he was reporting an independent tradition.

The most natural explanation of these facts is that there was a very strong connection in the disciples' minds between the events at Caesarea Philippi and those on the mountain of transfiguration, and that they did in fact take place within the space of a week. In

---

[1] In Mark, the only references to time, apart from 9.2, are the statement in 8.2 that the crowd had been with Jesus for three days, and the information given in 14.1 that certain events took place "two days before the Passover". Matthew follows Mark in these three statements (Matt. 17.1; 15.32; 26.2), and he and Luke both speak of forty days in connection with the temptation narrative (Matt. 4.2; Luke 4.2). Luke informs us that John the Baptist and Jesus were both circumcised "on the eighth day" (Luke 1.59; 2.21) and that Jesus was found in the temple "after three days" (Luke 2.46). In addition the evangelists sometimes remark that certain events took place "on the same day" (Mark 4.35; Matt. 13.1; 22.23) or "next day" (Mark 11.12, 20; Luke 9.37 and possibly 7.11 if we accept the reading in ℵ*, C, D, and many other MSS.). More generally, however, they use vague phrases such as "on the sabbath" (Mark 2.23; 6.2; Matt. 12.1; Luke 4.16, 31; 6.1—this may possibly be a more precise reference if we accept the reading δευτεροπρώτῳ in A, C, D and other Greek texts, the Vulgate and other Latin texts; Luke 6.6; 13.10; 14.1), "at that time" (Matt. 11.25; 12.1; 14.1), "in those days" (Mark 8.1; Luke 6.12), "after some days" (Mark 2.1), "one day" (Luke 5.17; 20.1), and "soon afterwards" (Luke 7.11, usual reading; 8.1). Even more frequently, they make no attempt to give a chronological reference at all, and introduce events with a simple καί or a participle. There is therefore little exact timing—and what there is can mostly be attributed either to tradition (the period of forty days) or legal requirements (circumcision on the eighth day—Lev. 12.3). Apart from the transfiguration, then, the only events which are "dated" are those which took place "two days before the Passover" (Mark 14.1; Matt. 26.2)—and even this expression may mean no more than "the day before", if the Jewish method of reckoning is being followed; cf. H. B. Swete, The Gospel According to St Mark, 1898, in loc., A. E. J. Rawlinson, Mark, in loc., V. Taylor, Mark, in loc.

this case, the slight difference between the Marcan and Lucan accounts is an understandable variation. An alternative explanation has traced Mark's period of six days to Ex. 24.16, and given it an entirely symbolic significance.[1] If this were the source of the phrase, however, then we should expect Jesus, like Moses, to spend these six days (during which, according to Exodus, the cloud covered Sinai) upon the mountain; if the "six days" are simply a deliberate echo of the Exodus story, then it is strange that they have been used so differently. It is also difficult to explain Luke's variant; we should have to suppose that he failed to see the significance of the Marcan phrase, but this in itself does not explain why he should alter it. On the other hand, it is possible that the gospel tradition contained from the beginning a temporal link of some kind, and that this was conformed to the six days of the Exodus story in the version which is given to us by Mark.

Whichever explanation we adopt, it is clear that for the evangelists at least there is a very close link between the transfiguration and the preceding events. There is therefore every reason to suppose that the clue to their understanding of the transfiguration is to be found in those events with which it is so closely connected in the gospel tradition. At Caesarea Philippi, Peter confessed that Jesus was the Messiah, and Jesus explained the nature of his Messiahship to the disciples in terms of the Son of man: as Son of man, he would ultimately receive "dominion and glory and kingdom", but until the moment of vindication the rejection of his rightful authority made suffering inevitable. Now Peter and his companions are given a confirmation of the Messiahship of Jesus which is also a glimpse of that authority: the things which they see and hear cannot be disclosed until the Son of man has "risen from the dead" because they are a revelation of the future "dominion and glory and kingdom" which belong to him by right, but which have not yet been finally delivered to him. When Mark and Matthew tell us that Jesus was "transformed", therefore, they must mean that he appeared to his disciples in the form which he would bear at his "coming" in glory.[2] Luke, indeed, specifically mentions

---

[1] E. Lohmeyer, *Markus*, in loc.; C. G. Montefiore, *The Synoptic Gospels*, I, 1927, in loc.; B. H. Branscomb, *Mark*, in loc.; P. Carrington, *According to Mark*, 1960, p. 196.

[2] See the discussion of Mark's interpretation of the transfiguration by G. H. Boobyer, in *St Mark and the Transfiguration Story*. Boobyer argues that the general outlook of Mark's Gospel, which looks forward to the revelation of Christ at the resurrection and parousia, together with the context of the transfiguration

glory in his account;[1] it is reflected also in the shining face and the dazzling white clothes.[2] Thus the form in which the disciples see him is the expression of the truth which Jesus has been trying to teach them: they see him for a moment in the glory which he will wear when he has passed through suffering. The things which they see and hear are foretastes of the "coming" of the Son of man in the glory of his Father which has been spoken of in 8.38. The connection between the glorious "coming" and the vision was clearly seen by the early Church, for Origen reports that certain commentators interpret the story as the actual fulfilment of Jesus' promise in Matt. 16.28 that some of those standing near by would live to see the Son of man coming in his kingdom.[3] The Marcan narrative suggests that this was the way in which Peter himself understood the transfiguration at the time: he thought that the eschatological day had dawned already, and that he was seeing the coming of the Son of man in glory (Mark 9.5).

Yet the account of the transfiguration itself does not mention the Son of man. If we are correct in linking it with Caesarea Philippi, then between Mark 8.29 and 9.7 we have moved from a confession that Jesus is "Messiah", via the title "Son of man", to the declaration that he is "Son of God". Does this represent a "heightening of Christology" on the part of the early Church— or is it a genuine part of the tradition? There are some signs of such a "heightening"—e.g. in the phrase τοῦ πατρὸς αὐτοῦ in Mark 8.38 and Matthew's addition of ὁ υἱὸς τοῦ Θεοῦ in 16.16—but the progression in titles is not one of them, for they all appear at the

---

story and the details of that story itself, all suggest that, for Mark, the transfiguration is "a manifestation of Christ in the glory of his second coming. . . . The transfiguration prophesies the parousia in the sense that it is a portrayal of what Christ will be at that day, and is in some degree a miniature picture of the whole second advent scene" (p. 87). Boobyer links the transfiguration with the parousia, and not with the resurrection (as is done, e.g. by J. Schniewind, *Markus*, in loc.), because he maintains that for Mark these are two separate events (pp. 20–6); but when we consider the pre-Marcan meaning of the transfiguration, it is probable that we should think simply of the future triumph of the Son of man, rather than in terms of *either* the resurrection *or* the parousia. See also A. M. Ramsey, *The Glory of God and the Transfiguration of Christ*, 1949, chapters 10 and 11, and E. Lohmeyer, *Markus*, in loc.—although the latter, of course, denies the historicity of the transfiguration.

[1] Luke 9.32.

[2] Mark 9.3; Matt. 17.2; Luke 9.29. In the New Testament, λευκός is used of clothing only in connection with heavenly beings—a fact noted by J. B. Bernadin in his article on "The Transfiguration" in *J.B.L.*, 52, 1933, pp. 181–9. See Matt. 28.3; Mark 16.5; John 20.12 and Acts 1.10, where it is used of angels; Rev. 3.4, 5, 18; 4.4; 6.11; 7.9,13, where it is used of saints.

[3] *Commentary on Matthew*, Book 12, 31.

Marcan stage of the tradition. Indeed, this progression reveals a consistent pattern, for the distribution of titles is logical: Peter uses the term "Messiah" (which is precisely what we should expect from him) Jesus prefers his own chosen self-designation "Son of man", and the phrase attributed to the voice from heaven—ὁ υἱός μου ὁ ἀγαπητός—is the same as that found in Mark 1.11. This, of course, may reflect Mark's own systematization rather than the original distribution of the titles, but the identification of the Son of man with the Son of God which has slipped into the Marcan text in 8.38 does not suggest that Mark has imposed this pattern on his material. Moreover, the use of the titles is remarkably in "character" with the speakers: however we explain the saying in Mark 9.7 it is significant that these words—spoken from heaven —express Jesus' "Messiahship" in terms of his relationship to God; Peter speaks, in human terms, of Jesus as Messiah and, in 9.5, as Rabbi; Jesus, who knows himself to fulfil man's obedience to God, prefers to speak in terms of the Son of man, whose authority is from God. Now, however, it is revealed to the three that the one who stands in this perfect relationship of obedience to God and who thus fulfils the Creator's intention expressed in Gen. 1.26 is none other than the Son of God: as Israel was called both Son of man and Son of God, so now is Jesus. This is the secret which will be revealed when the Son of man is vindicated—that he is also Son of God, and that the glory of which he has spoken is that of his Father. Once again, therefore, we find that Jesus is invested with the authority of God himself: not, this time, on the basis of his own claim, but according to the witness of the voice from heaven, which proclaims Jesus as the Son of God and commands the disciples to listen to him. Commentators generally trace the use of ἀκούειν here to Deut. 18.15, where it translates the Hebrew שָׁמַע—a root often conveying the meaning "to obey" as well as "to hear"—and refers to the obedience which the people will accord to the prophet like Moses whom God will raise up: in fact, however, שָׁמַע and ἀκούειν are used far more frequently of the obedience which is expected by Yahweh himself from his people, that given in Deut. 18.15 being, of course, an extension of this.[1]

---

[1] This meaning of שָׁמַע is especially frequent, according to Brown, Driver, and Briggs, in Deuteronomy and Jeremiah. See, e.g., the use of the command שִׁמְעוּ (ἀκούσατε) in Jer. 11.2–7, translated alternately in the R.V. by "hear" and "obey".

The use of the word in Mark 9.7 in connection with the statement that Jesus is the Son of God confirms that the authority with which Jesus is invested, and the obedience which is to be given to him, are both much greater than the authority and obedience which belonged to a prophet, however great.

The figures of Moses and Elijah have caused much trouble to all interpretations of the transfiguration, though they are most easily explained when the story is understood in relation to its eschatological setting. Elijah, at least, played an important rôle in Jewish eschatological speculation.[1] May not the clue to their presence be found in the teaching which is so often overlooked in discussion of the problem, but which nevertheless forms an integral part of the narrative—namely Jesus' warning to his disciples that they will have to face suffering for his sake? The way of the Messiah, he has told them, must lie through suffering and death; immediately he goes on to tell them that those who follow him must share in his sufferings; those who are "ashamed" of Jesus will in turn find that the Son of man is ashamed of them when he comes in glory. The obvious corollary to this last statement is, as we have seen, that the Son of man will not be ashamed of those followers who accept suffering and death for his sake:[2] in other words, they will have some share (as yet undefined) in the coming Kingdom.

When, therefore, the disciples see a vision of Jesus in the form which he will wear when he returns as the triumphant Son of man, we might expect to find that they see with him some of those who have shared suffering for his sake, and now share in his glory. As Jesus explains to James and John, those who appear at his right and left hands in glory will be those who have drunk his cup of suffering and who have been baptized with his baptism of death.[3] As yet, none of Jesus' followers has been through that experience; they cannot appear with him in this "preview" of his glory. There are others who *have* already suffered, however— namely the prophets and martyrs who preceded Jesus. Moreover, Jesus not only mentions their sufferings but apparently links them with his own: immediately after the transfiguration Jesus refers to the sufferings of "Elijah", and says that it was "written" that John the Baptist must suffer—just as it is written that Jesus him-

---

[1] See the discussion in G. H. Boobyer, op. cit., pp. 69–76.
[2] Implied in Matthew's quotation of Ps. 62.13(12) in 16.27.
[3] Mark 10.35–40; Matt. 20.20–3.

self must suffer; in the parable of the wicked husbandman[1] the
sufferings of Jesus are seen as the climax to a long line of persecution.[2] We should not be surprised, then, that two of these great
forerunners of Jesus, both of whom suffered persecution for their
faith, appear with Jesus in glory, not merely as representatives of
the Law and the Prophets, but as prototypes of those who suffer
for his sake.[3] If this is the correct explanation of the presence of
Elijah and Moses, we perhaps have also an explanation of the
puzzling order in which Mark mentions them: for it is Elijah who
figures in the ensuing conversation as the forerunner of the Son of
man in suffering, and who is therefore appropriately Jesus' com-
panion, "with Moses", in glory.

This interpretation is supported by the conversation which is recorded as taking place during the descent from the mountain, and
which returns to the subject of the Son of man's sufferings. It is, of
course, regarded as secondary by many scholars who fail to see its
relevance to its context: Mark 9.9f is interpreted as an editorial
device to explain why no one mentioned an event which either had
not yet occurred or in fact never happened at all;[4] the rest of the
conversation becomes a dispute between the Church and the
Jewish authorities.[5] There are many, however, who agree with the
judgement of F. C. Burkitt, that these verses read "like reminis-
cences of a real conversation".[6]

They open with the command to secrecy and the reaction of the
disciples to Jesus' words about the resurrection of the Son of man.
If we are right in interpreting the transfiguration as a genuine experience which looked forward to the vindication of the Son of man,
then there is no difficulty in accepting these two verses as historical:
the disciples have glimpsed the glory which belongs by right to the
Son of man, but which has not yet been revealed to men, and the

---

[1] Mark 12.1–12; Matt. 21.33–46; Luke 20.9–19.
[2] See the discussion in *Jesus and the Servant*, 1959, pp. 135f. Cf. also Matt.
23.29–36, Luke 11.47–51; Matt. 23.37–9, Luke 13.34f.
[3] We may compare Heb. 11.26, where Moses is said to have "considered
abuse suffered for the Christ greater wealth than the treasures of Egypt, for he
looked to the reward". See also Matt. 5.11f, where the future sufferings of the
disciples are linked with those of the prophets.
[4] B. H. Branscomb, *Mark*, pp. 163f; A. Loisy, *Synoptiques*, II, p. 40.
[5] R. Bultmann, *Geschichte*, pp. 131f, E.Tr. pp. 124f; E. Klostermann, *Markus*,
in loc.; E. Lohmeyer, *Markus*, in loc.; R. H. Lightfoot, *History and Interpretation of the Gospels*, 1935, pp. 92f.
[6] In *Christian Beginnings*, 1924, pp. 33f. See also V. Taylor, *Mark*, in loc.;
Jesus and His Sacrifice, 1937, pp. 91–7; C. E. B. Cranfield, *Mark*, in loc.; R.
Otto, *The Kingdom of God and the Son of Man*, pp. 249–51.

command to keep silent until the Son of man has been vindicated is therefore natural; so, too, is the bewilderment of the disciples when told that the Son of man will rise from the dead. Once again, it is possible that this reference to resurrection reflects the knowledge of the early Church, and that the original words of Jesus referred in much vaguer terms to his future vindication; in this case, the enigmatic phrase which caused their bewilderment has been replaced by one which clearly expresses what afterwards seemed the obvious interpretation. We may at least conclude, however, that Jesus spoke, as in 8.31, of final triumph for the Son of man after apparent disaster.

The following verses have caused much difficulty to those who, from Matthew onwards, have failed to understand Mark's sequence, and have resorted to rearrangement of the text.[1] There is, however, no need to make our interpretation depend on such conjectures. The disciples' question[2] about Elijah arises naturally out of their vision and their understanding of Jesus' person: they have been told to keep silent about what they have seen and heard, but if the scribes are right, then Elijah will appear publicly *before* the final time of judgement and vindication. In his reply Jesus confirms the truth of this teaching—unless, with Wellhausen,[3] we interpret his answer as a further question; this latter explanation seems highly unlikely, however, in view of the fact that Jesus' words are a quotation from Malachi. Commentators here almost unanimously refer to the scribes' teaching about the return of Elijah as the forerunner of the Messiah. In fact, however, neither the question of the disciples nor the reply of Jesus mentions the Messiah: the disciples speak of Elijah coming "first", but do not say before what, and the context would suggest that they meant before the glorification of the Son of man—or possibly before the coming of the kingdom of God referred to in 9.1. Now the three

---

[1] C. H. Turner in *A New Commentary on Holy Scripture*, ed. C. Gore, H. L. Goudge and A. Guillaume, II, 1928, suggests that verse 12b should follow verse 10; so, too, A. M. Hunter, *The Gospel According to St Mark*, 1948, in loc. F. C. Grant, *The Earliest Gospel*, 1943, pp. 101 and 114, and in *The Interpreter's Bible*, VII, p. 778, places 12b after 13. W. Bousset, *Kyrios Christos*, 1913, pp. 7f, and R. Bultmann, loc. cit., regard 12b as an interpolation into the Marcan text; H. E. Tödt denies that there is any support for this view, *Menschensohn*, pp. 181f, E.Tr. pp. 169, 196.

[2] Even if we do not interpret the first ὅτι in Mark 9.11 as the equivalent of τί, the sense is presumably still interrogative, the disciples expecting Jesus either to approve or to reject the tradition. Matthew replaces ὅτι with τί.

[3] *Ev. Marci*, p. 76. Cf. C. C. Torrey, *The Four Gospels*, note on p. 301.

disciples were no doubt thinking in "messianic" terms, but it
should be noticed that Jesus, by his answer, turns their attention
to a passage which relates the coming of Elijah to that of God himself; according to Mal. 4.5, Elijah was to come "before the great
and terrible day of the Lord".[1] This reference is undoubtedly the
origin and ground of most of the rabbinic speculation about
Elijah, and while it is undoubtedly true that he came to be thought
of as the forerunner of the Messiah, this was not his original position, but grew out of the association of the two figures in the eschatological scheme. The primary and essential thing about Elijah's
return is that he comes before the Day of Yahweh in order to
prepare his people and turn them to repentance.[2] There is no
indication in Mark, notwithstanding the opinion of numerous
commentators,[3] that Jesus uses the word "restore" here in order
either to question it or to qualify it: we may believe, rather, that
he used it in order to establish that the tradition about Elijah is
based on Old Testament scripture.

Following this reference to Malachi, we have the second reference to the Son of man in this paragraph, namely the declaration
that it is written of the Son of man that he must suffer many things.
This apparently abrupt change of subject has led many to understand it as a saying of the early Church: certainly, as it is normally
punctuated the verse creates difficulties, for we find Jesus asking a
question which would be more appropriate coming from the disciples, and leaving it unanswered. The clue to its presence in this
context, however, is to be found in the fact which we have just
noted—that the answer given by Jesus is a quotation from scripture.
In reply to the disciples' question about Elijah, he declares that
Elijah does indeed come—as it is written of him. Now, perhaps in
reply to the question which they did not dare to ask, he tells them
that the Son of man, too, must fulfil the words which were written

---

[1] Cf. also the messenger sent before Yahweh in Mal. 3.1, a passage interpreted messianically in Mark 1.2.

[2] See S-B, *Kommentar*, IV, pp. 784–98; J. Jeremias, "'Ηλείας", *T.W.N.T.*,
III, pp. 930–43. Elijah's return is mentioned frequently in Jewish writings,
e.g. Nu. R. 16.11; ʿEdhuyyoth 8.7; Pirkê R. Eliezer 43. Deut. R. 4.11, which
quotes various texts referring to the final triumph—Mal. 3.4, 23f; 3.1; Zech.
1.16f and 9.9—suggests the way in which the link between Elijah and the
Messiah grew. The two figures are found together, e.g. in Midr. Teh. 3.7;
42/43.5; Seder ʿOlam R. 17, and in B. ʿErubin 43b, where Elijah is the Messiah's
Forerunner.

[3] E.g. J. Wellhausen, loc. cit.; M.-J. Lagrange, *Marc*, in loc.; C. E. B. Cranfield, *Mark*, in loc.

of him. The meaning and relevance of verse 12b is clear if we understand it, not as one interrogative sentence, but as a question to which Jesus immediately gives the answer:[1]

'Ηλίας μὲν ἐλθὼν πρῶτον
ἀποκαθιστάνει πάντα.

καὶ πῶς γέγραπται ἐπὶ τὸν υἱὸν τοῦ ἀνθρώπου;
—ἵνα πολλὰ πάθῃ καὶ ἐξουδενηθῇ.

The connection between the two parts of the verse is now clear: Elijah does indeed come and so fulfils the scripture—but there are also things written about the Son of man.

If, nevertheless, we follow the punctuation which is normally accepted, then v. 12b should probably be regarded as taking up the question which we suggested would have been put by the disciples in response to the announcement of Mark 8.31.

In v. 13 we return to Elijah. Matthew, who prefers to group sayings about each subject together, disapproves of Mark's order and places this saying before the one concerning the Son of man. Nevertheless, Mark has preserved the original logic of the verses, for after the reference in v. 12 to the scriptural tradition regarding both Elijah and the Son of man, we come now to their fulfilment. Jesus announces that Elijah has already come—and, moreover, that they have done to him the things that they wished, as it is written of him. The difficulty arises here that canonical scripture does not, in fact, predict a disastrous fate for the returning Elijah, and commentators thus frequently infer the existence of some such prediction in a lost apocryphal book.[2] The phrase ὅσα ἤθελον, however, suggests that the thwarted desires of Jezebel recorded in 1 Kings 19.2–10 may be sufficient basis for Jesus' interpretation. Moreover, even if death itself did not overtake the historical Elijah, suffering and contempt certainly did, and to this extent we may say that John the Baptist endured the things which were written of his predecessor.

The obvious conclusion to be drawn from all this—that the things written about the Son of man will also be fulfilled—is not

---

[1] The text is punctuated in this way by Tischendorf. Cf. E. P. Gould, *The Gospel According to St Mark*, 1896, in loc. See also the translation in J. Schniewind, *Markus*.

[2] E.g. E. Lohmeyer, *Markus*, p. 183. Cf. also J. Jeremias, op. cit., pp. 941–3.

explicitly stated by Mark, but the inference is quite clear, and Matthew has made it obvious by his rearrangement: just as the things which were written about the coming of Elijah have been fulfilled in John the Baptist, so now what is written about the Son of man will also be fulfilled. At this stage we must ask what these things are which are written of the Son of man, and the answer is given in the words of Jesus—he must suffer many things and be treated with contempt. There is one significant difference between this passage and Mark 8.31—the absence of any specific reference to death and resurrection.[1] It is probably coincidence that in neither of the two Marcan passages which refer to the things which are written of the Son of man is there any mention of death, but the omission may possibly be significant: for the Old Testament passage which speaks of the suffering and contempt which Israel endures before being vindicated and given the glory and dominion which belongs to the Son of man also does not speak of death and resurrection. The words of Mark 9.12 are thus in complete accord with the picture drawn in Dan. 7.[2] There is, as we have shown elsewhere,[3] no evidence to support the often repeated view that Jesus' words here about what is written refer to the Servant Songs, and no reason, therefore, to suppose that he was thinking of any figure other than the Son of man. There is thus no need to resort to the extraordinary suggestion made by V. Taylor that the reference to death is omitted from this passage because the Old Testament does not speak of the death of Elijah, and that Jesus, wishing to stress the parallelism between Elijah and the Son of man, therefore omitted the death of the Servant from his description of the Son of man's sufferings:[4] it is only a fixed determination to trace every reference to suffering to Isa. 53 which envisages Jesus seeking for the highest common factor of various scriptural references, and which therefore fails to recognize that Dan. 7 points quite as clearly to the sufferings of the Son of man as 1 Kings 19 does to those of Elijah. It is certainly true that a parallel is drawn here between Elijah and the Son of man, but the point

---

[1] It should, however, be noted that if we take Mark 9.9 and 12 together, they form a close parallel to 8.31.

[2] Cf. C. F. D. Moule, in "From Defendant to Judge—and Deliverer", *S.N.T.S. Bulletin*, III, 1952, pp. 45f.

[3] *Jesus and the Servant*, pp. 93–7. Cf. also H. E. Tödt, *Menschensohn*, pp. 155f, E.Tr. pp. 168f.

[4] *Jesus and His Sacrifice*, pp. 94f.

of the comparison is not to be found via Isa. 53. Jesus agrees with the disciples that Elijah comes to restore—but goes on to point out that there is something else written about Elijah which they have failed to notice, namely that he had to endure suffering and contempt. So, too, the Son of man comes in glory—but again, there is something else written about him which nobody has noticed, and again it is suffering and contempt. Just as this less agreeable prediction was fulfilled in the case of Elijah, so too it will be fulfilled in the case of the Son of man, and the reason for both is the same—man's refusal to respond to God's summons: Elijah was unable to restore all things because men hardened their hearts, and the Son of man's authority goes unrecognized for the same reason. In this situation, both "Elijah"—i.e. John the Baptist—and the Son of man—i.e. Jesus—must suffer, and the suffering and contempt which are foreshadowed for them are inevitable: these things—and worse!—have already come upon John the Baptist, who has endured not only suffering and contempt, but death as well; the rejection of the forerunner not only foreshadows that of his successor but makes it quite certain that these things—and worse!—will come upon the Son of man also. One further point of comparison completes the parallel between the coming (rather than the sufferings) of Elijah and the sufferings of the Son of man: as in Mal. 4 it is the coming of Elijah which immediately precedes the Eschaton, so in Dan. 7 it is the sufferings of the saints. The disciples refer to the teaching of the scribes that Elijah must come "first", but Jesus points to something else which must happen "first"—his own suffering: this, too, must be fulfilled before the day of vindication and triumph.

There can be no doubt that the phrase "Son of man" in these two verses refers to Jesus himself, and not to some other eschatological figure. It is also clear that Mark understands it as denoting Jesus alone: nevertheless, it should be noted that the Son of man is very closely associated with others by the parallel which is drawn between his sufferings and those of Elijah. By the context of the saying, he is also closely linked with those who share his glory, for Jesus is seen in glorious form together with Elijah and Moses: it is those who share the sufferings of the Son of man who share also his glory. By this setting, also, we notice that the suffering and the vindication of the Son of man are held together, for though the "coming" of the Son of man is not mentioned, his suffering is related to the glory which cannot be spoken of until after his resurrection.[1]

4. MARK 9.31

For he was teaching his disciples, saying to them, "The Son of man will be delivered into the hands of men, and they will kill him; and when he is killed, after three days he will rise."

Cf. Matthew 17.22f; Luke 9.44

The initial prophecy of the passion, found in Mark 8.31, is repeated in a slightly different form in 9.31, and again in 10.33. It is possible that these three statements could all be traced to one original saying, and that the three-fold prophecy is the result of different traditions regarding words which, according to the evangelist, were not understood by the original hearers:[2] it would not be surprising if a saying which was heard with incomprehension and fear was remembered so inaccurately. Alternatively, the triple formula may be due to Mark's desire to emphasize the climax of his account. Yet if Jesus spoke of his sufferings and death to his disciples at all, as seems likely, then it is highly probable that he did so on more than one occasion, as the evangelists have supposed.[3]

Whether Mark 9.31 is a parallel account of the words in 8.31 or records a separate saying, its brevity and lack of detail give it a better claim to originality.[4] Only three points are made:

1. The Son of man is delivered into the hands of men.

2. They will kill him.

3. After three days he will rise.

Matthew's account gives the same three points—once again changing "after three days" to "the third day"; Luke's is even shorter, recording only the first item. This first statement is the most significant, since it is the only one not found in the earlier prediction.

---

[1] H. E. Tödt, *Menschensohn*, p. 181, E.Tr. p. 196.
[2] Cf. A. T. Cadoux, *The Sources of the Second Gospel*, 1935, pp. 25f, 167–9.
[3] So V. Taylor, *Mark*, p. 377.
[4] Cf. R. Otto, *The Kingdom of God and the Son of Man*, pp. 361f; A. J. B. Higgins, *Son of Man*, p. 34.

The verb παραδίδωμι used here is ambiguous: it may refer to the betrayal of Jesus by Judas, as in 3.19 and 14.18–21, but many commentators see in it a deeper significance, namely the idea that Jesus has been delivered into the hands of men by God himself.[1] The latter interpretation—which finds a parallel in Rom. 8.32— perhaps fits the general character of the passage better, since a specific reference to the betrayal seems out of place in a prediction where so little detail is given; in particular, the general term "men" seems more appropriate if the verb refers to the activity of God than if it refers to the betrayal by Judas, since in the latter case it would be more natural to speak of Jesus being betrayed into the hands of the chief priests. If the Son of man is delivered up by God, then the present tense used by Mark may be regarded as simple, rather than prophetic, for whereas Judas' act of betrayal lies in the future, the Son of man has already been delivered into the hands of men by God; in the imagery of Mark 12, the beloved son has been sent into the vineyard, and the tenants have already plotted how to destroy him. It is possible, of course, that Mark has in mind both meanings of the verb παραδίδωμι at this point, or that Jesus spoke of the divine activity and this has been interpreted in terms of the human betrayal in the light of that event.

Nothing is said in this passage about the authority of the Son of man—indeed he himself comes under the authority of the "men" with whom he stands in contrast. This paradox we have met already in 8.31, where we saw that when men deny the authority of the Son of man he is involved in suffering. This same pattern is found again in 12.1–9, in the story of the vineyard tenants who rebelled against the owner and thought they could usurp the authority of the son by killing him; their behaviour recalls that of the beasts in Dan. 7 who rebelled against God and usurped the authority he intended for his saints, represented by the one like a Son of man. Although paradoxical, therefore, this picture is in keeping with what we should expect of the Son of man in a hostile situation, provided also that he shows that obedience to God which is characteristic of him—an obedience reflected here in Jesus' acceptance of his destiny.

---

[1] E. Klostermann, *Markus*, in loc.; E. Lohmeyer, *Markus*, in loc.; V. Taylor, *Mark*, in loc.; M.-J. Lagrange, *Marc*, in loc.; J. Blinzler, *The Trial of Jesus*, 1959, p. 274.

Like the first prophecy of the passion, the teaching is addressed
to the disciples alone.[1] Mark and Luke record the disciples' incomprehension and fear, which Matthew has changed to sorrow.
Both Matthew and Luke follow Mark in placing the saying after
the healing of the epileptic boy, which follows the story of the
transfiguration; this renewal of the teaching comes quickly after
8.31 and 9.9–13, and it is possible that Mark has placed it here to
emphasize the necessity for its repetition after the demonstration
of the disciples' lack of faith in 9.14–19. More significant, however,
are the events which, according to the Marcan and Lucan accounts,
follow this teaching—namely a dispute regarding priority among
the disciples and the response of Jesus. We cannot, of course, rely
upon the connection being an historical one; indeed vv. 33–7 begin
a series of sayings which have been put together because of the
"catchwords". But Mark has apparently understood the relationship between the path which the Son of man must tread before he
is "raised up" and that to which he points his disciples. Greatness
in discipleship is not demonstrated by exercising authority over
others—quite the reverse: "If any one would be first, he must be
last of all and servant of all".[2] The relevance of vv. 36–7 to the
discussion on greatness is not clear, and the version given by
Matthew[3] is more intelligible: it is possible that Mark's account
represents a confusion between the saying about a child which he
records in 10.15 and that found in Matt. 10.40 about receiving a
disciple. Some have suggested that the reference to children in v.
37 is a misunderstanding and that here, as in v. 42, the saying
originally referred to humble believers.[4] In its present form,
Mark presumably regarded "receiving" a child in the name
of Jesus as a type of the lowly service expected of a
disciple.

---

[1] Mark 8.31 and Luke 9.43 refer specifically to the disciples; Matthew's
"them" (17.22) refers back to the disciples, mentioned in v. 19.
[2] It is possible that this saying, introduced by the words καὶ καθίσας ἐφώνησεν
τοὺς δώδεκα καὶ λέγει αὐτοῖς, is independent of the context into which Mark has
put it. Luke places a similar statement *after* the saying about the child given in
Mark 9.36f. If Mark is responsible for the connection between the "Son of man"
saying and the discussion of greatness, however, it is of no importance to our
discussion whether or not he has combined two or more sayings in the latter.
[3] Matt. 18.1–5. Matthew has separated the incident from the prediction of
the passion by the story of the half-shekel tax in 17.24–7.
[4] V. Taylor, *Mark*, in loc.

5. MARK 10.33f

Behold, we are going up to Jerusalem; and the Son of man will be delivered to the chief priests and the scribes, and they will condemn him to death, and deliver him to the Gentiles; and they will mock him, and spit upon him, and scourge him, and kill him; and after three days he will rise.

Cf. Matthew 20.18f; Luke 18.31ff.

This final prediction of the passion is by far the most detailed, and is for that reason the most open to suspicion.[1] This time παραδίδωμι is used in connection with the chief priests and scribes (who, in turn, deliver Jesus to the Gentiles) and should probably be understood of the betrayal by Judas. Details in Mark include the sentence of death passed by the priests and scribes, and the mocking and scourging by the Gentiles; Matthew includes the term "crucify", and both he and Luke change "after three days" to "the third day". In these detailed expressions we can see the influence of knowledge after the event,[2] yet it is highly probable that some such teaching—albeit in more general terms—was given at this stage of the ministry, when Jesus, now "on the road going up to Jerusalem", had taken the step which must lead irrevocably to his death.

Luke differs from Mark and Matthew in adding a reference to scripture; according to his account, Jesus tells his disciples: "Behold, we are going up to Jerusalem, and everything that is written of the Son of man by the prophets will be accomplished." It should be noted that there is no specific reference here to Old Testament passages which speak of the Son of man: rather Jesus declares that all things written by the prophets are now to be fulfilled in the Son of man. This is a favourite theme in Luke, taken up again in chapter 24, where the risen Christ expounds the scriptures to two of his disciples, "beginning with Moses and all the prophets", and explaining to them "in all the scriptures the things concerning himself". Once again, the reference is a broad one—πάσαις ταῖς γραφαῖς—and the teaching which Jesus finds there

---

[1] V. Taylor, *Mark*, pp. 436f.

[2] R. H. Lightfoot, *History and Interpretation in the Gospels*, 1935, pp. 170f, points out that Luke omits the condemnation by the Sanhedrin, and so brings the prediction into agreement with his narrative in chapter 23.

is that it was "necessary that the Christ should suffer these things and enter into his glory"—teaching found in πᾶσιν οἷς ἐλάλησαν οἱ προφῆται, but which his foolish and unbelieving followers have failed to understand. This same idea is repeated later in chapter 24, when Jesus reminds his disciples of his previous teaching "that everything written about me in the law of Moses and the prophets and the psalms must be fulfilled".

The context of this final prediction of the passion is, once again, illuminating. Mark, followed by both Matthew and Luke, places the saying immediately after the encounter with the rich man and the ensuing conversation between Jesus and his disciples. The rich man, although anxious to inherit eternal life, was nevertheless unable to pay the price—namely to give away all his possessions and follow Jesus. The disciples, on the other hand, have left everything and followed Jesus, and they will receive the eternal life which the rich man desired: "many that are first will be last, and the last first."[1] They are also promised a hundredfold return of what they have left—"with persecutions", an ominous reminder that following Jesus involves not only self-denial but also taking up the cross.[2]

The amazement of the disciples at Jesus' teaching in v. 24 is echoed in the use of the same word, ἐθαμβοῦντο, in v. 32, and the words which follow—οἱ δὲ ἀκολουθοῦντες—repeat the theme of following Jesus.[3] It is probable that Mark intended his description of Jesus walking ahead and leading his followers towards Jerusalem to convey more than a picture of the actual journey to the capital: Jesus is going before his disciples on a road which will bring him to suffering and death, and those who follow after him may expect the same fate.[4] This is perhaps why Mark distinguishes between the indefinite subject of ἐθαμβοῦντο and the definite subject (οἱ δὲ ἀκολουθοῦντες) of ἐφοβοῦντο, since although all who saw Jesus set out on this road to suffering were amazed, it was those who had left everything to follow him who were afraid, wondering to what

---

[1] Matthew here inserts the story of the labourers in the vineyard, 20.1–15, which he apparently considers illustrates this point about the first and last—a point which he repeats at the end of the parable, in v. 16.

[2] The addition of the words ἄρας τὸν σταυρόν (σου) at various places in Mark 10.21, found in A, W, f.1, f.13, TR, is probably traceable to 8.34. It is nevertheless probably a true interpretation of Mark's meaning.

[3] The verb ἀκολουθέω is used repeatedly in Mark 8–10: 8.34 (bis); 9.38 (bis); 10.21, 28, 32, 52.

[4] Cf. E. Schweizer, Lordship and Discipleship, 1960, pp. 14–16.

fate he was leading them. It was to the twelve that Jesus explained what lay before the Son of man, and once again the term "Son of man" is clearly associated with the disciples, and could even be interpreted as including them: the destiny of the Son of man extends beyond Jesus himself to those who follow him. This is brought out also in the incident which follows—the request of James and John to sit on either side of Jesus when he is glorified. The condition which precedes glory, however, is described as the "cup" and "baptism", and those who wish to share the glory of Jesus must drink from the same cup and undergo the same baptism: those who follow Jesus must take the same road through suffering. By their question, however, James and John show that they have not understood the teaching of Jesus concerning his own suffering, nor realized its implication for themselves. The disciples' failure to understand Jesus' teaching on the Son of man's suffering has been noted by Mark after each of the three predictions of the passion: after the second of these he writes, "They did not understand the saying, and they were afraid to ask him", and their misunderstanding is demonstrated in the dispute about greatness which follows; the first prediction is followed by Peter's protest, demonstrating his inability to grasp what Jesus has been saying; and now after the third prediction the other two witnesses of the transfiguration, James and John, are still thinking of the glory they had glimpsed, and failing to understand the nature of the suffering.[1]

The request of James and John and the indignation which it arouses in the other disciples lead into a discussion on the theme of greatness and priority very similar to that which followed the previous saying in Mark 9. Jesus contrasts the authority exercised by the "great" among the Gentiles with the behaviour he expects of his followers: the disciple who would be "great" must be the servant of the others, and the one who wishes to be first must be the slave of all. In this they will be following the example of the Son of man, who "came not to be served but to serve, and to give his life as a ransom for many".

We have seen, then, that all three of these predictions of the passion are followed by teaching on the subject of discipleship—

---

[1] Cf. Luke 24.25, which also notes the failure of two disciples (outside the circle of the twelve) to understand. This failure, however, is described before the teaching on the necessity for suffering, which is now a past event.

teaching where we find the same note of paradox as is contained in the sayings themselves. The Son of man ought to appear in glory and judge the rulers of the world; instead he is destined to suffer many things and be himself rejected by the rulers of Israel (Mark 8); the disciple of Jesus must deny himself, take up his cross and follow the same path, for, if he wishes to save his life, he must lose it. The Son of man ought to exercise authority over men; instead he is delivered into their power (Mark 9); the greatest of the disciples is the one who serves the others, and the first is the one who puts himself last. The Son of man ought to receive honour and service from men, but instead he meets only humiliation and death (Mark 10); the disciple who looks for glory should look instead for the cup of suffering, and remember that true greatness does not mean being served, but serving others. In this pattern Jesus and his followers are inextricably bound together: the necessity which is laid upon the Son of man is laid also upon the disciple. We must conclude that "the Son of man" is either a corporate term (as in Daniel) or a designation for one who is closely linked with his followers (as in Enoch).

We have seen that the idea of suffering, although paradoxical, is not inconsistent with the use of the term "Son of man". The fact that this paradox extends beyond the Passion predictions themselves to the teaching about discipleship supports the authenticity of the term in those sayings. The disciples find their lives by losing them, become first by being last, and greatest by being slaves, because the Son of man himself comes to glory via the path of suffering and humiliation.

6. MARK 10.45

For the Son of man also came not to be served
but to serve, and to give his life as a ransom for many.

Cf. Matthew 20.28; Luke 22.27

This relationship between master and disciples is summed up in the most complex of all the "Son of man" sayings in Mark 10.45. Placed by Mark at the conclusion of the account of the dispute between the sons of Zebedee and the ten, it demonstrates that the basis for the paradoxical behaviour required of disciples is to be found in the example of the Son of man himself; it is because the Son of man finds greatness through service, and authority through suffering, that his disciples must follow the same path. Mark 10.45 contains the supreme and fundamental paradox; whatever picture the disciples may have had of the Son of man, we may be quite sure that it was not the one given here. This is demonstrated by the use of the words οὐ . . . ἀλλά which, as C. K. Barrett has shown,[1] bring out a contrast between what might be expected of the Son of man and the facts. First, the expectation of Daniel and Enoch was certainly that the Son of man would come "to be served"—indeed, this is explicitly stated in Dan. 7.14:

> And to him was given dominion
>   and glory and kingdom,
>   that all peoples, nations, and languages
>   should serve him.[2]

As the inheritor of the dominion of Adam, the Son of man's destiny is to rule others and not to serve them. Secondly, the Son of man is not expected "to give his life"—rather, as in 1 Enoch, we might expect to find him taking the lives of others in his capacity as judge.[3] But he himself does not die; the passage from Daniel quoted above goes on to say:

> his dominion is an everlasting dominion,
>   which shall not pass away,
>   and his kingdom one
>   that shall not be destroyed.

As one who is obedient to God's Law, the Son of man reverses the transgression of Adam, and is not subject to death—an idea which has no difficulties in Daniel, where he signifies the nation, or 1 Enoch, where he is identified with Enoch, who was "taken" by God.

In order to explain the paradox in Mark 10.45, recourse has commonly been made to the Servant of Isa. 53—an idea which C. K. Barrett has demonstrated to be inadequate.[4] But if Jesus is not referring here specifically to Isa. 53, are we to look for a

---

[1] "The Background of Mark 10.45", *New Testament Essays*, ed. A. J. B. Higgins, 1959, p. 8.
[2] Cf. 1 Enoch 48.5; 62.9; and Ps. 8.5–9(4–8).
[3] C. K. Barrett, op. cit., p. 9.
[4] Op. cit., pp. 1–7. See also M. D. Hooker, *Jesus and the Servant*, pp. 74–9.

source elsewhere, or are we to trace the paradox solely to either Jesus' own originality or the faith of the early Church?

Once again, we must turn to Dan. 7 and ask whether in fact the idea is to be found in its essence there, and whether Jesus' words are not to be understood as a more profound interpretation of that passage. We have already seen that the necessity for suffering and death is, contrary to expectation, integral to the concept of the Son of man: are the ideas of service and of a ransom also to be traced to that figure? As before, we must remember the context and purpose of Daniel's vision: the triumph of the human figure is intended to bring comfort to those who are undergoing suffering for the sake of their faith. It must be remembered, too, that this "suffering" involved not only persecution and torture, but also in many cases death: to these martyrs the author offers the assurance that ultimately the cause of the saints will be vindicated and the people of God will triumph. To the individuals who are now faced with suffering and death is given the promise: the righteous who are left will be given the kingdom and glory. Now it is true that in Dan. 12.2 we have the further promise of resurrection, and it is said that the righteous will wake to everlasting life; it is possible that the author thinks of them as sharing in the glory of chapter 7. Nevertheless, because the Son of man is a corporate figure, we must recognize that while the destiny of the saints as a whole is to move through suffering to glory, the destiny of particular individuals may vary considerably: for some it meant death, and if the author's hope were ever fulfilled, it would be truly said of them that they served their fellows and gave their lives as a ransom that God might save his people. This is the basis of the idea found in 4 Maccabees that the sufferings and prayers of the martyrs atoned for Israel.[1] These are the few whose lives were given for the many, and whose deaths proved their obedience to God. Moreover, it is the martyrs of the Maccabees who are "the people of the saints of the Most High", symbolized by the one like a Son of man in Dan. 7.

If Jesus is now seen as fulfilling the rôle of the Son of man, the startling paradoxes of Mark 10.45 are, after all, comprehensible. As Son of man he is destined to pass through suffering and death to glory and authority; but since he alone is the Son of man, it is

---

[1] C. K. Barrett, op. cit., pp. 11–15.

part of his destiny also to serve others and to give his life as a ransom for them. The few have been narrowed down to the one, who stands over against the many. Yet *is* Jesus alone "Son of man"? Once again it is possible that the term may have been used in a corporate sense, though the present form of the saying has clearly been interpreted by the evangelists as referring to Jesus. Already the followers of Jesus have been urged to lose their life in order to find it; they have been told that for them, too, the path to glory lies through suffering and humility; they have been called to follow the path of service. Nevertheless, for the evangelist at least, there is a distinction between the Son of man and the disciples: they are closely related (as in Enoch), but not identified (as in Daniel). Those who now deny themselves and follow Jesus, who serve others and so copy the example of the Son of man, will find that they can stand without shame before the Son of man in his glory.

There now remains the fundamental question whether or not these words can, in fact, be treated as genuine words of Jesus. A large number of scholars regard the second part of the saying, at least, as the interpretation of the early Church.[1] A comparison with Luke 22.24-7, which appears to be a variant account of the same incident, suggests that Mark 10.45 may be a later version of a saying which has been preserved in a more original form by Luke:

> For which is the greater, one who sits at table, or one who serves? Is it not the one who sits at table? But I am among you as one who serves.

One difference between the Marcan and the Lucan forms of this saying is the fact that Luke uses the first person singular instead of the term "Son of man"; this perhaps supports the view that his version is closer to the original.[2] It is possible that Mark's version is a later, doctrinal modification of the one given by Luke.[3]

---

[1] E.g. H. Rashdall, *The Idea of Atonement in Christian Theology*, 1920, pp. 49-56; H. E. Tödt, *Menschensohn*, pp. 187-94, E.Tr. pp. 202-11.

[2] A. J. B. Higgins, *Son of Man*, p. 42, on the contrary, argues that Mark 10.45a "is more primitive than Luke 22.27, in that the subject is not 'I' but the Son of man". Yet he maintains also that the original saying behind Mark 10.45 is an "I"-word (p. 49). Are we to suppose that an "I"-word became a "Son of man" saying and then became an "I"-word again?

[3] R. Bultmann, *Jesus and the Word*, new edn, 1958, pp. 150f, describes Mark's words as a "Hellenistic variation of an older saying" preserved by Luke. Cf. also H. Rashdall, loc. cit. Contrast, however, E. Lohse, *Märtyrer und Gottesknecht*, 1955, pp. 117-22, who argues strongly that the language of Mark 10.45 is Palestinian. Similarly J. Jeremias, "παῖς Θεοῦ", *T.W.N.T.*, V, n. 474, regards the language of Mark 10.45 as Palestinian, and thinks that Luke 22.27 shows Hellenistic influence.

In support of this interpretation, it may be urged that the saying about the ransom in Mark introduces a new, extraneous idea—an idea, furthermore, which is not paralleled elsewhere in the gospel: to serve others is one thing, but to give one's life as their ransom is another. Nevertheless, there are certain factors which we must remember before dismissing too easily Mark's version.

First, we must question the assumption that the word λύτρον is totally foreign to the rest of the sentence. This judgement is in fact largely the result of interpreting λύτρον in the light of the guilt-offering, or אָשָׁם, in Isa. 53.10—an association for which, as we have shown elsewhere, there is no justification.[1] In the LXX, λύτρον and its cognate verb λυτρόω are used especially of God's acts of deliverance by which he freed his people from bondage, both at the Exodus[2] and at the long-awaited Return from Exile;[3] they are never used of a sin-offering or guilt-offering. The most likely background to the use of the word here is the Jewish hope that God himself would redeem his people—a hope expressed by the later prophets and by the apocalyptists. Yet this hope of redemption is the hope which has taken hold of Jesus' disciples:[4] it is one with the inbreaking of God's kingdom into the world, with the restoration of Israel, with the new era visualized in Dan. 7, and with the εὐαγγέλιον which Mark proclaims in 1.1. It is, in fact, the message of the whole ministry of Jesus, who restores men to wholeness, and casts out devils by the finger of God: the life that has

---

[1] *Jesus and the Servant*, pp. 76–8. See also C. K. Barrett, op. cit., pp. 5–7. A. J. B. Higgins, *Son of Man*, pp. 45f, attempts to defend the view that Mark 10.45 "sums up the general thought of Isa. liii" (Rawlinson) by maintaining that the distinction between λύτρον and אָשָׁם is open to question. Linguistic evidence may not be infallible, but why cling to an identification for which there is no evidence whatever, and ignore the Old Testament background of the term λύτρον altogether? Higgins apparently recognizes the weakness of his position, for he admits that it may "be judged an insufficiently exact approach", and appeals to the common use of λύτρον in the LXX; although never used to translate אָשָׁם it could, he feels, be so used in Mark 10.45, since "we cannot expect the New Testament writers always to be confined within the limits of Septuagintal usage, and they are not so confined". As an example, he quotes the varied translations of the verb עָרָה in Isa. 53.12, which is, he claims, rendered by παραδιδόναι in the LXX, διδόναι in Mark 10.45, and κενοῦν in Phil. 2.7. But to quote Mark 10.45, the verse under discussion, as a reference to Isa. 53 is to beg the question. So, too, is an appeal to Phil. 2.7, for κενοῦν is never used to translate עָרָה in the LXX, and this would therefore be another example of the very point which Higgins is trying to prove.

[2] E.g. Ex. 6.6; 15.16; Deut. 7.8; 9.26; Isa. 43.1; Mic. 6.4.

[3] E.g. Isa. 52.3; 62.12; Mic. 4.10; Jer. 15.21; 38(31).11.

[4] Luke 24.21.

been spent in freeing men from bondage is now given as their ransom. Far from introducing a foreign concept into the verse, therefore, the word λύτρον expresses the supreme example of the "service" which is spoken of in vv. 43–5a.

As far as the setting is concerned, it is difficult to decide whether Mark or Luke has the greater claim to reliability. Vincent Taylor supports the Marcan context, urging that a dispute over greatness is improbable after the Last Supper.[1] This dispute might have arisen, however, over the seating arrangements at the Supper (though in this case one might have expected it before the meal rather than after), and the details of Luke's account, with references to eating in vv. 27 and 30, suggest a conversation over a meal. A decision on this question does not, of course, decide the problem of the original form of the words themselves.[2]

More illuminating are the verses with which Luke follows the saying. These speak of the kingdom which God has "covenanted" to Jesus, and the share in that kingdom which he now in turn "covenants" to the disciples, although it remains his; the twelve are to eat and drink at the table of Jesus and to sit on twelve thrones judging Israel.[3] Such a pronouncement, almost immediately after the prophecy of betrayal in v. 21, is remarkable: either Judas' defection was a surprise to Jesus, or the present passage is misplaced, or the number "twelve" is a late development. Its connection here with the saying in v. 27 is important, but its meaning is not altogether clear. What is the significance of the verb διατίθημι? If it means "will" then there is a plain reference to the death of Jesus; but since the verb is used of God in the same sentence, it seems clear that we must understand it in the sense of "covenant"; even so, it would seem likely that Luke has linked the word with Christ's death, in view of the context which he has given to the saying. Moreover, the kingdom which is covenanted to Jesus by his Father must in some way be connected with the kingdom of God, which is linked in vv. 15f with Jesus' sufferings and with the Supper; the vow of abstention which Jesus takes in

---

[1] *Mark*, in loc.

[2] Thus A. J. B. Higgins, *Son of Man*, pp. 49f, supports the originality of the Lucan context, but regards the Marcan version as closer to Jesus' words. Mark's version would fit the Lucan setting better than Luke's own version.

[3] It is not clear in v. 29 whether or not βασιλείαν should be understood as the object of διατίθεμαι as well as of διέθετο. In either case, it is true to say that the disciples are covenanted a share in the benefits of Jesus' kingdom.

vv. 15f before his death looks forward to the consummation of the feast referred to in vv. 29f. If the "longer reading" of vv. 19b–20 is original, then this link is emphasized by the verb διατίθημι, which echoes the words spoken over the cup in v. 20—τοῦτο τὸ ποτήριον ἡ καινὴ διαθήκη ἐν τῷ αἵματί μου, τὸ ὑπὲρ ὑμῶν ἐκχυννόμενον. The present tense used in v. 29, διατίθεμαι, indicates that Jesus is accomplishing some new event; the earlier promises are fulfilled, and to those who have remained with him ἐν τοῖς πειρασμοῖς he now "covenants" that they will enjoy the benefits of the kingdom given to him by God. We are reminded again of the picture given us in Dan. 7 of the kingdom being presented to the Son of man, or saints of the Most High,[1] and we find that the Lucan narrative is not so far removed, after all, from the "ransom" saying of Mark 10.45: in some way the events in Jerusalem are the means whereby others (in Luke the twelve, in Mark the "many") are given a share in Jesus' kingdom. The connection between Mark's account and Luke's is confirmed when we remember that the covenant between God and Israel was made on the basis of the fact that he had redeemed them; again and again, the people are reminded that it was the saving events at the Exodus which are the basis of the covenant relationship established at Sinai.[2] The "covenant relationship" with the twelve representatives of the new Israel in Luke 22.29f is linked with the death of Jesus, which has already been described in 9.31 as an ἔξοδος, and so associated with the idea of God's redemption of his people. Moreover, in this covenant relationship Jesus stands in a vital mediating position between his Father, who has covenanted the kingdom to him, and his disciples, to whom he covenants a share in that same kingdom. The idea that Jesus' death is a λύτρον ἀντὶ πολλῶν, therefore, lies beneath the surface in Luke.

If our understanding of λύτρον is correct, then it was a true insight which linked the term "Son of man" with the idea expressed in Mark 10.45. Once again, it is *precisely because he is Son of man and as Son of man* that Jesus suffers. We have here, not a "fusion" between the term "Son of man" and some other concept, but an

---

[1] This idea is expressed clearly in Matthew's parallel to Luke 22.30b, where in Matt. 19.28 those who have followed Jesus are promised a share in the kingdom (sitting on twelve thrones) at the vindication of the Son of man —"when the Son of man shall sit on his glorious throne".

[2] E.g. Ex. 19.4f; 20.2; Lev. 26.13f; Deut. 29.1–15.

expression of something which is involved in being Son of man. This interpretation may be due to either Jesus or the early Church, but if we accept the view that Jesus used the term "Son of man" of himself at all, then it seems reasonable to suppose that the insight was his. Again, if Jesus recognized that the rejection of his authority must lead to suffering, and yet looked for a final vindication; if, moreover, he promised his followers that they would tread the same path of shame, and that they would share in the glory of the Son of man; then it would seem that their vindication, since it is dependent upon his, must necessarily be in some way dependent upon his suffering and death. So, then, it is because of his obedience "unto death, even death on a cross", that God will highly exalt him; and it is because of his obedience that he himself is able to share his glory with others—another way of saying that his life was given as a ransom for many.

8

Survey of the Material: C

1. MARK 13.26

And then they will see the Son of man
coming in clouds with great power and glory.

Cf. Matthew 24.30; Luke 21.27

Our interpretation of this particular verse in Mark 13 is closely
bound up with our understanding of the chapter as a whole. While
the majority of scholars regard the discourse as an artificial com-
pilation containing a high proportion of non-dominical sayings,[1]
there are those who trace its material to Jesus himself.[2] The really
crucial distinction, however, concerns the character of the material
rather than its authenticity: is it correct to describe the chapter as
an "apocalypse", or is it in fact closer to the spirit and form of Old
Testament prophecy than to apocalyptic writings?[3]

There has been a tendency in recent years to regard all eschatological literature as apocalyptic: but while apocalyptic writing is
normally eschatological, eschatology is by no means necessarily
always apocalyptic. As we have already noted,[4] apocalyptic grew
out of prophetic literature, and it is not always easy to draw the

---

[1] R. Bultmann, *Geschichte*, pp. 129f, E.Tr. pp. 122f; B. W. Bacon, *The Gospel
of Mark*, 1925, pp. 53–68, 120–34; T. F. Glasson, *The Second Advent*, pp. 76–
80; V. Taylor, *Mark*, pp. 498f, 636–44. These scholars vary, of course, in the
amount of material which they are prepared to attribute to Jesus himself.

[2] G. R. Beasley-Murray, *Jesus and the Future*, 1954, pp. 172–250; *A Commentary on Mark Thirteen*, 1957, pp. 1–18. Cf. C. E. B. Cranfield, *Mark*, pp.
387–90; J. Schniewind, *Markus*, p. 132.

[3] J. A. T. Robinson, *Jesus and His Coming*, p. 122, setting aside Mark 13.24–7,
writes of the rest of the chapter: "Thus reconstructed, the discourse ceases to be
an apocalypse in any proper sense of the term. It is rather a solemn warning in
the manner of the Prophets of the historical consequences of Israel's rejection
and of the attitude which the faithful must adopt to them." Cf. W. G. Kümmel,
Promise and Fulfilment, pp. 95–9; J. W. Bowman, *The Intention of Jesus*, pp. 55f.

[4] Above, p. 17.

dividing line between the two. In the present case, e.g., we may find parallels for the description of strife in v. 8, both in apocalyptic and in prophetic literature.[1] Although Mark 13 certainly resembles apocalyptic in its esoteric nature and in being concerned with future events, nevertheless it lacks many of the normal characteristics of apocalyptic literature. The so-called "Apocalyptic discourse" is *not* an account of visionary experiences; nor is it a revelation of the eschatological time-table: instead of mathematical calculations about the precise number of "weeks" before the End, we have the confession that no one, not even the angels or the Son, knows the time when that day will arrive; instead of promises that the End is coming soon, we have grim warnings of the disasters and sufferings which must first be endured because "the end is not yet".[2]

This question of the character of the material in the discourse is of vital importance to our study, because it affects our interpretation of the various sayings which make up the chapter. One of the great problems of the discourse is the curious juxtaposition of "historical" and "supernatural" events: on the one hand, we have what seems to be a prophecy of the fall of Jerusalem; on the other, we have verses which apparently predict the parousia. The fact that these two events are placed in sequence by Mark immediately raises two problems for the modern critic: (a) whereas the first event took place almost 1900 years ago, the second has not occurred; (b) the two events are totally different in character; one is a catastrophe which is now an historical fact, and the other is the break-up of the universe, which would bring history to a close. Yet it is doubtful whether either of these problems would have had meaning for Mark and his first readers. The gospel was probably written before the fall of Jerusalem; if not, it was written so soon after that event that the delay was not yet a cause of perplexity. As for the distinction between "historical" and "supernatural" events, that is foreign to the evangelists, as to the other biblical writers. The whole Hebrew understanding of God is grounded in the belief that he is a God who acts in history: it was he who brought up armies against Jerusalem, used kings as his

[1] Cf. Isa. 13.4f, 13; Jer. 14.12; 21.4–10; Ezek. 5.11f; Zech. 14.2–5; 2 Esdras 9.3; 13.31; 15.15.
[2] C. H. Dodd, "The Fall of Jerusalem and the 'Abomination of Desolation'", *The Journal of Roman Studies*, 37, 1947, pp. 47–54, prefers to describe Mark 13 as "a *Mahnrede* making use of apocalyptic motives".

instruments, raised Jesus from the dead, caused and controlled earthquakes and famines. It was therefore not incongruous to link together the activities of men and what today are termed "acts of God"; Roman armies were as much God's tools as were thunderbolts and falling stars.

This "confusion" of historical with supernatural events is by no means confined to Mark 13. The same phenomenon is found repeatedly in the Old Testament, in passages depicting the "Day of the Lord" and the judgement of the nation. The Old Testament prophets regularly use the imagery of darkened sun and falling stars to express the intensity of the suffering which is to fall upon the people.[1] At what point this kind of language becomes "apocalyptic" is debatable; probably at that stage where it ceases to be poetic imagery, and is taken literally of the break-up of the universe and the end of history.[2]

Influenced to a lesser or greater degree by Colani's "Little Apocalypse" theory, commentators on Mark 13 have endeavoured to separate the wheat of historical prophecy from the chaff of apocalyptic fancy; the former, it is felt, may fittingly be attributed to Jesus himself, while the latter is held to be unworthy. Yet scholars have perhaps been guilty of a literalism equal to that of the apocalyptic writers themselves. The very fact which appears to us so puzzling—the mixture of historical and supernatural events— is in many ways closer to Old Testament prophecy than to later apocalyptic. Moreover, the fact that Mark himself may have interpreted these events literally does not mean that the individual sayings were originally intended to be understood literally: we should not be misled by an apocalyptic veneer into assuming that the sayings are intrinsically apocalyptic.

Our first approach to the sayings, however, must be via the setting which has been given them by Mark. And here it is as well to remember the setting of the whole discourse in relation to the gospel. Appearing, at first sight, to stand in lonely detachment from the rest of the book, it is nevertheless closely linked both with what precedes and with what follows. The introductory words are more than an artificial link with the preceding narrative; they introduce the judgement of the Messiah upon his people, symbolized by the destruction of the sanctuary. The impending

---

[1] E.g. Amos 8.9; Joel 2.10, 31; 3.15.
[2] Cf. 2 Esdras 5.4; 1 Enoch 80.4–7; Ass. Moses 10.5.

fall of the temple had been one theme in the prophetic message about the Day of the Lord:[1] its destruction was an inevitable symbol of judgement and the severance of the relationship between Yahweh and his people. It is by no means surprising, therefore, to find a strong tradition that Jesus made a similar pronouncement.[2] The link between the teaching of Jesus and the teaching of the prophets has already been underlined for us by Mark in the parable of the vineyard in chapter 12. But it is the theme of rejection with which that parable—in common with the whole of chapters 11 and 12—is concerned. In his account of the triumphal entry Mark has depicted Jesus entering the capital city as its king. Yet according to the evangelist his kingship is barely recognized, acknowledged or understood. The only open declaration of his kingship comes from a blind beggar seated by the roadside, who is silenced by the crowd; even the entry itself is messianic only to those who realize its significance and understand the hidden meaning of the crowd's ambiguous greetings. Nor is Jesus' authority accepted in Jerusalem, as the question of the "authorities" in 11.27–33 shows: they have rejected the "only son", as their predecessors rejected the prophets, and the incidents which follow show them trying to trap Jesus. There is, however, another theme of rejection in these same chapters, and that is God's rejection of Israel. This theme, too, is found in the parable of the vineyard. Whatever may be the validity of the popular maxim that an authentic parable of Jesus can have only one point, there can be no doubt that in its present form this story has two: the rejection and death of the messengers and the only son is paralleled by the rejection and destruction of the tenants —indeed, the first rejection is the cause of the second. This rejection of Israel is expressed forcefully by the miracle of the withered fig-tree; recorded as it is in two parts, with Jesus' words of condemnation in the temple sandwiched between them, there can be little doubt that this story was understood by Mark as symbolizing the failure and rejection of Israel. The incident with which it is combined, the so-called cleansing of the temple, is primarily a word of judgement on Israel's failure to fulfil her mission, and Jesus' actions should perhaps be interpreted as a prophetic act symbolizing the coming destruction of the temple and the cessation

---

[1] Mic. 3.12; Jer. 26.6,18.
[2] Cf. Mark 14.58; 15.29; John 2.19.

of worship,[1] rather than as an attempt at the reformation of temple ritual. As the latter, the action must be regarded as ineffectual, for the moneychangers presumably soon set their tables to rights and recommenced their trade; as the former, the action has point, and links closely with the miracle of the fig-tree. It is worth noticing how these two incidents have been skilfully joined together, so that we have the following sequence of events:

1. Jesus enters the temple, and looks round, 11.11.

2. Jesus goes to the fig-tree and looks for fruit. He finds no fruit, and condemns the tree, 11.12–14.

3. Jesus drives the merchants out of the temple and condemns Israel for failing to make the temple a place of worship for all nations, 11.15–17.

4. The religious authorities seek a way to destroy Jesus, 11.18.

5. The fig-tree is found to have withered away, 11.20–1.

However we interpret the incident in the temple, it certainly involves the condemnation of Israel by her Messiah; as in the story of the fig-tree, and again in the parable of the vineyard, Jesus has looked for fruit, but found none; the sequel in both cases is inevitable.

Chapter 13 follows on, then, from what has gone before: the destruction which it foretells is the result of Israel's failure to respond to her Messiah. But the chapter is also linked with what follows: for the rejection of Jesus by his people is still to be carried through to its conclusion in the passion and crucifixion. Chapter 13 looks forward to the End which lies beyond the end of the story, to the wrath which Israel is storing up for herself, and to the vindication of Jesus, the rejected stone who is to be made the head of the corner.[2] Even the language of 13, as R. H. Lightfoot has shown, seems to "echo" the language of the passion narrative.[3] All this suggests that we should bear in mind the theme of rejection and its results in studying Mark 13.

The chapter begins with the exclamation of one of the disciples

---

[1] It is perhaps significant that the fourth evangelist links the incident with the saying about the destruction of the temple, even though he interprets this of the body of Jesus, John 2.13–22. Cf. also R. H. Lightfoot, *The Gospel Message of St Mark*, pp. 68f, 78f.

[2] Ps. 118.22, quoted in Mark 12.10.   [3] Op. cit., pp. 48–59.

at the sight of the temple. If the descriptions by Josephus[1] are accurate, there is no reason to doubt that the temple was an impressive sight, and likely to call forth comments, even from those familiar with it. But there may well be a deeper significance in the words. The impressive strength and solidity of the building may perhaps have encouraged the disciples in the belief that it would endure for ever, and they would have shared the general feeling of awe which equated the temple with the presence of God; their instinctive reaction to prophecies of the temple's destruction would probably resemble that of the Jews of earlier centuries, who refused to believe the words of Micah and Jeremiah, and declared, perhaps indignantly, perhaps complacently: "This is the temple of the Lord."[2] This interpretation of the disciples' words is supported by the setting which Matthew gives them, for in his narrative they follow immediately after the lament of Jesus over the city of Jerusalem.[3]

The words of Jesus concerning the temple in Mark 13.2, although they serve as the introduction to the discourse, are never taken up again. This may perhaps be a mark of the chapter's artificiality. Yet there is a real link between the destruction of the temple and ταῦτα πάντα accompanying it. The fate of the temple is inevitably associated with the fate of Jerusalem, and since both are seen as the judgement of God, they are accompanied by other eschatological events. For a similar pattern we need only turn once more to the prophets, where, for example, we find Micah prophesying the destruction of Jerusalem and the temple, events which he sees as the result of the nation's sin;[4] in 3.6 we find the imagery which was developed and taken literally by the apocalyptic writers:

> Therefore it shall be night to you, without vision,
>   and darkness to you, without divination.
> The sun shall go down upon the prophets,
>   and the day shall be black over them.

For Jeremiah, too, the fate of temple and city are bound up together: "This house shall be like Shiloh, and this city shall be desolate, without inhabitant."[5] Of particular interest is Jer. 7, where we find several links with the Marcan narrative. We have already

---

[1] *Antiquities*, XV,xi.3.   [2] Mic. 3.11; Jer. 7.4, 8–14.
[3] Matt. 23.37—24.1. Cf. G. R. Beasley-Murray, *A Commentary on Mark Thirteen*, pp. 20f.
[4] Mic. 3.12.   [5] Jer. 26.9; cf. 26.6; 7.14, 34.

noted the prophet's attack in v. 4 on the people's complacent trust in the temple of the Lord in their midst, and his prophecy in v. 14 of its destruction. The cause of the temple's coming destruction is the persistent sin of the people, vv. 8–13, and it is here, in v. 11, that we find the words recalled by Jesus in the temple:[1] "Has this house, which is called by my name, become a den of robbers in your eyes?" Another link with the gospel narrative is found in vv. 25f, which may perhaps have formed, with Isa. 5, the basis of the parable of the vineyard:

> From the day that your fathers came out of the land of Egypt to this day, I have persistently sent all my servants the prophets to them, day after day; yet they did not listen to me, or incline their ear, but stiffened their neck. They did worse than their fathers.

Finally, we may note the crowning sin in Jeremiah's eyes, described in v. 30:

> For the sons of Judah have done evil in my sight, says the Lord; they have set their abominations in the house which is called by my name, to defile it.

It is the desecration of the temple by the setting up of idols which seals its doom and the doom of the people. The term "their abominations", שִׁקּוּצֵיהֶם, is used in the same sense as the phrase שִׁקּוּץ מְשׁוֹמֵם/שֹׁמֵם in Dan. 11.31 and 12.11. It is the desecration of the temple by the "abominations" which unleashes the wrath of the Lord:[2]

> And the dead bodies of this people will be food for the birds of the air, and for the beasts of the earth; and none will frighten them away. And I will make to cease from the cities of Judah and from the streets of Jerusalem the voice of mirth and the voice of gladness, the voice of the bridegroom and the voice of the bride; for the land shall become a waste.

Finally, in 8.1–3 we read that the bones of all the inhabitants are to be spread out "before the sun and the moon and all the host of heaven, which they have loved and served, which they have gone after, and which they have sought and worshipped". The apocalyptic imagery of darkened sun and moon and falling stars may perhaps owe something to the idea of the overthrow of these celestial powers.

[1] Mark 11.17, in combination with Isa. 56.7.   [2] Jer. 7.33f.

It is perhaps worth noticing that, in its present form, this prophecy of Jeremiah shows another similarity with Mark 13. In spite of the reference to the setting up of abominations in the temple in 7.30, there is no mention of the destruction of the temple itself after 7.14, but only to the general catastrophe which overtakes the city and the nation, in which the temple may be presumed to be destroyed.

The association of the desecration of the temple with the destruction of the nation is found also in Ezek. 5, where the whole chapter describes the punishment which is coming. Once again, the desecration of the temple is the culminating sin, which leads to the total annihilation of the nation:[1]

> Wherefore, as I live, says the Lord God, surely, because you have defiled my sanctuary with all your detestable things and with all your abominations, therefore I will cut you down; my eye will not spare, and I will have no pity. A third part of you shall die of pestilence and be consumed with famine in the midst of you; a third part shall fall by the sword round about you; and a third part I will scatter to all the winds and will unsheathe the sword after them.

Finally, we may note Isa. 63.15—64.12, words spoken at a later date when the temple already lay in ruins. It is because of Israel's hardness of heart and iniquity that her adversaries have trodden down the sanctuary.[2] The anger of the Lord against his people is seen in her desolation:[3]

> Thy holy cities have become a wilderness,
>   Zion has become a wilderness,
>   Jerusalem a desolation.
> Our holy and beautiful house,
>   where our fathers praised thee,
> has been burned by fire,
>   and all our pleasant places have become ruins.

The prediction of the destruction of the temple must clearly be put into the category of prophecy rather than apocalyptic. The Old Testament background suggests that Mark is right in linking it with the theme of judgement.[4]

---

[1] Ezek. 5.11f.   [2] Isa. 63.18.
[3] Isa. 64.10f.
[4] This does not, of course, mean that the idea was not taken over into apocalyptic. Cf. 1 Enoch 90.28f.

According to Mark 13.3, the teaching of Jesus was delivered as he sat upon the Mount of Olives. It is not impossible that this setting is due to historical recollection;[1] even so, Mark would probably expect his readers to attach a deeper significance to it. A mountain has already served as the setting for the transfiguration, which prefigured the final glory of the Son of man. Moreover, according to Zech. 14.4, God was to "stand" upon the Mount of Olives at the judgement of Jerusalem. The mountain is therefore an appropriate setting for the discourse, and underlines the significance of Jesus' words, which are God's judgement upon his people; coming at the climax of the gospel, it is clear that Mark sees this judgement as the direct outcome of the Jews' failure to respond to Christ's ministry: it is the rejection of their Messiah which leads to the rejection of his people.

How far is this Mark's own understanding of the material, and how far is it justifiable to see it as a reflection of the mind of Jesus himself? In this particular case, we may perhaps claim with some certainty that the link between his rejection and the coming judgement is authentic, for it is already embedded in the "Son of man" saying in Mark 8.38, whose authenticity few would deny. Such a link is by no means surprising, when we remember that the Old Testament prophets also regarded the people's rejection of their message as intimately connected with God's judgement.[2]

We may perhaps conclude, then, that Mark is right in telling us that Jesus spoke of judgement on those who had rejected him. There is, however, another link between chapter 13 and 8.38: although chapter 13 begins with the theme of judgement upon Israel, it is equally concerned with the fate of the disciples; its theme, in fact, is very largely the trouble which is in store for those who are not ashamed of Jesus and who do not deny him. Before the time of judgement and condemnation for the enemies of Jesus, there is a period when they will be in a position to judge and condemn his followers; the disciples must be prepared for persecution before the final vindication. The whole of chapter 13 is thus an elaboration of the theme found in 8.34–8: those who wish to follow Christ must expect to follow the same path of suffering, for they will be hated by all because of his name; but those who are ashamed of Jesus, and who do not endure until the end, will not

---

[1] G. R. Beasley-Murray, *A Commentary on Mark Thirteen*, pp. 25f.
[2] E.g. Isa. 1.19f; Jer. 7.1–15. Cf. Jonah 3.

be saved. It is against this background that we must understand the climax of the chapter in vv. 24–7, the darkening of sun, moon, and stars, and the arrival of the Son of man. Its relevance to the general theme of the chapter is clear: the revelation of the Son of man is synonymous with judgement: for all who have rejected Jesus this means disaster; but for those who have been faithful it means vindication.

Most commentators have the gravest suspicions about the contents of Mark 13 in general, and about vv. 24–7 in particular. These verses have been described as "a patchwork of Old Testament testimonies" taken from the LXX, and therefore the product of the early Church;[1] at best, on this view, the saying about the Son of man is seen as "a distorted echo" of Jesus' words.[2] Some reject it on the ground that it differs from 8.38 and 14.62 in failing to hint at a relationship between Jesus and the Son of man.[3] Yet, when the saying is taken in its setting in St Mark's gospel, the relationship between Jesus and the Son of man is, in fact, parallel to that found in 8.38. This fact has perhaps been obscured by the recent tendency to analyse Mark 13 into sources, and to regard it as a conglomeration of pericopae, so isolating vv. 24–7 from their context. Moreover, the link and the distinction between the terms "Jesus" and "Son of man" in 8.38 are related to the link and the distinction between what happens "in this generation" and what happens at the End: it is precisely this link and distinction which are seen in the juxtaposition of historical and eschatological events in 13. Again, it is possibly this link and distinction which explain the apparent contradiction between the two sayings in 13.30 and 32, which because of their difficulties have a high claim to authenticity: the sufferings which Jesus predicts for his followers belong to the present era, and will be experienced by this generation, but the End belongs to the future era, and the time of its arrival is unknown.

It would be foolish to regard Mark 13.26 as a key passage in any attempt to recover the meaning of the term "Son of man" for Jesus; we cannot rely upon the authenticity of the saying or of its setting. Yet we should not be as hasty as some have been in dismissing it from the discussion. For even if saying and setting are

---

[1] T. F. Glasson, *The Second Advent*, p. 187.
[2] V. Taylor, *Mark*, in loc.
[3] E.g. A. J. B. Higgins, *Son of Man*, pp. 60–6.

both due to Mark or to the pre-Marcan Church tradition, yet the general picture is in remarkable agreement with 8.38.

The "Son of man" saying itself is clearly based on Dan. 7.13, though it is by no means a direct quotation; by comparison with Mark 14.62, we seem to have several secondary features: e.g. ὄψονται instead of ὄψεσθε, ἐν νεφέλαις for the phrase μετὰ τῶν νεφελῶν τοῦ οὐρανοῦ (which is closer to the LXX, and identical with Theodotion), and the generalizing summary μετὰ δυνάμεως πολλῆς καὶ δόξης.[1] As in Daniel, the "coming" of the Son of man follows a long period of tribulation, of which the last stage is the worst. From the context, it would seem that Mark has interpreted this event in terms of the parousia: it is perhaps unnecessary to discuss whether the Son of man goes up or down: since the stars have fallen from heaven, we are perhaps to understand that earth and heaven have fused into one. At any rate, Mark views this as the τέλος: the vindication of Christ's followers is the final act, and they are gathered by the angels from the corners of the earth.

Mark, like the author of 1 Enoch, has understood the details of Daniel literally. But was he correct in attributing this interpretation to Jesus? The very fact that these verses are based on Daniel suggests that Mark may have been wrong, for the vision of Dan. 7 is meant to be understood symbolically of the vindication of the saints of Israel. If Mark is right in attributing the use of Dan. 7.13 to Jesus, then we must conclude, either that Jesus himself is responsible for this literal interpretation of Daniel, and envisaged the arrival of the Son of man (whether himself or another) on earth; or that he, like Daniel, used this language symbolically to express his faith in the ultimate vindication of the one who was Son of man. It is perhaps significant that, although Mark has understood Dan. 7.13 of the parousia, the "arrival" of the Son of man is connected, as in Daniel, with the theme of present suffering and future vindication—with the sufferings of Jesus' disciples and their final vindication: by contrast, the Son of man in 1 Enoch and 2 Esdras has been detached from this theme, and the emphasis is on his judgement of the wicked. The theme of Mark 13 as a whole is thus closer to Dan. 7, where the Son of man is a symbolic figure, than it is to the later apocalyptic reinterpretation of that passage. Behind Mark's interpretation, therefore, there may well lie a stage in the

---

[1] Cf. A. J. B. Higgins, *Son of Man*, pp. 61–5.

tradition in which the coming of the Son of man was understood, as in Daniel, of a judgement scene before God, rather than of a parousia to earth.

2. MARK 14.21

For the Son of man goes as it is written of him, but woe to that man by whom the Son of man is betrayed! It would have been better for that man if he had not been born.

Cf. Matthew 26.24; Luke 22.22

The term "the Son of man" is used here twice by both Mark and Matthew. Luke has replaced the second reference by a relative pronoun, but retains the link and contrast between the two statements. The saying holds together two ideas which might seem to be contradictory but are in fact complementary. On the one hand, the Son of man "goes as it is written of him"—i.e. in accordance with the purpose of God. On the other hand, however, the Son of man is betrayed by "that man", who is responsible and culpable for his action.

This saying, with its appeal to the fulfilment of scripture, is often attributed to the early Church. Higgins, e.g., dismisses it in its present form as "a community creation", and writes: "the saying as it stands can hardly be regarded as the *ipsissima verba* of Jesus".[1] His reasons for this judgement are based, firstly, on the introductory ὅτι, and secondly, on the verb ὑπάγει. The introductory ὅτι he takes as evidence that this verse is an addition to vv. 19f from a separate sayings source—an addition made either by Mark or by a predecessor. This is possible, though it should be noted that Luke has either retained Mark's ὅτι or discovered it in another source, and apparently found no embarrassment in the word; it is possible that ὅτι is used here as a loose causal conjunction, and should be translated "for".[2] In any case, the fact that the saying may originally have been found in another setting

---

[1] *Son of Man*, pp. 50–2. Cf. R. Bultmann, *Geschichte*, p. 163, E.Tr. p. 152; C. G. Montefiore, *The Synoptic Gospels*, I, p. 325; J. Wellhausen, *Marc.*, in loc.

[2] As the R.S.V. Cf. Arndt-Gingrich, *Lexicon*, ὅτι, 3b; Blass-Debrunner, 456(1); also E. P. Gould, *Mark*, in loc., and A. Plummer, *The Gospel according to St Luke*, 1910, p. 500.

does not mean that it cannot be authentic.[1] The verb ὑπάγω in the sense of "to go to death" is found only here and in the fourth gospel, and it has been suggested that the Greek represents the Aramaic אזל, which could be used with this meaning;[2] in John, however, Jesus says "I go", and not, as here, "the Son of man goes". Higgins concludes that Jesus may well have spoken of "going", but that he used the verb in the first person singular, as frequently in John, and did not refer to the departure of the Son of man. This evidence is by no means conclusive, however. Certainly the fact that John also records this use of ὑπάγω "must be taken seriously", but it is risky to place too much weight on the number of these sayings in John, since their absence from the synoptic sayings (apart from our present text) suggests that John has multiplied them; his evidence can justifiably be used to support the general reliability of Mark 14.21a,[3] but is less convincing when used as an argument against the possibility that Jesus could have combined ὑπάγω with the term "Son of man".

In the second part of the verse we find "Son of man" linked once again with the verb παραδίδωμι. Here, as in 9.31 and 10.33, there is some ambiguity in the use of this word: although this time it refers primarily to the fact that Jesus is betrayed by Judas, it may perhaps also imply that ultimately Jesus is handed over into the hands of men by God, through the agency of Judas.[4] If so, then this word in itself conveys something of the tension between v. 21a and v. 21b.

Both parts of the verse can be attributed to the early Church, and interpreted as explanations of the passion placed into the mouth of Jesus; in this case they must be seen as attempts to show his acceptance of his fate and his foreknowledge of Judas' treachery. Nevertheless, the vocabulary of both suggests an early origin.[5] Moreover, the occurrence of the term "Son of man" is by no

---

[1] Higgins himself concludes that an original saying of Jesus (but in an "I"-form) lies behind Mark 14.21. His argument at this point seems to be motivated by the determination to get rid, at all costs, of the "Son of man" sayings.

[2] Cf. M. Black, *An Aramaic Approach to the Gospels and Acts*, 2nd edn, pp. 237f.

[3] V. Taylor, *Mark*, in loc., thinks it reasonable to regard ὑπάγει as "a mode of speech characteristic of Jesus".

[4] Cf. Origen, *Commentary on Matthew*, Book 13,8. See also C. E. B. Cranfield, *Mark*, in loc.; E. Lohmeyer, *Markus*, in loc.

[5] In addition to ὑπάγει and the phrase "the Son of man" itself we have the Semitic use of καλόν for the comparative (see M. Black, op. cit., p. 86).

means haphazard or fortuitous, since the double saying is an application and extension of the "Son of man" saying in 9.31. Taken together, these two statements about the Son of man bring out the significance of the saying in 9.31 by applying it to events within the setting of the passion narrative. We have already been told that the Son of man has been delivered into the hands of men; now we see what this statement entails: on the one hand, it means that the Son of man accepts his destiny, and "goes" as it is written of him; on the other, it means that he is betrayed by Judas. The irony of the situation is seen in the fact that the Son of man (who should be exercising authority) has come under the power of "that man" who has rejected his authority. Once again, the inevitability of suffering for the Son of man is linked with man's refusal to obey and acknowledge him.

3. MARK 14.41

And he came the third time and said to them, "Are you still sleeping and taking your rest? It is enough; the hour has come; the Son of man is betrayed into the hands of sinners."

Cf. Matthew 26.45

Once again, we find the title "Son of man" linked with the verb παραδίδωμι, but this time it is the verb and not the title which appears twice. Here, as in 14.21, the verb refers primarily to Judas, who is described as ὁ παραδιδούς με (v. 42): but once more παραδίδωμι may be used with a deeper significance, and the whole phrase in v. 41b certainly echoes the words of 9.31, ὁ υἱὸς τοῦ ἀνθρώπου παραδίδοται εἰς χεῖρας ἀνθρώπων. The idea that the Son of man is fulfilling a necessary destiny is contained also in the words ἦλθεν ἡ ὥρα. As in 14.21, the saying holds together the inevitability of the passion and the guilt of the betrayer.

Higgins refuses to consider this saying as even "approaching an authentic allusion of Jesus to his betrayal",[1] but the only reason he gives for this judgement is that it is very similar to a saying in John 12.23: ἐλήλυθεν ἡ ὥρα ἵνα δοξασθῇ ὁ υἱὸς τοῦ ἀνθρώπου. His argument seems inconsistent with the one he employed in dealing with Mark 14.21. There he found the "Johannine" ὑπάγω linked with "Son of man" in Mark but not in John, and so concluded

<hr/>

[1] Op. cit., p. 53. Similarly R. Bultmann, *Geschichte*, p. 163, E.Tr. p. 152. J. Wellhausen, *Marc.*, in loc., regards v. 41b as secondary.

that "Son of man" must be deleted from Mark; here he finds the "Johannine" ὥρα linked with "Son of man" in both Mark *and* John, and again concludes that "Son of man" must be deleted. Higgins may be right in his conclusions, but his argument is a feeble one, and can hardly be thought to warrant his dismissal of Mark 14.41 as "inauthentic", or his statement that "It illuminates the earlier Markan associations of the Son of man and παραδιδόναι, and in fact establishes that they are church formulations".[1] A more cogent argument in support of Higgins' view could be found in a comparison of Mark 14.41 with the saying which he regards as much closer to Jesus' words, i.e. Mark 14.18 and its exact parallel in John 13.21: ἀμὴν λέγω ὑμῖν ὅτι εἷς ἐξ ὑμῶν παραδώσει με. It is possible that an original statement by Jesus that he would be betrayed by one of his own followers has been transformed into a "Son of man" saying by the early Church. Yet the two predictions are not entirely parallel, for the sayings which combine the title "Son of man" with παραδίδωμι are not, as we have seen, simple references to the betrayal, but are linked with the idea that the suffering of the Son of man is in accord with the purposes of God. If the Church has substituted "the Son of man" for "me", it has also introduced this theme of divine necessity. The possibility that this association of the Son of man with his fate goes back to Jesus is, however, by no means excluded. Jesus may well have spoken of his betrayal by a disciple—in which case "one of you" and "me" form the natural antithesis; if so, however, then we have evidence that he expected to suffer, and it is reasonable to conclude that he considered the significance of that suffering and related it to his obedience to God's will. It is precisely these ideas which are brought out in the antithesis between "the Son of man" and "he who betrays me": here, "the Son of man" is, paradoxically, an appropriate one, since it expresses both obedience to the will of God and authority.[2] The irony of the situation is again found in the fact that this authority is denied: the Son of man is delivered into the hands of sinners, who refuse to acknowledge him; he is handed over into the power of those who do not obey God. As in Daniel, the usurping powers of evil are triumphant:[3] the Son of

---

[1] Loc. cit.   [2] Cf. H. E. Tödt, *Menschensohn*, p. 185, E.Tr. p. 200.

[3] It is possible that this idea is conveyed also by the phrase ἦλθεν ἡ ὥρα which is echoed in Luke 22.53 by αὕτη ἐστὶν ὑμῶν ἡ ὥρα καὶ ἡ ἐξουσία τοῦ σκότους. R. H. Lightfoot, however (*History and Interpretation in the Gospels*, 1935, p. 177), believes that in Mark the hour belongs to God, not to the power of darkness.

man is handed over into the hands of sinners—i.e. into the power of Gentiles,[1] who have appropriated an authority which does not belong to them.

4. MARK 14.62

And Jesus said, "I am; and you will see the Son of man sitting at the right hand of Power, and coming with the clouds of heaven."

Cf. Matthew 26.64; Luke 22.69

This verse is, for two reasons, possibly the most important and crucial of all the Marcan "Son of man" sayings: first, because these words form the answer given by Jesus to the question of Caiaphas regarding his messianic status; second, because they are the closest parallel in the gospel to Dan. 7.13, and so provide the strongest support for the belief that the New Testament use of the term "Son of man" is derived primarily from that chapter. Regarding the authenticity of this vital saying, however, there is the greatest divergence of opinion. On the one hand it can be argued that the entire account of the trial scenes is suspect, since it is unlikely that any of Jesus' followers were present to observe what happened, and the account may be based upon later beliefs regarding the person of Jesus and the reasons for his condemnation;[2] in particular, one may question the unexplained relationship between this trial and that before Pilate,[3] the relevance of the charge of blasphemy,[4] and the reply of Jesus, which combines two Old Testament quotations.[5] On the other hand, those who support the general credibility of the outline of the trial argue that the early Church would have sought information about the trial,[6] and may even have included members of the Sanhedrin who had been

---

[1] Cf. D. E. Nineham, *The Gospel according to St Mark*, 1963, in loc.

[2] Those who have followed H. Lietzmann in rejecting the Marcan account of the trial include R. Bultmann, *Geschichte*, pp. 290f, E.Tr. pp. 269f; cf. the *Supplement* to the 3rd edn, E.Tr. p. 433. See also D. E. Nineham, *Mark*, pp. 398–405.

[3] See D. E. Nineham, *Mark*, pp. 403f.

[4] See the discussion by V. Taylor, *Mark*, pp. 569f, and D. E. Nineham, *Mark*, pp. 402f.

[5] B. H. Branscomb, *Mark*, p. 280.

[6] A. J. B. Higgins, *Son of Man*, p. 67; V. Taylor, *Mark*, in loc.; W. G. Kümmel, *Promise and Fulfilment*, 1957, p. 50.

present; the reliability and logic of the particular events have also been vigorously defended.[1]

Even though the account in Mark 14.55–65 may contain secondary details, yet it is highly probable that Mark is correct in supposing that the charge brought against Jesus was connected with his Messiahship; even the account in 15.1, which Bultmann regards as an earlier source (and which may possibly be a doublet of the account in 14.55–65),[2] depicts the Jewish leaders as meeting in consultation, presumably to discuss the charge to be preferred against the prisoner, and the tradition that Jesus was brought before Pilate as a messianic pretender is too strong to be ignored.[3] It is no doubt true that the narrative reflects the belief of the early Church that Jesus was condemned by the Sanhedrin on account of his messianic claims.[4] Yet this does not necessarily imply that the Church was mistaken in its interpretation: the qualification in Jesus' reply to the high priest, as recorded in Matthew and Luke, and possibly also in the original version of Mark,[5] suggests a tradition going back behind the dogmatic interests of the Christian community. The epexegetic phrase ὁ υἱὸς τοῦ εὐλογητοῦ, however, may well reflect Christian belief.[6]

The messianic charge follows another, that of speaking against the temple. It is possible that these are two separate and unrelated accusations; Kilpatrick[7] interprets one charge as primarily religious, the other as political, the former intended by the high priest to demonstrate that Jesus was guilty according to Jewish law of an

---

[1] The general legal procedure is defended by G. D. Kilpatrick, *The Trial of Jesus*, 1953, and by A. N. Sherwin-White, *Roman Society and Roman Law in the New Testament*, 1963, pp. 24–47; Mark's understanding of blasphemy by J. Blinzler, *The Trial of Jesus*, 1959, pp. 105–7, and by O. Linton, "The Trial of Jesus and The Interpretation of Psalm cx", *N.T.S.* 7, 1961, pp. 258–62; and the authenticity of Jesus' reply by A. J. B. Higgins, *Son of Man*, pp. 66–75.

[2] R. Bultmann, *Geschichte*, pp. 290f, E.Tr. pp. 269f. Cf. V. Taylor, *Mark*, pp. 565 and 646. A. N. Sherwin-White, op. cit., pp. 44f, maintains that συμβούλιον ἑτοιμάσαντες (or ποιήσαντες) in Mark 15.1 cannot mean "held a council meeting" but has the more general meaning "to take a decision/form a plot" found in Mark 3.6; Matt. 12.14; 22.15; 27.7; 28.12; similarly Arndt-Gingrich, *Lexicon*.

[3] C. G. Montefiore, *The Synoptic Gospels*, I, 2nd edn, 1927, p. 357; B. H. Branscomb, *Mark*, pp. 279f, 284f.

[4] R. Bultmann, *Geschichte*, pp. 290–3, E.Tr. pp. 270–2.

[5] The variant reading σὺ εἶπας ὅτι ἐγώ εἰμι is attested by Θ fam.13 472 565 700 1071 geo arm Or. It would explain the readings in Matt. 26.64 and Luke 22.70, and would be in keeping with Mark's "messianic secret". It is supported by V. Taylor, *Mark*, in loc.

[6] J. Klausner, *Jesus of Nazareth*, 1928, p. 342, suggests that the title is not as Jewish as it sounds. In Matthew the phrase is replaced by ὁ υἱὸς τοῦ Θεοῦ.

[7] Op. cit., pp. 8–21.

offence punishable by death,[1] the latter preferred as a basis for an accusation before Pilate. Wellhausen[2] regards the messianic question as a later insertion, and believes that the original tradition referred to a charge of blasphemy arising from statements made regarding the temple; if this be the case, however, something is missing from the Marcan narrative, since the testimony of the witnesses is not established, and Jesus himself does not speak in reply, so that there is no basis for the high priest's declaration in v. 63. In the Marcan narrative the two accusations stand together, but the link between them is not made clear. We may conclude, either that Mark regarded them as two different ways in which "the chief priests and the whole council sought testimony against Jesus to put him to death", or that he understood the accusations of the false witnessses as a charge of claiming to be the Messiah.[3] It should be noted, however, that Mark regards the first accusation as false, whereas Jesus confesses the truth of the second. One of the puzzling features of Mark's account is his description of the witnesses as false; this detail can scarcely be regarded as accidental, for he twice uses the verb ψευδομαρτυρέω, and adds also that they were unable to agree in their accusations.[4] Yet Mark has himself recorded the tradition of Jesus' words against the temple in 13.2, and can hardly have forgotten that passage so quickly, especially if R. H. Lightfoot is right in suggesting a link between that chapter and the passion narrative.[5] Can this link be the clue to Mark's insistence that the testimony is false ? There is, of course, a significant

---

[1] The charge would then be comparable to that of speaking against the temple and the Law which is brought against Stephen by "false witnesses" in Acts 6.13.

[2] J. Wellhausen, *Marc.*, in loc.

[3] The Jewish hope of the End included the expectation of a new temple ,to be built at the inauguration of the messianic era. See W. Bousset, rev. H. Gressmann, *Die Religion des Judentums im Späthellenistischen Zeitalter*, 3rd edn, 1926, pp. 238–40. It was frequently supposed that God would rebuild the temple, but sometimes this activity was attributed to the Messiah. See G. Schrenk, "ἱερός", *T.W.N.T.*, III, p. 239; S.-B., *Kommentar*, I, p. 1005; M. Simon, "Retour du Christ et reconstruction du Temple dans la pensée chrétienne primitive", *Aux Sources de la Tradition Chrétienne*, Mélanges offerts à M. Goguel, 1950, pp. 347f; Y.M.-J. Congar, *The Mystery of the Temple*, E.Tr. 1962, p. 131; B. Gärtner, *The Temple and the Community in Qumran and the New Testament*, 1965, p. 17.

[4] Although Matthew refers to false witnesses in 26.60, he significantly does not refer this term to those who bring the charge about Jesus' words regarding the temple, which are changed to: δύναμαι καταλῦσαι τὸν ναὸν τοῦ Θεοῦ καὶ διὰ τριῶν ἡμερῶν οἰκοδομῆσαι. For Matthew, the testimony in this case is true, as is seen in the fact that it is brought by two men, in accordance with the requirement of Deut. 17.6; 19.15.

[5] *The Gospel Message of St Mark*, pp. 48–59.

difference between Jesus' words in 13.1f, and those which he is accused of saying in 14.58: in the former, Jesus prophesies the total destruction of the temple buildings, but in the latter it is he himself who will destroy the sanctuary and build another; it is this difference which enables Mark to describe the testimony as false.[1] But something more is involved; for the context of the words in 13.1f, as we have seen,[2] shows that Mark understood the fate of Jerusalem as God's judgement upon his people for the rejection of their Messiah. The full irony of the trial scene is brought home by this accusation of the false witnesses, for those who presume to judge Jesus will now in turn be judged by the Son of man, and it is they, and not Jesus, who are guilty of blasphemy against the temple, for it is their rejection of Jesus which sets the seal upon the fate of Jerusalem and its holy place.[3] In both chapters, the appearance of the Son of man[4] means the vindication of those who have suffered at the hands of the authorities.

Jesus' own statement opens with a quotation from Ps. 110.1, used here of the authority which is to be given to the Son of man; his exaltation to the right hand of God fulfils all that was implied regarding the Messiah's status in Mark 12.35-7. It is possible that Mark himself understood this as a reference to the parousia,[5] but there is no doubt that there was a tradition within the early Church which interpreted it of the exaltation of Jesus which had already taken place: according to the kerygma of the Church, Jesus was already exalted to the right hand of God.[6] The expectation of

---

[1] Cf. E. Meyer, *Ursprung und Anfänge des Christentums*, I, 1921, p. 192: "Nicht dass er die Zerstörung des Tempels verkündet hat, ist der Inhalt der Aussage und begründet die Anklage, sondern dass er von sich behauptet, er wolle ihn niederreissen und in drei Tagen wieder aufbauen. Dadurch erhebt er den Anspruch, der Messias zu sein." Does the Marcan account reflect a real difficulty encountered by the priests in trying to make Jesus' words imply more than they meant?

[2] See above, pp. 150-2.

[3] There is a further parallelism between Jesus' words in Mark 13 and the trial scene, which may or may not be deliberate. During the course of 13 Jesus refers to false messianic claimants, who come in his name saying ἐγώ εἰμι (v. 6; the theme is repeated in vv. 21f). Just as the words of the false witnesses at the trial are a distortion of the true words of Jesus, so the false claims of false messiahs echo but distort the ἐγώ εἰμι of Jesus. In the eyes of the Sanhedrin, Jesus is himself a ψευδόχριστος, but in fact he is no false claimant to the title, but the one whose testimony is true.

[4] The parallelism is brought out by the use of the same verb in the two passages, ὄψεσθε in Mark 14.62 echoing ὄψονται in 13.26.

[5] The saying is interpreted in this way by some modern commentators, e.g. C. E. B. Cranfield, *Mark*, in loc.; W. G. Kümmel, *Promise and Fulfilment*, pp. 50f.

[6] Cf. Acts 2.33; 5.31; Phil. 2.9.

immediate vindication which is conveyed already by Mark's
ὄψεσθε is made quite clear by both Matthew and Luke in their
accounts of the words of Jesus, for Matthew adds the words
ἀπ' ἄρτι, and Luke reads: ἀπὸ τοῦ νῦν δὲ ἔσται ὁ υἱὸς τοῦ ἀνθρώπου
καθήμενος ἐκ δεξιῶν τῆς δυνάμεως τοῦ Θεοῦ.[1] In the view of these
evangelists, the exaltation of Jesus follows immediately on his
death.

But this proclamation of the Son of man's exaltation to God's
right hand is linked with the declaration that he will "come".
Much of the debate in recent years regarding Mark 14.62 has
centred on the problem of this "coming": in which direction is the
Son of man to come—to God or to earth? Traditional exegesis has
interpreted it of the parousia, an event subsequent to and dis-
tinguishable from Christ's exaltation, and this interpretation receives support from the evangelists: for there can be little doubt,
in view of Mark 13.26, that Mark understood Jesus' words as a
reference to the End, and probably interpreted them, therefore,
of the parousia.[2] It is by no means certain, however, whether
Jesus, if he spoke these words, understood them in the same way,
and many scholars have argued strongly in recent years that their
original reference is to the exaltation of Jesus, and not to the
parousia.[3] The basis of this argument is, of course, the fact that in
their original context in Dan. 7.13 the words which are quoted
here do not refer to a movement from heaven to earth, but to the

[1] This agreement of Matthew and Luke is especially significant for two
reasons: (1) they agree in meaning, but the Greek phrase used is different; (2)
Luke appears to have been using a separate, independent source for the passion
narrative. It appears, therefore, that we have two independent witnesses to the
early Church's belief that Jesus spoke of an immediate exaltation of the Son of
man to the right hand of God. It is arguable, however, that the phrase "from
now on" originally stood in Mark's account, since this would explain its
appearance in both Matthew and Luke; this suggestion is supported by the
reading of Sy sin, and by one MS. of the Sahidic version. The phrase might
then have been omitted from Mark because of its difficulty. See T. F. Glasson,
The Second Advent, pp. 65–8. If this suggestion is correct, then the immediate
exaltation of Jesus (which is in any case implied in the text of Mark as it stands)
is explicit in the Marcan narrative also.
[2] Luke omits the words altogether; he may, of course, be following a tradition from which these words were absent. But it is possible that he has deliberately omitted them precisely because he understood them as a reference to the
parousia, and this seemed inappropriate in a context concerned with imminent
vindication. See below.
[3] See especially T. F. Glasson, The Second Advent, pp. 63–8, J. A. T. Robinson, "The Second Coming—Mark xiv.62", E.T., 67, 1956, pp. 336–40, and
Jesus and His Coming, pp. 43–53.

arrival of the Son of man before the throne of God:[1] the most
natural way of interpreting the phrase in the gospels is therefore
to understand it as indicating the approach of the Son of man to
God for judgement and vindication. In support of the traditional
interpretation it has been argued that it is precarious to determine
the meaning of a phrase in the New Testament by its Old Testament context, since rabbinic literature does not suggest that the
original meaning was necessarily decisive for the use made of it in
exegesis.[2] While it is undoubtedly true that both rabbinic and New
Testament writers tend to quote the Old Testament in an atomis-
tic way,[3] this does not mean that we must automatically reject the
original meaning of the Old Testament quotation, especially if that
meaning seems to be contained in the quotation itself: in the present
case, the fact that the New Testament omits to indicate the direction in which the Son of man was to be seen travelling does not
necessarily mean that the clouds have changed course and are now
moving from heaven to earth. Certainly the early Church understood their movement in this way; but this may have been a misunderstanding, fostered by their parousia hope: if one considers
the saying apart from this hope, however (and there is little evidence
in Mark that Jesus himself thought in these precise terms, and
certainly none that the Sanhedrin expected such a return), then
one must ask whether the words quoted from Daniel do not in
themselves suggest exaltation—not simply because that is the idea
conveyed in their original context,[4] but because the reference to
clouds in itself suggests an elevation. There is no basis for assuming
that the words must refer to a parousia and not to exaltation, simply
because the term "Son of man" is used of an individual.[5]

---

[1] Cf. the famous remark of T. W. Manson in "The Son of Man in Daniel,
Enoch and the Gospels", *B.J.R.L.*, 32, 1950, p. 174, reprinted in *Studies in the
Gospels and Epistles*, ed. M. Black, 1962, p. 126: "It cannot be too strongly
emphasized that what Daniel portrays is not a divine, semi-divine, or angelic
figure coming down from heaven, to bring deliverance, but a human figure
going up to heaven to receive it."

[2] H. K. McArthur, "Mark xiv.62", *N.T.S.*, 4, 1958, pp. 156–8.

[3] See J. W. Doeve, *Jewish Hermeneutics in the Synoptic Gospels and Acts*,
1953, pp. 95f, 132–5; H. J. Cadbury in *Beginnings*, Vol. V, p. 369; M. D.
Hooker, *Jesus and the Servant*, pp. 21–3.

[4] T. F. Glasson's statement that "It is unwarranted to assume that Jesus
would quote an Old Testament saying without knowing the remaining half of
the sentence" (*The Second Advent*, p. 64) does not justify us in assuming that
Jesus *did* have the rest of the sentence in mind.

[5] As is done by H. K. McArthur, op. cit. His objections are answered by
T. F. Glasson, in "The Reply to Caiaphas (Mark xiv.62)", *N.T.S.*, 7, 1961,
pp. 88–93. It should be noted that the principle which McArthur invokes (that

The interpretation of the coming with clouds in Mark 14.62 in terms of exaltation receives support from the structure of the sentence, for if Jesus is referring to two distinct events, separated by an interval of time, then he has bound them together in a strange way; as Glasson has pointed out, it is natural to assume that "two participles governed by the same verb describe simultaneous actions".[1] The difficulty of interpreting the "sitting" and the "coming" of separate events becomes acute in Matthew's version, where the phrase ἀπ' ἄρτι makes nonsense of the traditional interpretation: the event which the Sanhedrin will see "from now on" includes the "coming" as well as the "sitting", and the only logical explanation of this is to understand both verbs as referring to an immediate glorification.[2] The evidence of Matthew is the more remarkable, in view of his proclivity towards sayings of an eschatological nature; the phrase ἀπ' ἄρτι, in this context, does not agree with his own eschatology, and this suggests that he is not responsible for the phrase, a conclusion which seems to be confirmed by the evidence of Luke. The fact that Luke has omitted the reference to coming with clouds altogether suggests that he may have been aware of the difficulty: when this phrase is interpreted literally of the parousia it must be removed from the realm of what is imminent; similarly, we see that a literal understanding of the quotation from Ps. 110 causes him to change the verb ὄψεσθε to ἔσται.

This combination of Ps. 110.1 and Dan. 7.13 provides further support for the interpretation of the coming with clouds in terms of vindication when we remember that the words about exaltation to the right hand of God were probably understood originally in a

---

the meaning of a quotation is not determined by its original context) by no means proves the point that he is trying to prove (that Mark 14.62 *must* be understood of the parousia). For the examples of the Jewish exegesis of Dan 7.13 which he quotes, although they speak of a "coming with clouds", and although this phrase is wrested from its original context, nevertheless do not speak of a "parousia" of the Messiah; even B. Sanh. 98a, with its reference to the Messiah coming with clouds, is apparently to be understood, according to Jewish exegesis, as symbolic either of the magnificence and power which God will give him or of the speed of his arrival (Glasson, op. cit., p. 93). It should also be noted that there is no evidence that the "coming" of the Son of man with clouds was interpreted of the Messiah's arrival on earth in the time of Jesus. In 2 Esdras 13, the "Man" comes from the sea; in Enoch the clouds are not mentioned, and the Son of man seems to be permanently with God; in so far as there is any movement it is *to* God, when, in 70 and 71, Enoch is raised to heaven and revealed as the Son of man.

[1] Op. cit., p. 89.
[2] Cf. M.-J. Lagrange, *Évangile selon Saint Matthieu*, 1923, pp. clxv–vi.

metaphorical and not a literal way. If Jesus—or Mark, or the for-
mulator of the pre-Marcan tradition—was content to use the imagery
of exaltation of Ps. 110 *as* imagery, then there is no reason why he
should not have done the same with the imagery of exaltation in
Dan. 7; indeed, it is difficult to suppose that they were combined
together unless they *were* used in the same way:[1] either we may
believe that they were originally used of a literal ascension into
heaven and a "coming" on clouds; or we must suppose that
phrases which were originally intended to express in vivid language
the vindication of Jesus and his claims were understood literally
by the Church, which then interpreted the vindication hope in
terms of ascension and parousia.

The suggestion that both quotations should be understood as
primarily intended to convey a metaphorical meaning answers, to
some extent, the objection which has been made by some scholars
that the order of the quotations is incompatible with the interpretation of the coming with clouds in terms of exaltation.[2] Logically,
it is true, one might expect the "coming with clouds" to precede
the session at the right hand, but if the two phrases are both
images for the exaltation of Christ, then they are parallel expressions—though not necessarily identical in meaning—and there is
no necessity for them to be arranged in a sequence which seems to
us to be logical in terms of time and space. When the images are
interpreted literally, then one must, of course, have a logical sequence: it is possible, indeed, that the phrases were originally in
the opposite order,[3] and that they were reversed when the Church
separated the two expressions and interpreted them of the ascension and parousia; there is, however, no evidence for this supposition, nor is there any necessity for it. One explanation of the
present order could be that in Dan. 7 the placing of the "thrones"
is described before the arrival of the Son of man is mentioned;
indeed, this suggests that perhaps the present order is the logical
one after all, for judgement is a necessary preliminary to vindica-

---

[1] Cf. T. Preiss, *Le Fils de l'Homme*, 1951, pp. 35f. T. F. Glasson, in *N.T.S.*, 7,
1961, p. 93, quotes the opinion of Rabbi Isidore Epstein in support of his contention that the normal interpretation of Jewish commentators was to understand the passage symbolically.

[2] J. E. Fison, *The Christian Hope*, 1954, pp. 191f; H. E. Tödt, *Menschensohn*,
pp. 34f, E.Tr. p. 38.

[3] This is suggested by E. Schweizer, *Lordship and Discipleship*, 1960, p. 39,
and "The Son of Man", *J.B.L.*, 79, 1960, p. 120; cf. J. A. T. Robinson, *Jesus
and His Coming*, p. 45, n. 2.

tion, and takes place in Daniel before the "coming in clouds". No doubt it is paradoxical to find the Son of man himself sharing in judgement at this point, but this is a development which takes place both in the New Testament, where he is concerned (as he is not in Daniel) with the judgement of past activities,[1] and in 1 Enoch, where the Son of man (seated on God's throne) is revealed as the judge of the kings and mighty ones who have tormented Israel:[2] in both, the Son of man is God's agent in judgement, and it is only as he is revealed as sharing God's authority in judgement (whether this is expressed in terms of sitting on God's throne or at his right hand) that the Son of man can "come with clouds" or be fully vindicated.[3]

There is, then, much to support the view that the saying recorded in Mark 14.62 was originally intended to convey, like Dan. 7, the conviction that "the Son of man" will shortly be exalted and receive the authority proper to God's "right-hand man", and so be vindicated. Since such a vindication will be a reversal of the present human judgement upon Jesus, it implies some form of divine judgement, such as is described in Dan. 7 and Mark 12.1–12 and 13.[4] Nevertheless, the traditional view that the enthronement of Jesus and the "coming" of the Son of man are two separate events remains a tenable one. It is possible that from the very beginning the saying was intended as a reference to an immediate exaltation of Jesus and to a more distant and ultimate vindication, and that these events were understood either in a literal sense (as by the early Church in general) or as a metaphorical expression of Jesus' present exaltation and the hope that what was now a reality in heaven would ultimately become an actuality on earth also, in the setting up of the kingdom. Yet, however we interpret the time and manner of the "coming", it remains true that the saying is an expression of a confident hope of vindication, set in a context of present suffering.

---

[1] Mark 8.38.

[2] E.g. 1 Enoch 62.2–12; 69.26–9.

[3] An alternative explanation is offered by T. F. Glasson, in N.T.S., 7, pp. 90–2; he suggests that Ps. 110 is used of Jesus' personal exaltation, and Dan. 7 of the victory of the community.

[4] There is therefore no force in the objection of H. E. Tödt, loc. cit., who rejects the view that Mark 14.62 is parallel to Dan. 7.13 on the ground that in the latter, judgement is passed on the old aeon before the appearance of the Son of man; the whole context of the saying in Mark 14.62 implies the judgement of the present era, and this does not necessarily involve an interruption of history.

But is the context given to the saying by St Mark correct? Its authenticity as a word of Jesus has been denied on the ground that there is in fact no basis here for the high priest's charge of blasphemy. According to the Mishnah, the term "blasphemy" was applied in a highly technical sense, and could not be regarded as appropriate unless the name of God himself had actually been mentioned.[1] It has been suggested, however, that at the time of Jesus the term was not yet so closely defined and could include a verbal attack on the temple, the symbol of God's presence,[2] and certainly the author of Acts seems to have understood this as blasphemy and therefore a capital charge.[3] But according to St Mark's narrative it is not as a result of the charge about the temple (which in any case is not established) but in response to Jesus' own words, that the high priest declares him to be guilty of blasphemy. What is there, then, in these words, that can be described as blasphemous? According to the strict interpretation of the rabbis, nothing, since the name of God is avoided. But once again it is probable that the term "blasphemy" could have been extended at this time to include this kind of appropriation of the powers of God:[4] it could only have been regarded as blasphemy, of course, if Jesus was understood to be referring to himself when he spoke of the Son of man,[5] for there is nothing blasphemous in speaking of one

---

[1] Mishnah, Sanh. 7.5. Cf. W. Bousset, *Kyrios Christos*, p. 53.

[2] G. D. Kilpatrick, *The Trial of Jesus*, pp. 11–13. The temple represented the presence of God, and was apparently considered inviolable for this reason; cf. Jer. 7.4,14; Mic. 3.11.

[3] Acts 6.11–14; 7.54–60.

[4] J. Blinzler, *The Trial of Jesus*, E.Tr. 1959, pp. 105–7, describes blasphemy as: "a very elastic conception indeed. The post-Christian *Halacha* gives an unusually narrow definition. According to it, blasphemy was committed only if one cursed God explicitly, pronouncing the name Jahweh distinctly. . . . It may be taken as certain that this narrow definition had no validity in the time of Jesus . . . the narrowing of the conception of blasphemy is completely in line with the development of Jewish law. For after the elimination of the Sadducees, with their rigorous theory and practice of the law, the milder interpretation of the Pharisees gained ground progressively. But even in the rabbinical period, the narrow mishnic definition of blasphemy was not the only one prevailing. According to the rabbis, even one who spoke disrespectfully of the Torah or 'stretched out his hand to God' could be regarded as a blasphemer. Several incidents in the history of Jesus and the apostles show that the broader interpretation was current in the time of Jesus." Cf. S.-B., *Kommentar*, I, pp. 1008–19, especially p. 1017.

[5] This is perforce recognized by A. J. B. Higgins, *Son of Man*, p. 73, who regards Mark 14.62 as an "authentic" word of Jesus, yet denies that Jesus ever spoke of himself as Son of man. He is therefore compelled to suggest that Caiaphas mistakenly supposed that Jesus was referring to himself as Son of man. This is an extraordinary admission, and one which undermines Higgins' whole argument. Are we really to believe that Jesus spoke of another as Son of man,

who comes, whether in terms of Messiah or Son of man, as invested with God's authority. To claim for oneself a seat at the right hand of power, however, is to claim a share in the authority of God;[1] to appropriate to oneself such authority and to bestow on oneself this unique status in the sight of God and man would almost certainly have been regarded as blasphemy.[2]

The accusation of blasphemy in itself, therefore, is not incompatible with the reported words of Jesus. If we reject the latter on other grounds, then we must either find another basis for the charge, or else suppose that some other charge formed the basis of Jesus' condemnation by the Sanhedrin. As it stands, the saying is, like other "Son of man" sayings, a claim to authority. It is the ultimate claim, and it is a claim to ultimate authority.

but that Caiaphas condemned him to death because he mistakenly supposed him to be claiming to be this Son of man, and that his disciples equally mistakenly preached him in the same terms? If indeed both his friends and his enemies understood him to be referring to himself, it is difficult to maintain that both were mistaken.

[1] Cf. O. Linton, "The Trial of Jesus and the Interpretation of Psalm cx", *N.T.S.*, 7, 1961, pp. 258–62.

[2] Cf. Mark 2.5–7, where we have a situation which is exactly parallel: Jesus is accused of blasphemy because he claims to exercise an authority which belongs to God alone.

9

The Marcan Son of Man

1. THE SETTING OF
THE SAYINGS

It is now time to consider the relationship between the various "Son of man" sayings which we have been discussing, and their setting in the Marcan framework.

We must begin by considering the position of the two sayings in Mark 2.10 and 28. These two passages stand aloof from the remaining "Son of man" sayings, not only by their isolation in the Marcan narrative, but also by their apparent difference in character, and by their setting in public discussions. Any one of these three details is sufficient, in the view of many scholars, to discredit them. It may be, however, that taken *together* these characteristics contain the clue to the appearance of the sayings in this section; the separation in setting may perhaps be the explanation of the separation in meaning, and vice versa.

Both sayings fall in Mark 2.1—3.6, which is generally recognized to be a collection of "conflict stories". The fact that both of them are embedded in this kind of tradition is sufficient reason for them to be traced to the early Church by those scholars who regard all conflict stories as originating in the disputes between Palestinian Christians and their Jewish neighbours.[1] The fact that a story has a setting within the life of the early Church, however, does not necessarily mean that it could have no place in the life of Jesus as well; clearly at some point of his ministry Jesus must have

---

[1] E.g. R. Bultmann, *Geschichte*, pp. 12–15, E.Tr. pp. 14–17. Cf. H. E. Tödt, *Menschensohn*, pp. 117–24, E.Tr. pp. 126–33; A. J. B. Higgins, *Son of Man*, pp. 26–30.

come into conflict with the Jewish authorities. Moreover, though the disputes might be explained by the situation of the early Church, the sayings themselves are not. For this account of the origin of the conflict stories can offer no explanation of the use of the term "Son of man" in these contexts, unless we suppose either that the Palestinian Christians commonly referred to Jesus as "the Son of man" (a supposition which is contrary to the evidence of the whole New Testament) or that they believed it to be a natural way for Jesus to refer to himself. This latter suggestion, although the one commonly adopted, offers no explanation as to why the term "Son of man" should have been used in these particular sayings and not in others, or why it should have been regarded as appropriate in disputes with the Jewish community.

On this occasion, however, "radical" scholars are joined by the "conservatives" in denying these sayings to Jesus. Typical of the disquiet felt by conservative scholars regarding them are these words written by C. E. B. Cranfield, who is certainly not normally inclined to attribute dominical sayings to the early Church:[1]

> Would Jesus have used the term thus openly at this stage of his ministry and in conversation with his opponents?

It will be noticed that Cranfield's judgement here is based on two assumptions: (a) Jesus did not normally speak of the Son of man until a later stage in his ministry; (b) Jesus normally used the term "Son of man" only in conversation with his followers. Allowing for the moment the validity of these two assumptions, we must observe that Cranfield's argument here is somewhat curious. Firstly, he argues that the saying cannot be traced to Jesus because he would not have used the term "at this stage of his ministry". But at what stage? For both the saying in Mark 2.28, with which Cranfield is here concerned, and the saying in Mark 2.10 are found in the group of conflict stories in 2.1—3.6, which were probably already joined together in the pre-Marcan tradition, and were inserted *en bloc* by the evangelist at what he considered to be an appropriate point in his narrative.[2] If this is so, however, the fact that the two "Son of man" sayings in Mark 2 are separated by six

---

[1] *Mark*, p. 118.
[2] Cf. V. Taylor, *The Formation of the Gospel Tradition*, 2nd edn, 1935, pp. 15f, summarizing the work of M. Albertz.

chapters from the next saying is of no significance in the consideration of their origin. For the position of an incident in Mark can
tell us something significant about its origin only if we can fix that
position within the life of Jesus himself with some hope of accuracy[1]
—and this is obviously impossible in the case of sayings which are,
as Cranfield himself agrees, probably part of a pre-Marcan group-
ing on a topical basis.[2] The fact that St Mark has placed this block
of material, with its two "Son of man" sayings, in chapter 2 cannot be used in evidence against their reliability as authentic words
of Jesus. Secondly, Cranfield doubts the dominical origin of the
saying in Mark 2.28 on the basis that Jesus would not have used
the term "Son of man" "openly . . . in conversation with his
opponents". Once again, however, we may question the validity of
Cranfield's arguments on the basis of his own suppositions. For may
not the word "opponents" here perhaps be to some extent a
question-begging term? We, of course, inevitably think of the
scribes and Pharisees as Jesus' opponents; so, no doubt, did the
early Church. But unless the Jewish authorities were either completely indifferent to Jesus or consistently hostile to him from the
very beginning, then something very much like what Mark portrays must have taken place. For Mark presents us with a picture
of growing hostility on the part of the authorities—a hostility
which mounts, not simply in this early section, but throughout the
gospel. If Mark is correct, however—and Cranfield would no doubt
accept this outline—then we may question whether it is necessarily
correct to speak of the Pharisees as "opponents" of Jesus at what
Cranfield himself terms "this stage of his ministry", *before* they
have plotted to destroy him. As we have just noted, however, we
are not compelled to place this incident at the beginning of the
ministry. Nevertheless, we may still ask whether the term "opponents" is not a misleading one. For although the Pharisees here
take the initiative (in contrast to 2.1–12), we do not find the hostility between Jesus and the Pharisees which characterizes incidents
found later in the gospel narrative. These later accounts are of particular interest because of the changed attitude shown by Jesus; it
is as though the rôles are reversed, and it is the Pharisees who are
in fact condemned. In several cases Jesus turns the attack back upon

---

[1] An argument similar to Cranfield's is used (uncharacteristically) by D. E.
Nineham, in *Mark*, p. 102, about Mark 2.20.
[2] *Mark*, p. 12.

those who challenge him; in others, his anger with his opponents is mentioned.[1] These narratives can properly be described as "conflict stories" in which Jesus meets "opponents"; the hostility in 2.1–12 and 23–8 is certainly less marked.

But of course what Cranfield really means when he refers to "this stage of the ministry" is "the period before Caesarea Philippi"; and when he uses the terms "openly" and "opponents", what he primarily has in mind is the fact that Jesus' words are not addressed to his disciples, rather than the degree of hostility which is displayed by those who question him. We must therefore consider the validity of these two assumptions on which Cranfield's judgement is based.

The character of Caesarea Philippi as the pivotal point of the ministry has become the crucial test of the authenticity of the "Son of man" sayings for those scholars who regard Mark's outline as reliable; this test is founded on the fact that in twelve cases out of fourteen the Marcan "Son of man" sayings occur after Caesarea Philippi.[2] Once again, however, the argument used seems to be somewhat illogical. For the idea of the central importance of Caesarea Philippi, together with the belief that there is a link between Peter's declaration and the use of the term "Son of man", is derived from Mark himself. It is a curious procedure to build a theory about the distribution of a title upon Mark's usage, and conveniently eliminate the two passages which undermine it! For how are we to explain the fact that Mark himself used the term in chapter 2? Are we to suppose, with the older commentators, that Mark's tradition came to him in general in good historical order?[3] In this case presumably he himself did not notice the relationship between Caesarea Philippi and the title "Son of man" which he has preserved, and may be forgiven the two slips in chapter 2. Or

---

[1] In 3.1–6, Jesus is said to be angry with the Pharisees; his question may perhaps also be understood as a counter-attack on those who plan "to do harm" and "to kill" (so H. B. Swete, A. E. J. Rawlinson, V. Taylor). In 3.20–30 and 7.1–8 he turns the attack back on his accusers. In the latter passage, the Pharisees criticize the actions of Jesus' disciples—much as they do in 2.23–8—but the answer of Jesus here is quite different; instead of justifying their behaviour by a reference to his own authority, he returns to the attack and criticizes the Pharisees themselves for their false attitude and inner corruption. In 8.11f the Pharisees demand a sign, and meet with a peremptory refusal from Jesus, in contrast to 2.1–10. Similarly, Jesus refuses to answer the representatives of the Sanhedrin in 11.27–33 regarding his credentials.

[2] Notably T. W. Manson, *The Teaching of Jesus*, pp. 211–34. Matthew and Luke do not support the Marcan scheme.

[3] E.g. H. B. Swete, *Mark*, pp. liii–lvi.

are we to believe that he was well aware of the connection—but foolishly overlooked the fact that these two passages destroyed the pattern ?[1] It is a distortion of the evidence to ignore these two sayings in constructing a theory and then dismiss them because they do not fit the theory which we have produced. If we allow any significance to the Marcan pattern at all, then we ought to consider the part played by *all* the "Son of man" sayings, and not confine our attention to the majority. We must therefore reject the use of Caesarea Philippi as a yardstick for a saying's authenticity.

Similarly, we must question the basic assumption that the character of the audience is sufficient ground for denying a saying to Jesus. For once again, the belief that he used the term "Son of man" only in conversation with his disciples[2] is based upon the pattern which is provided by Mark, and once again the Marcan material itself belies the conclusion which has been drawn. In this case, not only do Mark 2.10 and 28 fall outside the accepted norm, but so does Mark 14.62 and, to some extent, so also does Mark 8.38. Mark 14.62 is allowed to stand as an exception; Mark 2.10 and 28 are not. As with the previous "norm" which depended upon the position of a saying in relation to Caesarea Philippi, so, too, the nature of the audience appears to be a standard which is based upon the majority evidence, and ignores the minority of sayings.

2. THE MARCAN PATTERN

Let us examine a little more closely the pattern with which Mark himself presents us. After the series of "conflict stories" in 2.1— 3.6 there is a definite break. Jesus, rejected by the Jewish authorities, who had now determined to destroy him, "withdrew" from the synagogues to the sea. When the crowds flocked to him, he chose twelve as his disciples, "to be with him, and to be sent out to preach and have authority to cast out demons". The next major break in the Marcan narrative comes in chapter 8, with the declara-

---

[1] H. E. Tödt, who also regards the scene at Caesarea Philippi as crucial for Mark in the revelation of the Son of man, suggests that he felt obliged to retain the "Son of man" sayings in 2.10 and 28 in spite of their awkward position (*Menschensohn*, p. 123, E.Tr. p. 132). If Mark had felt that these two sayings destroyed his scheme in their present position, however, would he not have placed the narratives containing them after Caesarea Philippi?

[2] This idea is based on the work of T. W. Manson, loc. cit.

tion at Caesarea Philippi; after this, Jesus begins to teach his disciples about his sufferings, concerning which there have hitherto been only vague hints. As has so often been recognized, Mark's distribution of the term "Son of man" does indeed have a clear relationship with this scheme, but if we take the total picture into account, then 3.6 appears to be quite as vital a turning-point as 8.27. What Mark himself depicts is an early period during which Jesus claims authority as the Son of man and uses the phrase openly in discussion with the Jewish authorities; when they reject him he ceases to appeal to them, for their hearts are hardened, and they have no desire either to see or to hear the truth. During this period Jesus does not use the term "Son of man", either to those who challenge him or to those who follow him: only after Peter's acknowledgement of Jesus' authority is the term found again. From now on it is used only in the company of those who have acknowledged Jesus, except in 8.38, where the crowd of potential followers listen-in "with his disciples"; in this case, however, we notice that the very subject under discussion is discipleship, of acknowledging the authority of Jesus or being ashamed of him. The final dramatic change comes during the passion narrative, following the point when "the hour has come; the Son of man is betrayed into the hands of sinners"; in reply to a direct challenge from the high priest Jesus acknowledges his authority and speaks of the future vindication of the Son of man.

The common factor which links these various sayings to the Marcan narrative cannot be expressed simply in terms of "after Caesarea Philippi and in the company of disciples". The majority of the sayings, certainly, can be covered by this formula, but the vital point with which they are *all* linked is the question of Jesus' authority—the authority which he claims and which his followers accept. The term "Son of man" can appropriately be used when the authority of Jesus is claimed or accepted, and this is why it is used in conversation with those who follow or challenge him. It is because he is Son of man that Jesus acts with the authority which characterizes his ministry, and it is to this fact, accordingly, that he appeals when his actions are first questioned; it is because he is Son of man that Jesus claims the allegiance of his followers, who recognize this authority; it is because he is Son of man that he claims authority in the presence of the high priest, and confidently affirms the imminent vindication of that claim; it is, as we have seen,[1] paradoxically, precisely because he is Son of man that he must suffer, for the authority which is his has been denied by the Jewish authorities. Against this background, Mark's scheme is seen as completely logical; it no longer seems strange that he should place two "Son of man" sayings in chapter 2, cut off from the other twelve. Rather we see that here he sets out for us the claims of Jesus at the beginning of the ministry—the "secret" of the Son of man (like that of the Son of God) is already revealed. Mark's placing of these two sayings is not, then, an unfortunate and embarrassing slip; they are as closely related to the rejection of 3.6 as the later sayings are to 8.27, for they are addressed to those who ought to acknowledge his authority and have not yet rejected him, just as the sayings following 8.27 are addressed to those who have accepted him and acknowledged his authority. Moreover, as we have seen already, the sayings about the necessity for the Son of man to suffer follow on from the rejection in 3.6—in other words, from the refusal of the Jewish leaders to recognize the authority of the Son of man which has been demonstrated to them. Because they are blind and deaf, the truth remains hidden from them, and they do not hear of the Son of man again until the high priest demands to know Jesus' identity in 14.61.

From our examination of the Marcan "Son of man" sayings, then, a pattern has begun to emerge. In spite of the classifications into various groups, they are found to have certain characteristics in common. The first is this theme of authority,[2] which determines both the audience and the content of the saying: all are expressions of this authority, whether it is an authority which is exercised now, which is denied and so leads to suffering, or which will be acknowledged and vindicated in the future. This theme binds the three "groups" of "Son of man" sayings together, for each, paradoxically, implies the other two. The sayings in chapter 2 do not in themselves involve the others, but because they are rejected by the Jewish leaders they are inevitably followed by the sayings about suffering and final vindication. These two themes of suffering and vindication are also linked together. It is sometimes maintained that the two groups of sayings are entirely separate and are never combined.[3] Here, however, we see one of the

[1] Above, pp. 107–14.
[2] The importance of the ἐξουσία of the Son of man is stressed also by H. E. Tödt, *Menschensohn, passim.*
[3] R. Bultmann, *Theology of the New Testament,* I, pp. 29f.

dangers of dividing the sayings into groups, for this statement is an over-simplification which conceals the truth. It is true that nowhere in Mark is there a saying which holds together the necessity for suffering with the imagery of coming in glory. But the belief in the ultimate vindication of the Son of man is contained in every one of the Marcan passion predictions, expressed in terms of the resurrection.[1] Equally significant is the fact that all three of the sayings which are usually classified under the heading of "parousia" sayings are found in contexts which are concerned with suffering: the coming of the Son of man in Mark 8.38 and 13.26 represents the vindication of those who have suffered for Jesus' sake, and the shame of those who have not been prepared to share in his suffering; in 14.62 it signifies the vindication of Jesus himself, now standing before the high priest, about to bear the sufferings which he has foretold for the Son of man. The vision of the triumphant Son of man always appears in contrast to a more imminent expectation of suffering, either for Jesus himself or for his followers, and it must be understood in that context, not abstracted from it; the triumph of the Son of man is thus no isolated event, but is firmly linked with the present sufferings of Jesus and his disciples.[2] The remaining "Son of man" sayings, Mark 10.45, 14.21 and 41, also contain within themselves the paradox of the Son of man, for each depicts the Son of man in a situation in which he does not exercise the authority which is properly his.

We see, then, that the three "groups" of sayings in Mark offer together three aspects of the Son of man's authority—an authority which is in turn proclaimed, denied and vindicated. There is another common factor, however, and this is the way in which the context of each saying implies, to a greater or lesser degree, a corporate significance for the term "Son of man". It is this phenomenon, of course, which led scholars such as T. W. Manson to maintain that the Son of man was in fact a corporate figure, as in Daniel.[3] The Son of man in the gospels, however, is not a truly corporate figure: rather, it is true to say that the consequences of the Son of man's authority always extend to others; that, as in Enoch, he is no isolated figure, but the one on whom the fate of

---

[1] Mark 8.31; 9.31; 10.34.
[2] A similar situation is, of course, found in Dan. 7, where the triumph of the one like a Son of man in v. 13 is set in the context of Israel's present suffering.
[3] T. W. Manson, "The Son of Man in Daniel, Enoch and the Gospels", B.J.R.L., 32, 1950, pp. 171–93.

others depends. The consequences of his authority for others in Mark 2.10 and 28 are obvious; in 10.45, also, he is linked with those for whom he gives his life. In all the sayings which predict suffering for the Son of man, Jesus is linked in the context with his followers, who are expected to share both his suffering and his glory. Similarly, the fate of those who have followed Jesus or been ashamed of him is linked with the vindication of the Son of man in 8.38 and 13.26. Only in the context of the passion narrative does the Son of man emerge as a solitary figure. Even the saying in 14.21, however, is set within the context of the Last Supper, and is immediately followed by the breaking of the bread and the pouring of the wine, symbols of the share which the disciples have both in the death of the Son of man and in his place of honour in the coming kingdom. Only in 14.41 and 62 is the Son of man found alone —both in the sayings and in fact—for in 14.41 he is found in company only with those who have failed to share his agony, and before 14.62 all his disciples "forsook him and fled". The Son of man stands alone. Nevertheless, the words of 14.41 echo and fulfil those given in 9.31, for "the hour has come; the Son of man is betrayed into the hands of sinners"; similarly 14.62 affirms the vindication spoken of in 8.38; Mark 10.45 stands between to remind us that the solitary Son of man is not in fact alone, and that the events of the passion finally link the Son of man and "the many" firmly together.

Mark's pattern of "Son of man" sayings is revealed, then, as a logical and coherent whole. But how far is this the result of Mark's own interpretation of the term "Son of man"? Or to what extent may we trace it back into the pre-Marcan tradition or even to Jesus himself? It is possible, as Mark affirms, that Jesus spoke of himself in terms of "Son of man"?

3. JESUS' OWN USE OF THE TERM

As we have already noted, it has become almost axiomatic in recent work on the Son of man that Jesus could not have spoken of himself in terms of the Son of man, and that only the eschatological sayings about the coming of the triumphant Son of man can be considered as authentic words of Jesus. These conclusions are based on two main arguments, the first of which is form-critical, and the second psychological.

The form-critical approach rejects the majority of sayings on the basis that it has found their *Sitz-im-Leben* in the faith of the early Church, and unravelled the process by which they came to be attributed to Jesus.[1] The argument that these sayings *originated* in the early Church can be convincingly maintained, however, only if it can be shown that the early Church possessed a living "Son of man" theology which might create such sayings, and if it is impossible to set the sayings within the life of Jesus himself. There is no sign (unless we believe the sayings themselves to be such) of a creative "Son of man" theology in the Church; and the pattern which we have discovered in the Marcan sayings suggests that they are more coherent, and therefore less likely to be the accidental products of the community, than is often supposed.

Can we, however, place them within the life and thought of Jesus? Here we meet the so-called "psychological argument" that it is impossible to believe that Jesus could have thought of himself as "the Son of man", and that if he used the term at all, therefore, he must have been referring to the advent of another. This argument has been put most persuasively by John Knox:[2]

> How could [so sane a person] have identified himself with the essentially superhuman personage of the apocalypses—with him who, "sitting at the right hand of power", will come "with the clouds of heaven"?

Now the point of Knox's "psychological" difficulty is that he finds it impossible to think of a sane man identifying himself with an eschatological supernatural figure travelling on the clouds. Here, however, we must question his assumption—and that of many other scholars—that this is what Jesus must have meant if he spoke in these terms. Once again we meet a case where the evidence appears to have been manipulated to fit the theory. It is first assumed that the Son of man is a supernatural cloud-borne figure; next, any saying in the gospels which does not fit into this category is eliminated as a creation of the early Church; finally, the picture which remains, of Jesus claiming to be the future eschatological supernatural Son of man, is found incredible, and

---

[1] E.g. R. Bultmann, *Geschichte*.   [2] *The Death of Christ*, p. 58.

it is therefore concluded—contrary to the evidence of those sayings which have been eliminated—that Jesus spoke of another, coming Son of man. This whole procedure is based on the assumption that "the Son of man" was necessarily and exclusively interpreted at the time of Jesus as meaning "the eschatological redeemer who will appear at the end of time riding upon clouds", and it can therefore be justified only if this assumption is proved to be correct.

At first sight the evidence seems to support this assumption. For the gospels seem to point firmly to Dan. 7 as the source of the sayings in the mouth of Jesus, and the reference there is to the Son of man coming in the clouds. The only explanations of Dan. 7 which we have (in 1 Enoch and 2 Esdras) both understand the term "Son of man" in this way. Moreover, the largest group of "Son of man" sayings in the gospels can be classified as eschatological. Closer examination of the evidence, however, shows that the basis for the assumption that "Son of man" would necessarily be understood in this manner is very shaky indeed.

Firstly, our investigation of Daniel has shown that the description of the Son of man there does not support Knox's interpretation. For in Dan. 7 the one like a Son of man represents Israel, and the vision is not meant to be taken literally. The author does not expect an eschatological redeemer to appear on clouds at the end of the world; he expects the saints in Israel to be vindicated by God and given the kingdom promised to them. Obviously this does not necessarily mean that Jesus (if he used the term) applied it in the same sense; but it does leave the possibility open that he, too, used it symbolically, rather than interpreting the details (such as travelling on clouds) literally.

Secondly, the support which is given to Knox's understanding of the term "Son of man" by 1 Enoch and 2 Esdras is of very dubious value. Certainly, these books indicate that in some circles the vision of the Son of man was interpreted literally. There is no other evidence for this understanding, however, and we do not know how widespread this interpretation was, or whether it was the normal one during the first half of the first century A.D.[1]

---

[1] Among those who doubt whether the kind of interpretation which we meet in 1 Enoch was the normal one are M. Black, "The Son of Man Problem in Recent Research and Debate", *B.J.R.L.*, 45, 1963, p. 312, and C. H. Dodd, *According to the Scriptures*, 1952, pp. 116f, and *The Interpretation of the Fourth Gospel*, 1953, p. 242.

Moreover, 1 Enoch 37—71 are of uncertain date, and may well be later than the time of Jesus;[1] 2 Esdras was certainly not yet written.[2] We should also note that 2 Esdras interprets the details of Daniel's vision in a more crude and literal sense than 1 Enoch, a fact which suggests that this kind of literal interpretation was still developing after the time of Jesus.

Thirdly, the assumption is not supported by the evidence of the gospels. We have a considerable number of sayings in which "the Son of man" is quite clearly *not* equivalent to "the eschatological redeemer coming on the clouds". In order to support the view that the term was normally understood in that sense, one must regard these other sayings as inventions of the early Church. The explanation given is that the Church made two false assumptions: firstly, it mistakenly supposed that when Jesus used the term "Son of man" he was referring to himself, not to another, and so it came to identify him with the Son of man; secondly, it concluded that Jesus commonly used the term "Son of man" to designate himself in contexts where he might well have said "I". There are thus two stages in the development of these sayings—(a) the equation of Jesus with the Son of man in the "original" sayings and (b) the formation of new "Son of man" sayings, which are either community products or sayings where an original personal pronoun has been changed to "the Son of man". There are, however, very grave difficulties with this explanation.

1. The supposed development must have taken place during a very short period of time—i.e. during the Aramaic-speaking period of the Church.[3] It is doubtful whether there was, in fact, sufficient time for both these steps to be taken.

2. It is presupposed that the term "the Son of man" is a symbol for "the eschatological redeemer coming on the clouds"; it is this identification which makes Jesus' use of the term as a self-designation incredible to Knox. If "the Son of man" was necessarily and invariably understood in this sense, however, how are we to explain the fact that the Church so quickly forgot the "proper"

---

[1] See above, pp. 47f.

[2] Cf. W. O. E. Oesterley, 2 *Esdras*, pp. xliv–xlv, G. H. Box, *The Ezra-Apocalypse*, pp. xxviii–xxxiii.

[3] Bultmann believes that the second step was made by the Hellenistic Church, but this suggestion is rejected as impossible by scholars who in other ways agree with his position, e.g. H. E. Tödt, *Menschensohn*, pp. 105f, 109, 197f, E.Tr. pp. 114, 117, 214.

eschatological meaning of the term, and used it freely in other contexts where, *ex hypothesi*, it so obviously did not fit? The theory that the Church is responsible for all the non-eschatological "Son of man" sayings involves the further supposition that the community in which these sayings were created was unfamiliar with the eschatological figure of the Son of man. In other words, the term was by no means always interpreted as designating a supernatural eschatological redeemer who comes to earth on the clouds.

3. There is a tendency within the gospel tradition to develop and emphasize the apocalyptic and eschatological element in the "Son of man" sayings. This is most clearly seen by comparing the Marcan sayings with those in Matthew. If there is a development *towards* the eschatological interpretation, however, this suggests that the "original" Son of man in the gospel tradition may in fact have been *less* supernatural than the evidence now suggests, not more. In this case, it is a distortion of the evidence to eliminate the non-eschatological sayings altogether.

4. It is questionable whether the early Church was quite so ready to put Christological terms into the mouth of Jesus as is supposed. A comparison with the term "Christ" suggests a certain reticence. Certainly "Christ" is found occasionally in the words of Jesus in the gospels, and may well have been put there by the early Church. There is, however, a marked contrast between the scanty references to Christ in the gospels, and the large number of references to the Son of man, as also between the vast number of references to Christ in the rest of the New Testament, and the almost complete absence of references to the Son of man.

The Son of man whom Knox finds a psychological stumbling-block is a figure which has been created out of part of the evidence. Once again, we see the danger of separating the various kinds of saying and eliminating one or more groups from the discussion. The total evidence does not support the view that the Son of man must be viewed as a supernatural redeemer-figure descending from heaven; it is not necessarily true to say (as did Bousset[1]) that as soon as the Danielic symbol is interpreted messianically the

---

[1] W. Bousset, *Kyrios Christos*, p. 16.

Messiah must become a supernatural figure. The possibility of an interpretation which was messianic but *not* "supernatural" deserves consideration.

It is unlikely that agreement will ever be reached on the question of Jesus' own use of the term "Son of man". The fact that the evidence has come to us via the evangelists leaves it open both to their interpretation and to ours. Inevitably, the answer which we give to the question is determined largely by our attitude to the nature of the gospel evidence and to certain theological problems. On the one hand, we have a group of scholars who believe that it is still possible to use the gospels as a source for a reconstruction of the mind as well as the life of Jesus, and who attempt to trace his "messianic self-consciousness".[1] This approach is normally linked with an attitude which regards the question as one which is of vital importance for Christology and the faith of the Church; J. W. Bowman,[2] for example, writes: "*The Church cannot indefinitely continue to believe about Jesus what he did not know to be true about himself!*" At the other extreme we have scholars who cut the Christian faith loose from the life and thought of Jesus, and who deny that the recovery of Jesus' "self-consciousness" is either possible or important;[3] for them, the gospels are evidence of the faith and thought of the early Church, not of Jesus. Such widely differing approaches inevitably lead to very different answers to the question of the origin of the term "Son of man" in the gospels: it can either be regarded as the expression of Jesus' inner conviction about his person and mission, or be seen as a declaration of the early Church's faith in him.

Neither of these explanations is without its difficulties. The traditional position, which understands "the Son of man" as Jesus' own self-designation, offers little real explanation as to why he should have used that term. The popular belief that Jesus regarded himself as Messiah, preferred the term "Son of man" to "Messiah" because it was less political, and reinterpreted the whole concept in terms of the Suffering Servant,[4] is a singularly

---

[1] E.g. V. Taylor, in *Jesus and His Sacrifice*, 1937, and C. J. Cadoux in *The Historic Mission of Jesus*, 1941.

[2] *The Intention of Jesus*, 1945, p. 108.

[3] E.g. J. Knox, *The Death of Christ*. Contrast with Bowman's attitude, Knox's argument that Jesus' true humanity excludes the possibility that he was conscious of being "Son of man", pp. 70–3.

[4] Held, e.g., by V. Taylor; see *Mark*, pp. 119f.

tortuous but unsatisfying explanation, and one which does not fit
the facts. The term "Son of man" is left unrelated to the majority
of the contexts in which it appears, apart from hypothetical links
with other terms which do not appear. A real attempt to see the
term as appropriate and relate it to the gospel situation was made
by R. H. Fuller,[1] but at the cost of interpreting it as a "proleptic"
term: he saw Jesus "not as the one who is already Son of man, but
as the one destined to be the Son of man, as the Son of man designate".[2] Fuller thus agreed with those scholars who regard the
"eschatological" meaning of "Son of man" as the basic one, but
differed from many of them in believing that Jesus used the term
of himself, and that the extension to other uses took place during
the ministry of Jesus, not after his death and resurrection. His ingenious theory founders on the difficulties of understanding how
—or why—Jesus should have acted "proleptically" as the Son of
man.[3] There is nothing in the Marcan sayings to suggest that
Jesus believed that he was destined to "become" Son of man;
the "future" sayings all refer to "coming", not "becoming", and
none of the other sayings contains a hint that Jesus regards himself as acting only as the Son of man *designatus*. If Jesus "acts as
the one destined to be the triumphant Son of Man already during
his ministry and humiliation"[4] it is, we suggest, not because he is
"one destined to be the triumphant Son of Man", but because he
is already "the Son of Man", and is therefore "destined to be . . .
triumphant".

Yet it must not be forgotten that the explanations which escape
the difficulties involved in understanding "Son of man" as Jesus'
self-designation themselves encounter difficulties which are perhaps as grave. We have already noted some of the problems which
are raised by the position held by Bultmann and Knox. To these
we may add the further query of the possibility of such a radical
change in the disciples' view of Jesus: was even the resurrection
sufficient to change one who had claimed only to be a prophet into
a supernatural Son of man ?[5] A further problem is the position of

[1] *Mission and Achievement*, pp. 95–108.
[2] Op. cit., p. 103.
[3] Fuller himself now describes this solution as "a rather artificial attempt to
paper over the undeniable inconsistency within the Son of man sayings", *The
Foundations of New Testament Christology*, p. 122.
[4] Op. cit., p. 108.
[5] See E. Schweizer, "The Son of Man Again", *N.T.S.*, 10, 1963, pp. 257f.
Cf. W. C. van Unnik, "Jesus the Christ", *N.T.S.*, 8, 1962, pp. 101–7.

Jesus himself, if he proclaimed another as coming Son of man.[1] This difficulty has been pointed out by H. Conzelmann, who suggests that the relationship which exists between Jesus and the coming Kingdom leaves no room for another figure to inaugurate the end.[2] Conzelmann's own solution, however—he follows P. Vielhauer[3] in denying to Jesus any reference to the Son of man— raises enormous difficulties: it would be extraordinary if the early Church (even via "prophets" speaking in the name of Christ) had put the term so often into the mouth of Jesus, and yet refrained almost without exception from using it in other contexts; it is also extremely unlikely that the Church would ever have created a saying in the form found in Mark 8.38.[4]

4. JESUS: THE SON OF MAN

Any attempt to deal with this problem of Jesus' own understanding adequately would obviously require a consideration of all the gospel sayings, and not those in Mark alone. Yet this examination has been made so often that it is worth enquiring whether our study of the Marcan sayings can shed any light upon the problem.

Our examination of Daniel's imagery suggested that the vision of "one like a Son of man" was not used simply as apocalyptic symbolism, but was intended to express a very real and fundamental truth about the righteous nucleus of Israel. The vindication of those who were faithful to God was certain, because he had acknowledged them as his chosen people, destined to inherit the rule once given to Adam; their present suffering was due to the fact that this authority was at the moment unacknowledged by the rebellious nations over whom they should be ruling. This same theme of Israel's divine right to rule the earth, a right usurped by other nations, was found in much of the inter-testamental literature, expressed sometimes in terms of Adam, though the phrase "Son of man" is not used. In 1 Enoch, in spite of the fact that the Son of man has become an individual of supernatural character,

---

[1] This is illustrated by the tortuous and obscure explanation to the problem given by A. J. B. Higgins, *Son of Man*, pp. 200–2.
[2] "Gegenwart und Zukunft in der synoptischen Tradition", *Z.Th.K.*, 54, 1957, pp. 281f. Cf. R. Schnackenburg, *God's Rule and Kingdom*, E.Tr. 1963, pp. 160–7.
[3] "Gottesreich und Menschensohn in der Verkündigung Jesu", *Festschrift für Günther Dehn*, ed. W. Schneemelcher, 1957, pp. 51–79.
[4] Cf. F. Hahn, *Christologische Hoheitstitel*, 1963, p. 38.

he is still closely associated with the themes of election and obedience. Both he and the community which is so closely linked with him are defined as the "elect" and "righteous".

The supernatural events which characterize the appearance of the Son of man in Daniel and 1 Enoch have distracted our attention from the more fundamental features of this figure. The Son of man is not simply one who appears at the end of time to act as judge: rather it is because he is Son of man now—i.e. elect, obedient, faithful, and therefore suffering—that he will be vindicated as Son of man in the future: the eschatological rôle of the Son of man is based upon his obedient response to God now. This is true not only in Daniel but also in 1 Enoch, where the Son of man who will be enthroned at the End is the Son of man "who is born unto righteousness", who in fact is found to be the humble and righteous Enoch, who "walked with God".

If this is indeed the basic meaning of the Danielic image of "one like a Son of man", then it offers us a background against which we may understand the Marcan sayings. This picture is, in fact, significantly close to that which E. Schweizer finds in the gospel sayings themselves:[1]

> The Son of man described in those sayings which seem to be original is a man who lives a lowly life on earth, rejected, humiliated, handed over to his opponents, but eventually exalted by God and to be the chief witness in the last judgment.

Schweizer links this picture primarily with the suffering, righteous man in Wisd. 2—5, but he compares also the exaltation of the righteous Enoch in Enoch 70—71, and the representative character of the Son of man in Daniel.

As used in St Mark, the title "Son of man" expresses the fundamental truth about Jesus' person and work, and the corollaries involved in being Son of man are the same as in Daniel. Jesus' authority as Son of man is grounded in his election by God, and in his obedience to him, ideas which are expressed in the words from heaven in Mark 1.11, where Jesus is addressed in terms used in the Old Testament of Israel.[2] It is because he is the Son of man that Jesus claims authority; it is his obedience as Son of man that involves him in suffering; it is the fact that he is Son of man that is

---

[1] "The Son of Man", *J.B.L.*, 79, 1960, pp. 121f. For his analysis, see "Der Menschensohn", *Z.N.T.W.*, 50, 1959, pp. 188–202.
[2] M. D. Hooker, *Jesus and the Servant*, pp. 68–73.

the ground of his faith in his ultimate vindication. The sayings are found to have a coherence and unity; moreover, the term is seen to be related to the sayings, and also to the ministry of Jesus: it is not merely a title which has been arbitrarily substituted for the pronoun "I".

The term "the Son of man" is thus seen to be appropriate in precisely those contexts where it is found in St. Mark. The relevance of the various sayings to the figure of the Son of man, and the coherent pattern which they form, are strong support for the traditional belief that the majority of the sayings go back to Jesus himself; we must at least trace the various types of sayings to one source, and not to the indiscriminate creation of the early Church. Further support for the view that it is his own self-designation is found in the fact that, although the term "Son of man" is appropriate to the contexts in which it is found *within the ministry of Jesus*, it is inappropriate apart from that setting. It would have been meaningful for Jesus himself to claim authority, accept the necessity for suffering, and confidently affirm ultimate vindication, on the basis that he was the Son of man, of whom these things were "written", for "the Son of man" denotes primarily one to whom authority belongs and who can confidently expect vindication. For the early Church, however, the term was inappropriate: Jesus had already been vindicated and exalted by God. He had been made "Lord and Christ", and his authority could best be expressed in these terms; the necessity for his sufferings could best be understood in terms of the fulfilment of Old Testament scripture; only the future, final manifestation of his glory, an expectation based on the imagery taken from Daniel, was now expressed, as was natural, in terms of "the Son of man". It is thus far easier to explain the origin of many of the "Son of man" sayings within the ministry of Jesus, than in the life and faith of the early Church. The fact that the term "Son of man" was meaningful within the ministry of Jesus, but lost its relevance at the moment when the Son of man was glorified, explains the absence of the term from the rest of the New Testament.[1]

---

[1] Cf. C. F. D. Moule, "From Defendant to Judge", *S.N.T.S. Bulletin*, III, 1952, p. 49, who suggests that the reason why the term "Son of Man" recedes is that "there were better words than 'Son of Man', when once the Son of Man had been glorified—'Christ', 'Lord', 'Son of God' . . . That is, the Son of Man, *on earth*, is predominantly thought of as *to be vindicated in the future*; and when once he is actually *with the clouds* then a more exalted title is suitable."

The Marcan sayings, then, present us with an interpretation of the Son of man which is consistent, and which would make sense within the life of Jesus. As such, this interpretation deserves consideration as possibly a reasonably reliable representation of Jesus' own use and understanding of the term. Its consistency and appropriateness add weight to the view that Jesus used the term "Son of man" of himself, not, however, as a convenient "messianic" term, or as a claim to supernatural powers, but as an expression of the basis and meaning of his person and destiny: it expresses his position in the world, a position founded upon his relationship with God, for it is his relationship with God (expressed in terms of choice, obedience and "Son of God") which explains his relationship with men (expressed in terms of authority, rule and "Son of man"); Jesus, like Israel, can be termed "Son of man" only because his relationship with God is such that he can also be described as "Son of God".

The authority, necessity for suffering, and confidence in final vindication, which are expressed in the Marcan sayings, can all be traced to Dan. 7. The importance of that chapter for Jesus' use of the term is supported by the quotation in Mark 14.62: we are not precluded from attributing a reference to that chapter to Jesus by the arbitrary and somewhat circular argument of Tödt[1] that Jesus never quoted from Dan. 7, and therefore any reference to that chapter in his mouth cannot be genuine; the fact that the early Church was fond of Old Testament quotations does not exclude the possibility that Jesus himself used and quoted scripture in endeavouring to understand and express his own mission and faith in God. Nor need the fact that in Daniel "the one like a Son of man" is a corporate term occasion any difficulty. Daniel itself, and the interpretation given by Enoch, are evidence of the oscillation between corporate and individual. The apparent distinction between Jesus and the Son of man in Mark 8.38 is explained if, as in Dan. 7.13, the "coming" of the Son of man in glory is symbolic of the vindication of one who has, in fact, been truly Son of man all along. There is no psychological problem involved in Jesus' use of the term for himself; for it is not taken with $\ddot{v}\beta\rho\iota\varsigma$ as a claim to supernatural power and position, but is the consequence of his obedient relationship to God and his acceptance of the will of

---

[1] *Menschensohn*, pp. 32f, E.Tr. pp. 35f, on Mark 13.26 and 14.62.

God, and it expresses, not self-aggrandizement, but rather his faith in God, who will fulfil his purposes and vindicate those who are faithful to him. Jesus himself is the embodiment of this ideal, the one true Israelite who is able to accept the mission and destiny of his people; but, as in 1 Enoch, he is closely linked with those who are prepared to join themselves to him. Jesus proclaims the kingdom of God, the kingdom which he himself accepts and embodies, and calls other men to accept the same yoke of obedience, which will involve them in the same experience of suffering and vindication; yet he stands apart from them by the fact that it is in him that men are faced by decision, and ultimately the path which they take is determined by their attitude to him.

The three strands of sayings in the Marcan tradition belong together, therefore, and present us with a coherent interpretation of "the Son of man" which may well go back to Jesus himself. This obviously does not mean, of course, that all the sayings which we have examined are necessarily "authentic" sayings of Jesus; it does suggest, however, that we are more likely to discover the truth about the Son of man by considering the total picture which emerges (even though there may be minor distortions in that picture) than by classifying and eliminating various types of sayings, so using only half the evidence available to us. Valuable as the study of the history of tradition may be, the analysis of individual sayings can sometimes conceal the truth, for the attempt to classify the different strata of tradition can divide the material to such an extent that one can no longer see the whole pattern.

How far Mark himself was aware of the significance of the term "Son of man" in the pattern which he has preserved it is difficult to say. In view of the content and context of the two sayings in chapter 2, it seems clear that he understood the term as a claim to authority by Jesus—a theme which is in any case dominant in St Mark's gospel. The distribution of the sayings suggests that he also intended to contrast the present rejection of that claim by the Jewish authorities (2.10; 2.28; 3.6; 14.62) and the acknowledgement which would be made in the future (8.38; 13.26; 14.62). The association between the sufferings of the Son of man and the path which the disciple is expected to tread, together with the link between the appearance of the Son of man and the vindication of the elect, suggests that Mark recognized that the term signified one who was the leader of a community which was closely bound to him. This corporate link remains, in spite of the fact that the references to rejection have been influenced by knowledge of the unique event of the crucifixion, and in spite of Mark's own literal interpretation of the eschatological sayings, which has shifted the emphasis to some extent from vindication to judgement, and from the resurrection to the parousia: the vindication which is now expected includes the followers of Jesus, and their sufferings are not yet completed.

It seems unlikely, on the other hand, that the pattern which we have discerned has been imposed upon the material entirely by Mark himself, for he was using tradition older than himself. It is true that the pattern is discerned much more clearly in Mark than in the other gospels, but there are traces of it in other sources. We cannot examine these other sources in detail here, but we may perhaps mention briefly some of the points which deserve attention. It is often maintained that the absence from Q of any sayings which predict the passion of the Son of man is significant.[1] This fact is, however, largely explained by their irrelevance apart from a passion narrative;[2] there is, in fact, almost no reference of any kind to Jesus' suffering in Q;[3] yet the saying in Luke 9.58 = Matt. 8.20 certainly implies the rejection of the Son of man. The theme of rejection is also found in Luke 17.25, where the Son of man's suffering is said to be the necessary preliminary to his glory.[4] References to the present activity of the Son of man are found in Q. It is noteworthy that two recent writers who attribute these sayings in their present form to the early Church have nevertheless stressed that these references are not to be explained simply as examples of the random substitution of the term "Son of man" for the first person singular pronoun.[5] These sayings refer not merely to the present *activity* of the Son of man but to his present *authority*: they imply either the authoritative behaviour of Jesus or the rejection of his authority. Thus we find his authority expressed in the form of a

---

[1] Cf. A. J. B. Higgins, *Son of Man*, pp. 132f. If, as seems probable, Q did not exist as a single document, the force of this argument is lessened.

[2] This is admitted by Higgins, loc. cit. See also R. H. Fuller, *Mission and Achievement*, p. 104; M. Black, in *B.J.R.L.*, 45, 1963, p. 310.

[3] The one possible exception is the lament for Jerusalem, Luke 13.34f = Matt. 23.37–9; the reference here, however, is indirect and subordinate to the main theme, the fate of Jerusalem.

[4] This association is not sufficient justification for dismissing the saying as an "editorial insertion", as Higgins, *Son of Man*, pp. 78f.

[5] H. E. Tödt, *Menschensohn*, pp. 105–16, E.Tr. pp. 113–25; A. J. B. Higgins, *Son of Man*, p. 121.

contrast between John the Baptist and the Son of man;[1] the rejection of his authority is expressed in the form of a contrast between the animals and the homeless Son of man,[2] and in terms of blasphemy against the Son of man.[3] These occurrences of the term "Son of man" are explained by Bultmann as originating in a linguistic misunderstanding by the Hellenistic community,[4] and by Tödt as an extension of the authority of the Son of man into the earthly ministry of Jesus;[5] whereas Bultmann sees no link between the "eschatological" and the "earthly" sayings, Tödt regards the latter as arising logically out of the former. Tödt is surely right in stressing that the link between the two groups of sayings is found in the concept of authority: but the difference between them which he himself notices—namely that "the transcendent attributes, rights, functions and limitlessness of the heavenly Son of Man are not at all transferred to Jesus on earth"[6]—suggests, not that the earthly activity of the Son of man is an extension of his heavenly authority, but that it is the idea of ἐξουσία which is basic, and his transcendent attributes possibly secondary. The authority which the Son of man exercises on earth is not "supernatural" or "proleptic"; it is the activity of one who claimed an authority which was relevant to the particular situation in which he found himself, and which was rejected by those among whom he lived.

In the gospels of Matthew and Luke the proportion of "eschatological" sayings is much higher than in Mark. This probably reflects the interest and situation of the Church: in a community which expected the consummation of the era and the appearance of Christ, the eschatological references to the Son of man would, we have suggested, be meaningful, for they would be transferred

---

[1] Luke 7.33f = Matt. 11.18f. Cf. H. E. Tödt, *Menschensohn*, p. 107, E.Tr. p. 116: "That action of the Son of Man for which this generation reproaches him here is a specific act of sovereignty superior to the restraints of the Law by virtue of the authority of a direct mission. It is action which befits only an authorized person."

[2] Luke 9.58 = Matt. 8.20. Cf. H. E. Tödt, *Menschensohn*, p. 114, E.Tr. p. 122: "The very one who summons men to follow with full authority is the same whom this generation refuses to receive, thus depriving him of a home. Again it is men's hostility to Jesus' claim to full authority which refuses a home to the Son of man as well as to Jesus' followers."

[3] Luke 12.10 = Matt. 12.32. Cf. H. E. Tödt, *Menschensohn*, p. 112, E.Tr. p. 120: "The designation Son of Man . . . means the claim to full authority uttered by Jesus on earth which the opponents resist."

[4] *Theology of the New Testament*, I, p. 30.

[5] *Menschensohn*, pp. 105–30, 248f, E.Tr. pp. 113–40, 272–4.

[6] *Menschensohn*, p. 130, E.Tr. p. 140; cf. p. 112, E.Tr. p. 120.

from the exaltation of Christ which had already taken place to the final establishment of God's kingdom; there would therefore be a tendency to increase the number of such sayings, to interpret them of a literal "coming", and to embroider them with apocalyptic detail drawn from the Old Testament. Many of these sayings are concerned with the theme of crisis and judgement, e.g. Luke 17.30; 18.8; 21.36; Matt. 13.41; 19.28; 25.31. This last passage is of particular interest, because of the change in title from ὁ υἱὸς τοῦ ἀνθρώπου in v. 31 to ὁ βασιλεὺς in v. 34, a fact which leads many scholars to regard v. 31 as editorial.[1] It is worth noticing, however, that Matthew here presents us with a picture similar to that found in both Daniel and Mark; the Son of man comes in glory, he is enthroned, and he then acts as "king" or judge: in spite of his own editing, it is possible that Matthew here preserves a tradition which is older than his own understanding of the Son of man as an eschatological figure—namely, that "the Son of man" is an appropriate designation for one who *will be* vindicated, rather than for one who has already been enthroned; when the Son of man has come in glory, then other terms are more appropriate for him.

In the Johannine tradition, we find the term "Son of man"—still used by Jesus alone[2]—connected closely with the theme of glorification; the glory of the Son of man is not linked with his parousia but with his exaltation,[3] and both exaltation and glorification are linked so closely with Jesus' death, that the verbs ὑψοῦν and δοξάζειν can be used of the crucifixion.[4] The Son of man is also the source of spiritual food,[5] and Jesus is said to have been given authority by his Father to execute judgement because he is Son of man.[6] It is interesting to find that the Johannine tradition, although so different from the Marcan, also expresses the theme of the Son of man's vindication beyond suffering, though in Johannine thought the exaltation has so transformed the humiliation that the two have become fused. The Johannine sayings convey, in Johannine terms, the theme of vindication which lies behind both the "eschatological" sayings in St Mark—where it is expressed in terms of the parousia—and the "passion" sayings—

---

[1] E.g. J. Jeremias, *The Parables of Jesus*, 1954, p. 142; H. E. Tödt, *Menschensohn*, p. 68, E.Tr. pp. 73f; A. J. B. Higgins, *Son of Man*, pp. 115–18.
[2] John 12.34 cannot be regarded as an exception.
[3] John 1.51; 3.13; 6.62.   [4] John 3.14f; 8.28; 12.23; 13.31f.
[5] John 6.27,53.   [6] John 5.27.

where it is expressed in terms of the resurrection. Since it is unlikely that Johannine thought here has been influenced by Mark,
it seems possible that both rely ultimately on a common tradition
which spoke both of the suffering and of the victory of the Son of
man. It is, indeed, possible that the Johannine form is sometimes
closer than the Marcan to the original saying.[1]

The solitary reference to the Son of man in Acts is an enigma
which has received many different explanations.[2] We may simply
note here that its use in the particular context which is given to it
seems entirely appropriate in the light of our study of Mark. Here
we have, for the first and only time in Acts, an account of the
sufferings and death of one who is prepared to follow Jesus;[3] like
his Master, he suffers at the hands of a disobedient and stiff-necked
people, and is put to death because of his own obedience to God.
As the Son of man had been vindicated by his exaltation after his
death, so now Stephen confidently awaits the vindication promised
to those who are not ashamed of Jesus. The vision of the Son of
man at the right hand of God is parallel to the declaration of Jesus
before the high priest, and both occasions are "double trial
scenes":[4] although Jesus and Stephen are condemned by the
Jewish court, in the heavenly court both are vindicated, and it is
their judges who are condemned. The much debated question of
the posture of the Son of man is in fact no problem if this interpretation is correct, for in Mark 14.62 "sitting at the right hand"
is an expression of the exaltation and vindication of the Son of man
himself, whereas in Acts 7.56 he stands as the vindicator of Stephen,
acknowledging before God the disciple who has acknowledged him
before men.[5]

In the rest of the New Testament the Son of man does not
appear, apart from a reference to the Danielic vision in Rev. 1.13,
and a quotation of Ps. 8. in Heb. 2.6ff. This latter passage is of considerable importance, for it appears to embody a "Son of man"
Christology which has as its fundamental features the authority of
the Son of man, to whom God has subjected all things (though in

---

[1] Cf. M. Black, *B.J.R.L.*, 45, 1963, p. 317, on John 3.14.
[2] See the latest study of the problem, by C. K. Barrett, "Stephen and the
Son of Man", *Apophoreta*, Festschrift für Ernst Haenchen, ed. W. Eltester,
1964, pp. 32–8, and the literature quoted there.
[3] Cf. C. K. Barrett, op. cit., p. 36.
[4] Cf. C. F. D. Moule, *S.N.T.S. Bulletin* III, 1952, p. 47.
[5] Similarly C. F. D. Moule, loc. cit.; O. Cullmann, *The Christology of the
New Testament*, p. 183.

fact all things are not yet subject), his humiliation and suffering, the glory and honour which have come to him "because of the suffering of death", and the fact that through this suffering and death he has been made the pioneer of salvation by whom many sons are brought to glory. We see here the same features of authority, humiliation, vindication and corporate participation which are found in Mark. Equally important are the passages in the Pauline epistles which express, directly or indirectly, the idea of Christ as the Second Adam.[1] As an example we may refer to Phil. 2, which may possibly be pre-Pauline, where we find the same pattern once again: Christ, in the form of God, and therefore entitled to authority, was nevertheless humble and obedient, accepting even the consequence of that obedience, which was crucifixion. As a result God has exalted him and given him lordship and dominion over everything in heaven and on earth and under the earth.[2] A further consequence is that Christian believers share his mind, and exhibit in their own community the same pattern of obedience and even suffering, confidently awaiting the time of vindication, when they will share in Christ's glory.[3] Such passages suggest that, though the title "Son of man" itself may not be used in the New Testament epistles, the ideas which are associated with it have nevertheless played a very important part in the formation of New Testament theology: this theme, however, is a subject which demands a study to itself.

[1] E.g. Rom. 5.12–21 (and throughout Romans), 1. Cor. 15.21f, 42–50, and the references to Christ as εἰκὼν τοῦ Θεοῦ, 2 Cor. 4.4; Col. 1.15ff.

[2] Cf. M. Black, op. cit., p. 315.

[3] Phil. 2.5; 1.29; 2.1f; 3.20f.

BIBLIOGRAPHY
INDEX

Bibliography

TEXTS

Biblia Hebraica, ed. R. Kittel, Stuttgart, 3rd edn, 1950.
Septuaginta, ed. A. Rahlfs, 2 vols., Stuttgart, 1935.
The Old Testament in Greek according to the Septuagint, ed. H. B. Swete, 3 vols., Cambridge, 4th edn, 1934.
Novum Testamentum Graece, ed. E. Nestle, Stuttgart, 20th edn, 1950.
The Revised Standard Version of the Bible, London, 1952.
The Apocrypha and Pseudepigrapha of the Old Testament in English, 2 vols., ed. R. H. Charles, Oxford, 1913.
Lévi, I. *The Hebrew Text of the Book of Ecclesiasticus*, Semitic Study Series III, Leiden, 1904.
Midrash Rabbah, ed. H. Freedman and M. Simon, 10 vols., London, 1939.
The Midrash on Psalms, Midrash Tehillim, Yale Judaica Series, vol. XIII, 2 vols., trans. W. G. Braude, New Haven, 1959.
The Mishnah, trans. H. Danby, Oxford, 1933.
The Babylonian Talmud, ed. I. Epstein, London, 1948–52.
Le Talmud de Jérusalem, trans. M. Schwab, new edn, Paris, 1932–3.
The Fathers according to Rabbi Nathan, trans. J. Goldin, Yale Judaica Series, vol. X, New Haven, 1955.
Pirkê de Rabbi Eliezer, trans. G. Friedlander, London, 1916.
Mekilta de-Rabbi Ishmael, ed. J. Z. Lauterbach, Schiff Library of Jewish Classics, Philadelphia, 1949.
Vermes, G., *The Dead Sea Scrolls in English*, London, 1962.
Origen, *Commentary on Matthew*, trans. J. Patrick, *Ante-Nicene Christian Library*, additional vol., ed. A. Menzies, Edinburgh, 1897.
Philo, trans. F. H. Colson and G. H. Whitaker, Loeb Classical Library, London, 1949.
The Works of Flavius Josephus, trans. W. Whiston, London.

OTHER BOOKS AND ARTICLES

Abbott, E. A., "The Son of Man", *Diatessarica VIII*, Cambridge, 1910.
Abbott, E. A., *The Message of the Son of Man*, London, 1909.

Allen, W. C., *The Gospel According to St Matthew*, Edinburgh, 1907.

Andel, C. P. van, *De Structuur van de Henoch-Traditie en Het Nieuwe Testament*, with summary in English, pp. 114–27, Utrecht, 1955.

Arndt, W. F., and Gingrich, F. W., *A Greek-English Lexicon of the New Testament and Other Early Christian Literature*, translation of W. Bauer's *Wörterbuch*, Chicago and Cambridge, 1957.

Ashby, E., "The Coming of the Son of Man", *E.T.*, 72, 1961, pp. 360–3.

Bacon, B. W., *The Gospel of Mark*, U.S.A., 1925.

Bacon, B. W., "The 'Son of Man' in the Usage of Jesus", *J.B.L.*, 41, 1922, pp. 143–82.

Barr, J., "Daniel", *Peake's Commentary on the Bible*, new edn, ed. M. Black and H. H. Rowley, London, 1962.

Barrett, C. K., "The Background of Mark 10.45", *New Testament Essays*, ed. A. J. B. Higgins, Manchester, 1959, pp. 1–18.

Barrett, C. K., *The Gospel According to St John*, London, 1955.

Barrett, C. K., *The Holy Spirit and the Gospel Tradition*, London, 1947.

Barrett, C. K., "New Testament Eschatology", *S.J.T.*, 6, 1953, pp. 136–55, 225–43: I—"Jewish and Pauline Eschatology"; II—"The Gospels".

Barrett, C. K., "Stephen and the Son of Man", *Apophoreta*, Festschrift für Ernst Haenchen, ed. W. Eltester, Berlin, 1964, pp. 32–8.

Bartlett, J. Vernon, and Carlyle, A. J., *Christianity in History*, London, 1917.

Baumgartner, W., "Ein Vierteljahrhundert Danielforschung", *Theologische Rundschau*, Neue Folge, 11th Jahrgang, 1939, Tübingen, pp. 59–83, 125–44, 201–28.

Beare, F. W., "The Sabbath was Made for Man?" *J.B.L.*, 79, 1960, pp. 130–6.

Beasley-Murray, G. R., *A Commentary on Mark Thirteen*, London, 1957.

Beasley-Murray, G. R., *Jesus and the Future*, London, 1954.

Beer, G., article on 1 Enoch in E. Kautzsch, *Die Apokryphen und Pseudepigraphen des Alten Testaments*, Tübingen, 1900.

Bentzen, A., *King and Messiah*, London, 1955, E.Tr. of *Messias-Moses Redivivus-Menschensohn*.

Bernadin, J. B., "The Transfiguration", *J.B.L.*, 52, 1933, pp. 181–9.

Black, M., *An Aramaic Approach to the Gospels and Acts*, 2nd edn, Oxford, 1954.

Black, M., "The Eschatology of the Similitudes of Enoch", *J.T.S.*, new series, 3, 1952, pp. 1–10.

Black, M., "Servant of the Lord and Son of Man", *S.J.T.*, 6, 1953, pp. 1–11.

Black, M., "The Son of Man Problem in Recent Research and Debate", *B.J.R.L.*, 45, 1963, pp. 305-18.

Black, M., "Unsolved New Testament Problems: The 'Son of Man' in the Old Biblical Literature", *E.T.*, 60, 1949, pp. 11-15.

Black, M., "Unsolved New Testament Problems: The 'Son of Man' in the Teaching of Jesus", *E.T.*, 60, 1949, pp. 32-6.

Blass, F., and Debrunner, A., *Grammatik des neutestamentlichen Griechisch*, 8th edn, Göttingen, 1949, E.Tr. by R. Funk, Chicago and Cambridge, 1961.

Blinzler, J., *The Trial of Jesus*, Westminster, U.S.A., 1959, trans. from 2nd German edn by I. and F. McHugh.

Boobyer, G. H., *St Mark and the Transfiguration Story*, Edinburgh, 1942.

Bornkamm, G., *Jesus of Nazareth*, London, 1960, E.Tr. of *Jesus von Nazareth*.

Bousset, W., *Kyrios Christos*, Göttingen, 1913.

Bousset, W., and Gressmann, H., *Die Religion des Judentums in Späthellenistischen Zeitalter*, 3rd edn, rev. Gressmann, Tübingen, 1926.

Bowman, J., "The Background of the Term 'Son of Man'", *E.T.*, 59, 1948, pp. 283-8.

Bowman, J. W., *The Intention of Jesus*, London, 1945.

Box, G. H., *The Ezra-Apocalypse*, London, 1912.

Box, G. H., and Oesterley, W. O. E., "Ecclesiasticus", in R. H. Charles, *Apocrypha and Pseudepigrapha*, I, Oxford, 1913.

Branscomb, B. H., *The Gospel of Mark*, London, 1937.

Brown, F., Driver, S. R., and Briggs, C. A., *A Hebrew and English Lexicon of the Old Testament*, Oxford, 1907.

Brownlee, W. H., *The Meaning of the Qumran Scrolls for the Bible*, New York, 1964.

Bultmann, R., *Die Geschichte der synoptischen Tradition*, 2nd edn, Göttingen, 1931; E.Tr. by J. Marsh, Oxford, 1963.

Bultmann, R., *Jesus and the Word*, new edn, London, 1958, E.Tr. of *Jesus*.

Bultmann, R., *Theology of the New Testament*, vol. I, London, 1952, trans. K. Grobel.

Burkill, T. A., *Mysterious Revelation*, New York, 1963.

Burkitt, F. C., *Christian Beginnings*, London, 1924.

Burkitt, F. C., "Four Notes on the Book of Enoch", *J.T.S.*, 8, 1907, pp. 444-7.

Burkitt, F. C., Review of Charles' edn of the Testaments of the Twelve Patriarchs, *J.T.S.*, 10, 1909, pp. 135ff.

Cadbury, H. J., "The Titles of Jesus in Acts", *Beginnings*, vol. V, London, 1933, pp. 354-75.

Cadoux, A. T., *The Sources of the Second Gospel*, London, 1935.

Cadoux, C. J., *The Historic Mission of Jesus*, London, 1941.

Cadoux, C. J., "The Imperatival Use of ἵνα in the New Testament", *J.T.S.*, 42, 1941, pp. 165–73.

Campbell, J. Y., "The Origin and Meaning of the term Son of Man", *J.T.S.*, 48, 1947, pp. 145–55.

Campbell, J. Y., "Son of Man", *A Theological Wordbook of the Bible*, ed. A. Richardson, London, 1950, pp. 230–3.

Carrington, P., *According to Mark*, Cambridge, 1960.

Casey, R. P., "The Earliest Christologies", *J.T.S.*, new series 9, 1958, pp. 253–77.

Charles, R. H., *The Apocrypha and Pseudepigrapha of the Old Testament in English*, 2 vols., Oxford, 1913.

Charles, R. H., *The Book of Enoch*, new edn, Oxford, 1912.

Charles, R. H., *The Book of Jubilees*, London, 1902.

Charles, R. H., *A Critical and Exegetical Commentary on the Book of Daniel*, Oxford, 1929.

Charles, R. H., *The Greek Versions of the Testaments of the Twelve Patriarchs*, Oxford, 1908.

Charles, R. H., *The Testaments of the Twelve Patriarchs*, London, 1908.

Congar, Y. M.-J., *The Mystery of the Temple*, E.Tr., London, 1962.

Conzelmann, H., "Gegenwart und Zukunft in der synoptischen Tradition", *Z.Th.K.*, 54, 1957, pp. 277–96.

Cooke, G. A., *Ezekiel*, Edinburgh, 1936.

Coppens, J., "Le chapitre VII de Daniel", *Ephemerides Theologicae Lovanienses*, 39, 1963, pp. 87–94.

Coppens, J., "Le Fils d'homme Daniélique, vizir céleste?", *Ephemerides Theologicae Lovanienses*, 40, 1964, pp. 72–80.

Coppens, J., "Le Serviteur de Yahvé et le fils d'homme daniélique sont-ils les figures messianiques?", *Ephemerides Theologicae Lovanienses*, 39, 1963, pp. 104–13.

Coppens, J., "Les Saints dans le Psautier", *Ephemerides Theologicae Lovanienses*, 39, 1963, pp. 485–500.

Coppens, J., "Les Saints du Très-Haut sont-ils à identifier avec les Milices Célestes?", *Ephemerides Theologicae Lovanienses*, 39, 1963, pp. 94–100.

Coppens, J., "L'Origine du symbole 'Fils d'homme'", *Ephemerides Theologicae Lovanienses*, 39, 1963, pp. 100–4.

Coppens, J., and Dequeker, L., *Le Fils de l'homme et les Saints du Très-Haut en Daniel VII, dans les Apocryphes et dans le Nouveau Testament*, Louvain, 1961.

Cranfield, C. E. B., *The Gospel according to Saint Mark*, Cambridge, 1959.

Creed, J. M., *The Gospel According to St Luke*, London, 1930.
Creed, J. M., "The Heavenly Man", *J.T.S.*, 26, 1925, pp. 113–36.
Cross, F. M., and Freedman, D. N., "The Blessing of Moses", *J.B.L.*, 67, 1948, pp. 191–210.
Cullman, O., *The Christology of the New Testament*, London, 1959.
Dalman, G., *The Words of Jesus*, Edinburgh, 1909, trans. D. M. Kay.
Davies, W. D., *Paul and Rabbinic Judaism*, 2nd edn, London, 1955.
Davies, W. D., "Unsolved New Testament Problems: 'The Jewish Background of the Teaching of Jesus: Apocalyptic and Pharisaism'", *E.T.*, 59, 1948, pp. 233–7.
Dibelius, M., *From Tradition to Gospel*, London, 1934, trans. B. Lee Woolf.
Dodd, C. H., *According to the Scriptures*, London, 1952.
Dodd, C. H., "An Essay in Form Criticism", *Studies in the Gospels*, ed. D. E. Nineham, Oxford, 1955, pp. 9–36.
Dodd, C. H., "The Fall of Jerusalem and the 'Abomination of Desolation'", *The Journal of Roman Studies*, 37, 1947, London, pp. 47–64.
Dodd, C. H., "The Framework of the Gospel Narrative", *E.T.*, 43, 1932, pp. 396–400.
Dodd, C. H., *The Interpretation of the Fourth Gospel*, Cambridge, 1953.
Dodd, C. H., *The Parables of the Kingdom*, 3rd edn, London, 1936.
Doeve, J. W., *Jewish Hermeneutics in the Synoptic Gospels and Acts*, Assen, 1953.
Driver, S. R., *The Book of Daniel*, Cambridge, 1900.
Drummond, J., "The Use and Meaning of the Phrase 'The Son of Man' in the Synoptic Gospels", *J.T.S.*, 2, 1901, pp. 350–8, 539–71.
Duncan, G. S., *Jesus, Son of Man*, London, 1948.
Dupont-Sommer, A., *The Essene Writings from Qumran*, Oxford, 1961, trans. G. Vermes.
Easton, B. S., *Christ in the Gospels*, New York and London, 1930.
Emerton, J. A., "The Origin of the Son of Man Imagery", *J.T.S.*, new series 9, 1958, pp. 225–42.
Engnell, I., *Studies in Divine Kingship in the Ancient Near East*, Upsala, 1943.
Engnell, I., "The 'Ebed Yahweh Songs and the Suffering Messiah in 'Deutero-Isaiah'", *B.J.R.L.*, 31, 1948, pp. 54ff.
Evans, C. F., "Sabbath", *A Theological Wordbook of the Bible*, ed. A. Richardson, London, 1950, pp. 205f.
Farrer, A. M., *A Study in St Mark*, London, 1957.
Fascher, E., "Theologische Beobachtungen zu δεῖ", *Neutestamentliche Studien für Rudolf Bultmann*, Beihefte zur *Z.N.T.W.*, 21, 1954, pp. 228–54.

Feuillet, A., "Le Fils de l'homme de Daniel et la tradition biblique", *Revue Biblique*, 60, 1953, Paris, pp. 170–202, 321–46.

Fison, J. E., *The Christian Hope*, London, 1954.

Frey, J. B., "Apocryphes de l'Ancien Testament", *Dictionnaire de la Bible*, Supplément Vol. 1, ed. L. Pirot, Paris, 1928, cols. 354–459.

Fuller, R. H., *The Foundations of New Testament Christology*, London, 1965.

Fuller, R. H., *The Mission and Achievement of Jesus*, London, 1954.

Gärtner, B., *The Temple and the Community in Qumran and the New Testament*, Cambridge, 1965.

George, A. R., "The Imperatival Use of ἵνα in the New Testament", *J.T.S.*, 45, 1944, pp. 56–60.

Glasson, T. F., *The Second Advent*, London, 1945.

Glasson, T. F., "The Reply to Caiaphas (Mark xiv.62)", *N.T.S.*, 7, 1961, pp. 88–93.

Gould, E. P., *The Gospel according to St Mark*, Edinburgh, 1896.

Grant, F. C., *The Earliest Gospel*, New York and Nashville, 1953.

Grant, F. C., "The Gospel According to St Mark, Notes on Exegesis", *The Interpreter's Bible*, vol. VII, New York and Nashville, 1951, pp. 647–917.

Grant, F. C., *The Gospel of the Kingdom*, New York, 1940.

Gunkel, H., *Schöpfung und Chaos in Urzeit und Endzeit*, Göttingen, 1895, 2nd edn, 1921.

Gurney, O. R., "Hittite Kingship", *Myth, Ritual and Kingship*, ed. S. H. Hooke, Oxford, 1958, pp. 105–21.

Hahn, F., *Christologische Hoheitstitel, Ihre Geschichte im frühen Christentum*, Göttingen, 1963.

Hart, J. H. A., *Ecclesiasticus* (The Greek Text of Codex 248), Cambridge, 1909.

Heaton, E. W., *The Book of Daniel*, London, 1956.

Hebert, A. G., *The Throne of David*, London, 1941.

Heidel, A., *The Babylonian Genesis*, 2nd edn, Chicago, 1951.

Héring, J., *Le Royaume de Dieu et Sa Venue*, Paris, 1937.

Higgins, A. J. B., *Jesus and the Son of Man*, London, 1964.

Higgins, A. J. B., "Son of Man-*Forschung* since 'The Teaching of Jesus'", *New Testament Essays*, ed. Higgins, Manchester, 1959, pp. 119–35.

Hooke, S. H., "The Myth and Ritual Pattern in Jewish and Christian Apocalyptic", *The Labyrinth*, ed. Hooke, London, 1935, pp. 211–34.

Hooke, S. H., ed., *Myth and Ritual*, Oxford, 1933.

Hooke, S. H., ed., *Myth, Ritual and Kingship*, Oxford, 1958.

Hooker, M. D., *Jesus and the Servant*, London, 1959.

Hoskyns, E. C., "Jesus the Messiah", *Mysterium Christi*, ed. G. K. A. Bell and A. Deissmann, London, New York, and Toronto, 1930, pp. 67–89.

Hunter, A. M., *The Gospel according to Saint Mark*, London, 1948.

Jackson, F. J. Foakes, and Lake, K., *The Beginnings of Christianity*, Part I, vols. I and V, London, 1920 and 1933.

Jeremias, J., "Die aramäische Vorgeschichte unserer Evangelien", *Theologische Literaturzeitung*, 74, 1949, Leipzig, pp. 527–32.

Jeremias, J., *The Parables of Jesus*, London, 1954, trans. S. H. Hooke.

Jeremias, J., "'Ηλ(ε)ίας", *T.W.N.T.*, II, pp. 930–43.

Jeremias, J., "παῖς Θεοῦ", *T.W.N.T.*, V, pp. 676–713.

Jervell, J., *Imago Dei: Gen. 1.26f im Spätjudentum, in der Gnosis und in den paulinischen Briefen*, Göttingen, 1960.

Johnson, A. R., "Divine Kingship and the Old Testament", *E.T.*, 62, 1951, pp. 36–42.

Johnson, A. R., "Hebrew Conceptions of Kingship", *Myth, Ritual, and Kingship*, ed. S. H. Hooke, Oxford, 1958, pp. 204–60.

Johnson, A. R., "The Role of the King in the Jerusalem Cultus", *The Labyrinth*, ed. S. H. Hooke, London, 1935, pp. 71–112.

Johnson, A. R., *Sacral Kingship in Ancient Israel*, Cardiff, 1955.

Kahle, P., *The Cairo Geniza*, Schweich Lecture for 1941, London, 1947,

Kallas, J., *The Significance of the Synoptic Miracles*, London, 1961.

Käsemann, E., *Essays on New Testament Themes*, London, 1964, trans. from *Exegetische Versuche und Besinnungen*, 1 Band, 2nd edn, 1960.

Kautzsch, E., *Die Apokryphen und Pseudepigraphen des Alten Testaments*, Tübingen, 1900.

Kilpatrick, G. D., *The Trial of Jesus*, Oxford, 1953.

Klausner, J., *Jesus of Nazareth*, London, 1928.

Klostermann, E., *Das Markusevangelium*, 2nd edn, Tübingen, 1926.

Knox, J., *The Death of Christ*, London, 1959.

Kraeling, C. H., *Anthropos and Son of Man*, New York, 1927.

Kümmel, W. G., *Promise and Fulfilment*, London, 1957, E.Tr. of 3rd edn of *Verheissung und Erfüllung*.

Lagrange, M.-J., *Évangile selon Saint Marc*, 4th edn, Paris, 1947.

Lagrange, M.-J., *Évangile selon Saint Matthieu*, Paris, 1923.

Langhe, R. de, "Myth, Ritual and Kingship in the Ras Shamra Tablets", *Myth, Ritual and Kingship*, ed. S. H. Hooke, Oxford, 1958.

Liddell, H. G., and Scott, R., *A Greek-English Lexicon*, rev. H. Stuart Jones, 9th edn, Oxford, 1958.

Lietzmann, H., *Der Menschensohn*, Freiburg and Leipzig, 1896.

Lightfoot, R. H., *The Gospel Message of St Mark*, Oxford, 1950.

Lightfoot, R. H., *History and Interpretation in the Gospels*, Bampton Lectures for 1934, London, 1935.

Linton, O., "The Trial of Jesus and the Interpretation of Psalm cx", *N.T.S.*, 7, 1961, pp. 258–62.

Lohmeyer, E., *Das Evangelium des Markus*, 11th edn, Göttingen, 1951.

Lohmeyer, E., *Gottesknecht und Davidsohn*, Upsala, 1945.

Lohmeyer, E., "Die Verklärung Jesu nach dem Markus-evangelium", *Z.N.T.W.*, 21, 1922, pp. 185–215.

Lohse, E., *Märtyrer und Gottesknecht*, Göttingen, 1955.

Loisy, A., *L'évangile selon Marc*, Paris, 1912.

Loisy, A., *Les Évangiles Synoptiques*, 2 vols., Paris, 1907.

McArthur, H. K., "Mark xiv.62", *N.T.S.*, 4, 1958, pp. 156–8.

McCown, C. C. "Jesus, Son of Man: A Survey of Recent Discussion", *Journal of Religion*, 28, 1948, Chicago, pp. 1–12.

McNeile, A. H., *The Gospel According to St Matthew*, London, 1949.

Manson, T. W., "Mark ii.27f", *Coniectanea Neotestamentica XI in honorem Atonii Fridrichsen*, Lund and Copenhagen, 1947, pp. 138–46.

Manson, T. W., "Realized Eschatology and the Messianic Secret", *Studies in the Gospels*, ed. D. E. Nineham, Oxford, 1955, pp. 209–22.

Manson, T. W., *The Sayings of Jesus*, London, 1949.

Manson, T. W., *The Servant Messiah*, Cambridge, 1953.

Manson, T. W., "The Son of Man in Daniel, Enoch and the Gospels", *B.J.R.L.*, 32, 1950, pp. 171–95. Reprinted in *Studies in the Gospels and Epistles*, ed. M. Black, Manchester, 1962.

Manson, T. W., *The Teaching of Jesus*, 2nd edn, Cambridge, 1935.

Manson, W., *Jesus the Messiah*, London, 1943.

Manson, W., "The Son of Man and History", *S.J.T.*, 5, 1952, pp. 113–22.

Meecham, H. G., "The Imperatival Use of ἵνα in the New Testament", *J.T.S.*, 43, 1942, pp. 179f.

Messel, N., *Der Menschensohn in den Bilderreden des Henoch*, Beihefte zur *Z.A.T.W.*, 35, 1922.

Meyer, E., *Ursprung und Anfänge des Christentums*, I, Stuttgart and Berlin, 1921.

Milik, J. T., *Ten Years of Discovery in the Wilderness of Judaea*, E.Tr. by J. Strugnell, London, 1959.

Montefiore, C. G., *The Synoptic Gospels*, 2 vols., 2nd edn, London, 1927.

Montgomery, J. A., *A Critical and Exegetical Commentary on the Book of Daniel*, Edinburgh, 1927.

Moore, G. F., *Judaism in the First Centuries of the Christian Era*, 3 vols., Cambridge, U.S.A., 1927–30.

Morgenstern, J., "The King-God among the Western Semites and the Meaning of Epiphanes", *V.T.*, 10, 1960, pp. 138–97.

Morgenstern, J., "The 'Son of Man' of Daniel 7.13f", *J.B.L.*, 80, 1961, pp. 65–77.

Moule, C. F. D., *An Idiom Book of New Testament Greek*, 2nd edn, Cambridge, 1959.

Moule, C. F. D., "From Defendant to Judge and Deliverer", *S.N.T.S. Bulletin*, III, 1952, Oxford, pp. 40–53.

Moulton, J. H., and Milligan, G., *The Vocabulary of the Greek Testament*, London, 1930.

Mowinckel, S., *He That Cometh*, Oxford, 1956, trans. G. W. Anderson.

Mowinckel, S., *The Psalms in Israel's Worship*, 2 vols., Oxford, 1962, trans. D. R. Ap-Thomas.

Muilenburg, J., "The Son of Man in Daniel and the Ethiopic Apocalypse of Enoch", *J.B.L.*, 79, 1960, pp. 197–209.

Mundle, W., "Die Geschichtlichkeit des messianischen Bewusstseins Jesu", *Z.N.T.W.*, 21, 1922, pp. 299–311.

Nineham, D. E., *The Gospel According to St Mark*, London, 1963.

Nineham, D. E., ed., *Studies in the Gospels*, essays in memory of R. H. Lightfoot, Oxford, 1955.

North, C. R., "The Religious Aspects of Hebrew Kingship", *Z.A.T.W.*, 50, 1932, pp. 8–38.

Noth, M., "Die Heiligen des Höchsten", *Gesammelte Studien zum Alten Testament*, 2nd edn, Munich, 1960, pp. 274–90; reprinted from Mowinckel Festschrift, 1955.

Oesterley, W. O. E., *II Esdras*, London, 1933.

Oesterley, W. O. E., *The Wisdom of Jesus the Son of Sirach or Ecclesiasticus*, Cambridge, 1912.

Otto, R., *The Kingdom of God and the Son of Man*, London, 1938, E.Tr. of *Reich Gottes und Menschensohn*, rev. edn, 1934.

Parker, P., "The Meaning of 'Son of Man'", *J.B.L.*, 60, 1941, pp. 151–7.

Paul, L., *Son of Man*, London, 1961.

Peake, A. S., "The Messiah and the Son of Man", *B.J.R.L.*, 8, 1924, pp. 52–81.

Plummer, A., *An Exegetical Commentary on the Gospel According to St Matthew*, 2nd edn, London, 1910.

Plummer, A., *The Gospel according to St Luke*, 5th edn, Edinburgh, 1922.

Porteous, N. W., *Das Danielbuch*, Göttingen, 1962.

Porter, F. C., *The Messages of the Apocalyptical Writers*, London, 1905.

Preiss, T., *Le Fils de l'Homme*, Montpellier, 1951.

Preiss, T., "The Mystery of the Son of Man", in *Life in Christ*, London, 1957, pp. 43–60.

Ramsey, A. M., *The Glory of God and the Transfiguration of Christ*, London, 1949.

Rashdall, H., *The Idea of Atonement in Christian Theology*, London, 1919, Bampton Lectures for 1915.

Rawlinson, A. E. J., *St Mark*, 3rd edn, London, 1931.

Richardson, A., *An Introduction to the Theology of the New Testament*, London, 1958.

Riesenfeld, H., *Jésus Transfiguré*, Copenhagen, 1947.

Riesenfeld, H., "The Mythological Background of New Testament Christology", *The Background of the New Testament and Its Eschatology*, ed. W. D. Davies and D. Daube in honour of C. H. Dodd, Cambridge, 1956, pp. 81–95.

Robinson, J. A. T., "Expository Problems: The Second Coming—Mark xiv.62", *E.T.*, 67, 1956, pp. 336–40.

Robinson, J. A. T., *Jesus and His Coming*, London, 1957.

Rowley, H. H., *Darius the Mede and the Four World Empires in the Book of Daniel*, Cardiff, 1935.

Rowley, H. H., *The Relevance of Apocalyptic*, London, 1944.

Russell, D. S., *The Method and Message of Jewish Apocalyptic*, London, 1964.

Ryssel, V., article on Ecclesiasticus in E. Kautzsch, *Die Apokryphen und Pseudepigraphen des Alten Testaments*, Tübingen, 1900.

Schenke, H.-M., *Der Gott "Mensch" in der Gnosis*, Göttingen, 1962.

Schmidt, N., "The 'Son of Man' in the Book of Daniel", *J.B.L.*, 19, 1900, pp. 22–8.

Schmidt, N., "Was בר נשא a Messianic Title?", *J.B.L.*, 15, 1896, pp. 35–53.

Schnackenburg, R., *God's Rule and Kingdom*, Freiburg, 1963, trans. from *Gottes Herrschaft und Reich*, 1959.

Schniewind, J., *Das Evangelium nach Markus*, 9th edn, Göttingen, 1960.

Schrenk, G., "ἱερός", *T.W.N.T.*, III, pp. 221–84.

Schweitzer, A., *The Mystery of the Kingdom of God*, London, 1914.

Schweizer, E., *Lordship and Discipleship*, London, 1960, E.Tr. of *Erniedrigung und Erhöhung bei Jesus und seinen Nachfolgern*, 1955.

Schweizer, E., "Der Menschensohn", *Z.N.T.W.*, 50, 1959, pp. 185–209.

Schweizer, E., "The Son of Man", *J.B.L.*, 79, 1960, pp. 119–29.

Schweizer, E., "The Son of Man Again", *N.T.S.*, 9, 1963, pp. 256–61.

Scott, R. B. Y., "Behold He Cometh With Clouds", *N.T.S.*, 5, 1959, pp. 127–32.

Sharp, D. S., "Mark ii.10", *E.T.*, 38, 1927, pp. 428f.

Sherwin-White, A. N., *Roman Society and Roman Law in the New Testament*, Sarum Lectures for 1960–1, Oxford, 1963.

Sidebottom, E. M., "The Son of Man as Man in the Fourth Gospel", *E.T.*, 68, 1957, pp. 231–5, 280–3.

Simon, M., "Retour du Christ et reconstruction du Temple dans la pensée chrétienne primitive", *Aux Sources de la Tradition Chrétienne*, Mélanges offerts à M. Goguel, Neuchatel and Paris, 1950, pp. 247–57.

Simon, M., *St Stephen and the Hellenists in the Primitive Church*, Haskell Lectures for 1956, London, 1958.

Sjöberg, E., *Der Menschensohn im Äthiopischen Henochbuch*, Lund, 1946.

Sjöberg, E., *Der Verborgene Menschensohn in den Evangelien*, Lund, 1955.

Stauffer, E., "Messias oder Menschensohn", *Novum Testamentum*, I, 1956, Leiden, pp. 81–102.

Stauffer, E., *New Testament Theology*, E.Tr. J. Marsh, London, 1955.

Strack, H. L., and Billerbeck, P., *Kommentar zum Neuen Testament aus Talmud und Midrasch*, Munich, 1922–8.

Swete, H. B., *The Gospel According to St Mark*, London, 1898.

Taylor, V., *The Formation of the Gospel Tradition*, 2nd edn, London, 1935.

Taylor, V., *The Gospel According to St Mark*, London, 1952.

Taylor, V., *Jesus and His Sacrifice*, London, 1937.

Taylor, V., "The 'Son of Man' Sayings Relating to the Parousia", *E.T.*, 58, 1947, pp. 12–15.

Taylor, V., "Unsolved New Testament Problems: The Messianic Secret in Mark", *E.T.*, 59, 1948, pp. 146–51.

Thompson, G. H. P., "The Son of Man: The Evidence of the Dead Sea Scrolls", *E.T.*, 72, 1961, p. 125.

Tödt, H. E., *Der Menschensohn in der synoptischen Überlieferung*, Gütersloh, 1959; E.Tr., *The Son of Man in the Synoptic Tradition*, trans. of 2nd edn, 1963, London, 1965.

Torrey, C. C., *The Apocryphal Literature*, New Haven, U.S.A., 1945.

Torrey, C. C., *The Four Gospels*, London, no date.

Turner, C. H., "St Mark", *A New Commentary on Holy Scripture*, ed. C. Gore, H. L. Goudge, and A. Guillaume, London, 1928.

Turner, H. E. W., *Jesus Master and Lord*, London, 1953.

Unnik, W. C. van, "Jesus the Christ", *N.T.S.*, 8, 1962, pp. 101–16.

Vielhauer, P., "Gottesreich und Menschensohn in der Verkündigung Jesu", *Festschrift für Günther Dehn*, ed. W. Schneemelcher, Neukirchen, 1957.

Vielhauer, P., "Jesus und der Menschensohn", *Z.Th.K.*, 60, 1963, pp. 133–77.

Volz, P., *Die Eschatologie der jüdischen Gemeinde im neutestamentlichen Zeitalter*, Tübingen, 1934.

Wellhausen, J., *Das Evangelium Marci*, Berlin, 1903.

Widengren, G., "Early Hebrew Myths and Their Interpretation, *Myth, Ritual and Kingship*, ed. S. H. Hooke, Oxford, 1958, pp. 149–203.

Wrede, W., *Das Messiasgeheimnis in den Evangelien*, 3rd edn, Göttingen, 1963.

Zimmern, H., *The Babylonian and the Hebrew Genesis*, London, 1901.

Index of Biblical, Apocryphal, and Other Ancient Writings

OLD TESTAMENT

(References here are normally to the Hebrew text, and where necessary references to the English or the Septuagint version are given in brackets.)

15—S.O.M.

JEWISH APOCRYPHAL AND PSEUDEPIGRAPHICAL WRITINGS

OTHER ANCIENT WRITINGS

Index of Greek Words

Index of Modern Authors

Index of Subjects

A

Adam, 24, 26, 29, 50–2, 54–6, 57, 60, 61f, 62–5, 66, 67, 69, 70, 71f, 73, 93, 95f, 100, 141, 189
Apocalyptic, character of, 13f, 17, 29, 43, 148–55, 189
Abraham, 25, 52, 63, 64, 65, 67, 70, 74
Anthropos, *see* Primal Man.

B

Babylonian cultus, 18, 20, 21, 25
Babylonian Epic of Creation, 18, 20
Beasts, imagery of, 11–30, 53, 60, 63, 66, 67–9, 70, 71
Blasphemy, 84, 86, 88, 89, 166, 172f

C

Creation mythology, 17–23, 25f
Caesarea Philippi, 81, 103–6, 109, 110, 122f, 124, 125, 177–9
Church, early, 6–8, 77–80, 81–3, 87, 92, 94, 104, 107, 129, 143f, 157f, 159, 162, 163f, 166, 168, 170, 171, 174f, 183, 185–9, 191

D

David, 74, 97f, 102
Divine kingship, 21f

E

Elect One, 34–46
Elijah, 74, 127f, 129–33
Enoch, 42, 47, 60, 63, 141
Enthronement festival, 17f
Exodus, the 25, 74, 124, 146

F

Form-criticism, 5–7, 81, 85f, 90, 183

I

Israel, as inheritor of God's promises, 13, 19, 21, 27–30, 50–6, 58, 61f, 62–6, 68f, 70, 71, 73, 74, 93, 95f, 189

J

Jerusalem, destruction of, 149–55
Judgement, 23, 151–8, 170
John the Baptist, 127f, 131–3

K

Kingdom of God, 90, 145f

L

Last Supper, 145f, 182
Law, the, 57f, 60, 63, 71, 74, 102
Leviathan, 17, 18, 20

M

Marduk, 20
Messiah, 66f, 68f, 73, 129, 187
  Jesus as, 104–7, 110–13, 124, 126, 152, 165f, 187f
Messianism, 78f, 112f
Messianic secret, 106f
Michael, 14
Moses, 15, 74, 95, 124, 126, 127f
Mount of Olives, 156
Myth and ritual pattern, 18, 21

N

Nebuchadnezzar, 15f
New Year festival, 25
Noah, 15, 58, 63, 64, 67
Noah, fragments of the Book of, 34, 36f, 39

P

Primal man, 12f, 23, 43, 45, 49, 72